Adult Attachment and Couple Psychotherapy

'This book is a perfect illustration of the creativity that can be released when different disciplines begin to talk to one another within a common setting.'

From the Foreword by Jeremy Holmes

Attachment theory has triggered an explosion of research into family relationships, and provided a conceptual basis for the work of practitioners. *Adult Attachment and Couple Psychotherapy* brings research and practice perspectives to bear on the adult couple relationship, and provides a framework for assessing and working with secure and insecure partnerships.

Divided into three parts, the book

- looks at what is meant by secure and insecure attachment in the couple;
- describes how theory and research have been applied to practice, and how practice has added to the understanding of the complex problems that couples bring to therapy;
- examines the significance of training and the organisation of work for effective practice with couples.

Using vivid illustrations from clinical and community work, *Adult Attachment and Couple Psychotherapy* offers stimulating reading for all who wish to reassess their models of practice in this field.

Christopher Clulow is Director of the Tavistock Marital Studies Institute, London, where he practises as a couple psychotherapist, teacher and researcher. He has published extensively on working with couples undergoing change, and about marriage and family life.

Adult Attachment and Couple Psychotherapy

The 'secure base' in practice and research

Edited by Christopher Clulow

Brunner-Routledge
Taylor & Francis Group

HOVE AND NEW YORK

First published 2001
by Brunner-Routledge
27 Church Road, Hove, East Sussex BN3 2FA

Simultaneously published in the USA and Canada
by Taylor & Francis Inc
325 Chestnut Street, 8th Floor, Philadelphia, PA 19106

Reprinted 2001 and 2002

Reprinted 2003
by Brunner-Routledge
27 Church Road, Hove, East Sussex BN3 2FA
29 West 35th Street, New York NY 10001

Brunner-Routledge is an imprint of the Taylor & Francis Group

Typeset in Times by RefineCatch Limited, Bungay, Suffolk
Printed and bound in Great Britain by
Biddles Ltd, Guildford and King's Lynn

This publication has been produced with paper manufactured
to strict environmental standards and with pulp derived
from sustainable forests.

British Library Cataloguing-in-Publication Data
A catalogue record for this book is available from the British Library

Library of Congress Cataloging-in-Publication Data
Adult attachment and couple psychotherapy: the 'secure base' in
practice and research/edited by Christopher Clulow.
     p. cm.
   Includes bibliographical references and index.
    ISBN 0–415–22415–2—ISBN 0–415–22416–0 (pbk.)
    1. Attachment behaviour. 2. Marital psychotherapy.
  3. Interpersonal relations. 4. Personality disorders—Etiology.
  5. Psychology, Pathological. I. Clulow, Christopher F.

RC455.4.A84 A35 2000
616.89′156—dc21
                           00–044648

ISBN 0–415–22416–0 (pbk)
    0–415–22415–2 (hbk)

Contents

Notes on the contributors

Kim Bartholomew, Ph.D., is an Associate Professor in the Department of Psychology at Simon Fraser University, in Vancouver, BC, Canada. She received her Ph.D. in Personality Psychology from Stanford University in 1989. Her research interests relate to attachment processes in adult intimate relationships. Recent projects have focused on gender differences in experiences of partner violence and the applications of attachment theory to abusive heterosexual and same-sex relationships.

Christopher Clulow, Ph.D., is Director of the Tavistock Marital Studies Institute, where he works as a senior couple psychotherapist, teacher and researcher. He has directed action research projects on the transitions to parenthood and out of marriage, and published extensively on marriage and couple work for professional and lay readers. He is Therapies Editor of *Sexual and Relationship Therapy*, a Full Member of the Society of Psychoanalytical Marital Psychotherapists, and advisor to other professional journals and organisations in the field. For eight years he chaired the Commission on Marriage and Interpersonal Relations of the International Union of Family Organisations. He is a qualified rater of the Adult Attachment Interview and currently heads up the Institute's attachment-based research programme on couples' approaches to managing conflict.

Carolyn Pape Cowan, Ph.D., is an Adjunct Professor of Psychology at the University of California, Berkeley. A clinical psychologist, she has co-directed two longitudinal research and intervention studies, the first on the transition to parenthood and the second on the first child's transition to elementary school. She is co-editor with Phyllis Bronstein of *Fatherhood Today: Men's Changing Role in the Family* (Wiley, 1988) and co-author with Philip Cowan of *When Partners Become Parents: The Big Life Change for Couples* (second edition, Erlbaum, 2000).

Philip Cowan, Ph.D., is Professor of Psychology and Director of the Institute of Human Development at the University of California, Berkeley. A clinical psychologist, he has co-directed two longitudinal research and intervention studies, the first on the transition to parenthood and the second on the first child's transition to elementary school. He is co-editor of *Family Transitions: Advances in Family Research* and *Family, Self and Society: Towards a New Agenda for Family Research*, and co-author with Carolyn Pape Cowan of *When Partners Become Parents: The Big Life Change for Couples* (second edition, Erlbaum, 2000).

Lisa Crandell, Ph.D., is a research psychologist who trained in child and family clinical psychology at Michigan State University, receiving her doctorate in 1994. In 1995 she was awarded a grant from the National Institute of Health to conduct a longitudinal study on mother–infant relations at the Tavistock Clinic. During her attachment to the Tavistock Clinic she worked with the Tavistock Marital Studies Institute on a pilot research project that aimed to conceptualise couple functioning in attachment terms. Her research interests include developmental psychopathology, infant mental health and attachment across the life-span.

Judith Crowell, MD, is an Associate Professor of Psychiatry and Behavioural Sciences, and the Director of Training of Child and Adolescent Psychiatry at the State University of New York at Stony Brook. She graduated from the University of Vermont College of Medicine in 1978 and completed her training in psychiatry at the University of Wisconsin, Madison, and Stanford University. Her research in developmental psychology has explored narrative assessments of adult attachment representations and their relations to parenting and child behaviour, and applied this to couple functioning. She is co-principal investigator on two longitudinal studies, one on the development of adult attachment models after marriage and the other on intergenerational influences on family life and mental health.

Lynne Cudmore, BA, originally qualified as a social worker and worked for seven years in an inner city social services department. She has worked at the Tavistock Marital Studies Institute since 1978, where she is a senior marital psychotherapist and lecturer in marital studies. Her research interests include the impact of infertility on the couple relationship and the impact of child death on the parental partnership. She is a Full Member of the Society of Psychoanalytical Marital Psychotherapists and is currently training to be a child psychotherapist at the Tavistock Clinic.

Donald Dutton, Ph.D., is Professor of Psychology at the University of British Columbia. He completed his doctorate in social psychology at the University of Toronto, Canada, in 1974. He is a group therapist who has developed a psychological model for understanding the behaviour of perpetrators of intimate abuse. He has published extensively in the field and serves as an expert witness in civil and criminal trials involving domestic abuse.

James Fisher, Ph.D., is a past staff member of the Tavistock Marital Studies Institute, where he practised as a clinician, teacher and researcher. He is an Associate Member of the British Association of Psychotherapists and a Full Member of the Society of Psychoanalytical Marital Psychotherapists. He is now working in full-time private practice in London. He is the author of *The Uninvited Guest: Emerging from Narcissism towards Marriage* (Karnac, 1999), co-editor of *Intrusiveness and Intimacy in the Couple* (Karnac, 1995), and is currently working on a study of Shakespeare and contemporary psychoanalytic thinking.

Antonia Henderson, Ph.D., received her doctorate in psychology from Simon Fraser University, Vancouver, BC, Canada, in 1998. Her research has focused on attachment processes and relationship abuse in both clinical and community samples. She works as a research consultant in the area of health psychology, looking at attitudes, belief systems and motivational processes of kidney donors. She continues to conduct research on close relationships, and teaches courses on sports psychology and the psychology of equine behaviour.

Dorothy Judd, Ph.D., is a past staff member of the Tavistock Marital Studies Institute, where she worked as a couple psychotherapist, teacher and researcher. After teaching art, she trained and worked as an art therapist, and then as a child psychotherapist at the Tavistock Clinic. While working for sixteen years in child guidance clinics and teaching hospitals, she specialised in working with terminally ill children, their families and medical staff. Most of her publications are on this subject, including *Give Sorrow Words: Working with a Dying Child* (Free Association Books, 1989) and a co-edited book, *The Imaginative Body: Psychodynamic Therapy in Health Care* (Whurr, 1994). She currently teaches infant observation and has a private practice.

Anton Obholzer, MB, F.R.C.Psych., is Chief Executive of the Tavistock and Portman Clinics National Health Service Trust, a consultant psychiatrist and psychoanalyst. He originally trained as a medical doctor and worked for some years in general practice. He has held senior clinical and executive positions in the Tavistock Clinic since 1980, and has a particular interest in the application of psychoanalytic and group relations concepts to management and organisation consultancy. Since 1980 he has been Chair of the Tavistock Consulting to Institutions Workshop and has written, lectured and consulted extensively to organisations in Europe and further afield.

Felicia Olney, Dip.Soc.Studies, is a senior marital psychotherapist and clinical lecturer in marital studies at the Tavistock Marital Studies Institute, where she co-ordinates the Institute's training and consultation services. Her background includes social work in local authority and child guidance settings. She has worked on group relations conferences and currently teaches on the Tavistock Clinic's MA in social work. A major work interest has been the application of psychoanalytic and systemic thinking to organisational issues, and has included staff supervision work with social services departments and other public and voluntary sector organisations. She is an Associate Member of the British Association of Psychotherapists and a Full Member of the Society of Psychoanalytical Marital Psychotherapists.

Jenny Riddell, MA, is a marital psychotherapist and clinical lecturer in marital studies at the Tavistock Marital Studies Institute. She has worked as a counsellor, supervisor, trainer and clinical manager for Relate, a national couple counselling organisation, and has taught on adult and further education courses.

Avi Shmueli, B.Sc., first trained as a clinical psychologist before joining the staff of the Tavistock Marital Studies Institute and training as a couple psychotherapist. He is completing his doctorate studies at University College London, and has a particular interest in developing empirical approaches to research in psychoanalysis.

Dominique Treboux, Ph.D., is a Research Associate in the Department of Psychology at the State University of New York at Stony Brook. She received her doctorate in developmental psychology at Fordham University in the Bronx, New York, and is a member of Judith Crowell's research team at the State University of New York.

Christopher Vincent, MA, is a senior marital psychotherapist and clinical lecturer in marital studies at the Tavistock Marital Studies Institute, where he co-ordinates the Institute's research and publications activities. His clinical and research interests have focused on work with individuals and couples who are separating or divorcing, and he currently is part of the research team looking at the relationship between attachment patterns and couples' conflict management tactics. He is an Associate Member of the British Association of Psychotherapists and a Full Member of the Society of Psychoanalytical Marital Psychotherapists.

Foreword

Jeremy Holmes

Coupling is where all human life starts. From a Bowlbian perspective, the search for, establishment, maintenance and mourning of couple relationships are central themes of adult existence. Yet theorising couplehood is not easy. Within psychotherapy there are three major contenders, each of which, in varying degrees, is represented in this volume.

The first is the psychoanalytic tradition, and especially the Klein–Bion contribution. Here the basic concepts are those of projection and projective identification, and by extension from the therapeutic situation, transference. Each member of a couple is both a source and a receptacle of projections, and of transferential perceptions. One member of a dyad may, for example, express primitive feelings of rage and disappointment that 'belong' to and originate from the unconscious of the other. If the relationship is threatened, the individuals who comprise it will then rightly fear that they will lose these split-off parts of themselves if they separate. Equally, each member of a couple can perceive and will treat the other as though they represent a primitive internal object – such as an uncaring mother or a seducing father. Not infrequently, partners are chosen because they appear to be the very opposite of the parental introject, and then turn out, through the unconscious mutual shaping that is part of coupledom, to be either uncannily similar to that which is avoided or unsatisfactory because they are so unlike what is expected and known.

Since these processes are probably universal, theory needs normative criteria by which couples in difficulty can be distinguished from those that are functioning well. Here, the Kleinian tradition relies on the distinction between paranoid-schizoid and depressive position functioning. Where each member of the dyad treats the other as an extension of themselves, where there is rigid splitting and division of roles, or where one member feels persecuted by his or her partner, especially if he has unconsciously provoked that persecution, problems are likely to arise. When the members of the partnership can see one another as whole human beings, a mixture of good and bad, and can accept the inevitable differences and separations that are the counterpart of intimacy and passion, things are likely to go well.

This interpersonal perspective in psychoanalysis has been hard won. Freud's theorising started from isolated monads that only gradually encounter the 'other' as they emerge from a dream-world of drive-driven primary narcissism. One response to this was the emergence of the systemic tradition based on cybernetics and an anthropological/sociological perspective which takes as its starting point the couple as a system in which individual members are merely sub-units. Here the major themes include:

- maintaining a boundary around the couple – one that is sufficiently permeable for children and others to have access to their parents yet close-woven enough for the couple to protect their privacy and distinctness as a unit;
- the power relationship within the dyad – the resulting contractual relationship and the extent to which negotiations around it are based on mutual respect or driven by dominance and submission;
- roles – how they are parcelled out between the couple and how rigidly they are adhered to;
- communication between the members of the couple – how open or restricted it is, the major channels through which it is conducted, and whether it is predominantly instrumental or affective in nature.

From this tradition the normative perspective depicts the well-functioning couple as protected by a semi-permeable boundary, able to share power and roles but in a flexible and interchangeable way, having a clearly adhered-to overt and implicit contract, with broad and open channels of communication – especially of feelings – and with the capacity for mutual enjoyment.

As a third force in psychotherapy, attachment theory has had a long gestation, partly because of its ambivalent relationship with psychoanalysis, which, with ethology, was one of its principal forebears. Attachment theory is both monistic *and* systemic, and so seems an ideal vehicle for thinking about couples. Its starting point is two separate individuals who are, at the same time, inescapably in relationship to one another. The original dyad studied by Bowlby and Ainsworth and their students was, of course, not the adult couple, but that of parent and child. Ainsworth's Strange Situation Test provided a way of classifying different patterns of security and insecurity. Later, researchers such as Hazan, Shaver and Bartholomew (one of the distinguished contributors to this volume) began to apply attachment ideas to their research on adult couples. At this stage attachment theory remained more of a research tool than a therapeutic modality. The same was true of the next significant step, Main's development of the Adult Attachment Interview, a research instrument that mirrors the Strange Situation Test producing a similarly broad classification of attachment patterns, but in this case for adults.

Attachment ideas are at last beginning to percolate into psychotherapeutic practice. This volume is an example of the exciting possibilities that can come from the cross-fertilisation of ideas between researchers and therapists. As a means of orienting readers I will outline the current state of attachment theory as a guide to clinical practice as I see it. Six main attachment domains are delineated, each of which can be applied to individuals, couples and families. These comprise the secure base, exploration and play, protest and assertiveness, loss, internal working models, reflective function and narrative competence.

Secure base   The first, and most important domain is that of the secure base, the domain that constitutes the conceptual anchor for this book. Early attachment thinkers tended to see the secure base in behavioural terms, and defined as the caregiver to whom the infant visibly turns when threatened or ill, and who is able, to a greater or lesser extent, to provide the essential protection needed if the infant is to survive. The concept seemed to have limited application to adults until it was realised that the secure base can be seen not just as an external figure, but also as a *representation* of security within the individual psyche.

The original caregiver/child secure base experience can be thought of as comprising:

- a set of behaviours activated by threat;
- a response to those behaviours by the caregiver;
- a psycho-physiological state which is the end result of those behaviours.

Caregiver responses associated with the secure base include responsiveness, sensitivity, consistency, reliability, attunement, the capacity to absorb protest, and what Meins (1999) calls 'mind-mindedness': the ability to see the distressed child as an autonomous and sentient being with feelings and projects of her or his own. The psycho-physiological state includes such physiological elements as relaxedness, warmth, closeness, feeling soothed, satiation, a full stomach, steady breathing, a reduced pulse rate and calmness. Psychological components include thoughts such as 'all's well with the world', 'everything will be all right', 'where there was chaos and confusion there is now order' and 'all is under control'.

Adults, however seemingly autonomous, will, as well as making physical contact with loved ones, have an internal secure base zone to which they turn at times of stress, especially as part of affect regulation. This zone can also be conceptualised as a schema or object relationship. Activating the internal secure base may come about through comforting thoughts or images, and behaviour such as resorting to hot baths, bed, favourite foods, alcohol, duvets, music, books or television programmes. Security must be achieved whatever the cost: psychological survival requires some kind of secure base experience, compromised though this may be by the limitations of the caregiver and the recipient's capacity to elicit appropriate care. The internal representation of the secure base can be activated by different parts of the cycle: that is presumably why baths, bed and warmth produce the desired state of calmness.

Pathological variants of secure base behaviour include comfort eating, substance abuse, compulsive masturbation or deliberate self-harm. These create some element of the secure base cycle described above, and this, in turn, can have a soothing function however self-destructively it has been achieved. For example, experiences of escalating chaos followed by relief are characteristic of self-harming episodes in people suffering from borderline personality disorder. Many will describe how soothed they feel when they see the blood flow after cutting themselves, or when they lie down after taking an overdose of tablets, or following a stomach wash-out. Ingredients of these behaviours are to be found in couples who are in severe difficulties, such as those for whom a sexual relationship is only possible after a major row.

The Strange Situation Test and Adult Attachment Interview, both of which are described in this book, delineate insecure patterns of attachment security. Although both are categorical measures as used in research, it is possible to imagine two separate axes: one describing a bipolar continuum from dismissing/avoidant through secure base to preoccupied/ambivalent strategies for managing threat, the other describing a unipolar axis running from coherent/autonomous to incoherent/disorganised representational worlds. Insecure variants are essentially trade-offs. The avoidant individual stays close enough to a rejecting caregiver to get a measure of protection, but not so close as to feel the full pain of rejection. The ambivalent person will cling to a caregiver as a way of compensating for inconsistency. Neither achieves the full secure base state of security, and so a sacrifice has to be made: for infants exploratory play is inhibited, for adults intimacy is compromised or autonomy restricted in the service of security.

Similarly, disorganisation and incoherence are so disruptive of the caregiving environment that people will go to great lengths to create some sort of order, however problematic and sub-optimal their efforts may be. For example, there may be attempts at control through obsessional behaviour, the use of dissociative strategies (in which overall chaos is reduced by splitting), delusional attempts to impose coherence from within on an inchoate external environment, or the predictability of a sick role.

As this volume so well testifies, both secure and insecure variants of secure base phenomena are to be found within couple relationships. In couples each partner acts as a secure base for the other, and each brings her or his own internal secure base representations and expectations – with varying degrees of in-built insecurity – into the partnership. If the relationship is stable, a 'third element' can be forged out of these representations: the partnership itself, and the pattern of mutual expectations it implies. This provides far greater security than either member of the couple can achieve on their own.

Seeing the relationship as separate from each of its component parts is a key point of contact between psychoanalytic and attachment perspectives. Coupledom offers the possibility of moving from a two-person, pre-oedipal position, to a three-person oedipal constellation. From a neo-Kleinian perspective, the oedipal situation is seen as a developmental step where, if the child can tolerate the parental couple and the loss of exclusive possession of mother that implies, s/he gains a decentered perspective and a freedom of thought essential for interpersonal success. The attachment analogue of this process is the establishment of a secure base *representation* – and especially representation in language – so that the child is no longer wholly dependent on the physical presence of the caregiver but can be comforted by the thought of 'mum-and-dad', or 'home'. This, in turn, depends on the caregiver's ability to represent her child's representations: to see the child as a separate and sentient being (Fonagy, 1999a). Similarly, healthy functioning in couples depends on the capacity to see, think and talk about their relationship as an entity in its own right, separate from the two individuals who comprise it.

Exploration and play   Companionable interaction, and the capacity for mutual pleasure – whether sexual, playful or intellectual – is central to coupledom. Attachment theory postulates that there is a reciprocal relationship between secure base behaviour and exploration. When people feel threatened they will seek out their secure base, and, for the moment, fun and play will be correspondingly inhibited. Anxiety is the enemy of enjoyment. If one member of a couple does not feel secure – worrying, for example, that the other will abandon her at any minute – it is unlikely that s/he will be able to enjoy their sexual relationship. Helping couples to grasp this very simple concept is often a gateway to understanding sexual difficulties, or an inability to profit from the 'quality time' so beloved of agony aunts and informal advice givers.

Protest and assertiveness   Rows, violence and rage are among the commonest reasons for couples seeking help. From an attachment perspective, anger is triggered when there is a threat of separation and has the function, in what is essentially a negative reinforcement schedule, of ensuring that the attachment bond remains intact. This can be seen in many different ways in couples. If one member of a couple threatens the bond by having an affair, this will evoke straightforward rage in the betrayed one as their security and self-esteem is so bound up with their partner. More subtly, anger is often provoked when one member of a couple fails to be considerate, or to take into account the other's point of view. As we have seen, a crucial component of the secure base is mind-mindedness, the capacity to see the other as having a mind and feelings of his or her own.

Inconsiderateness ignores the other's feelings, threatens this aspect of the secure base and so inevitably triggers protest. Assertiveness training, which in a formal or informal way is an important component of working with couples, helps people to escape from the traps of submission or uncontrollable rage, to use anger effectively to restore attachment bonds and to maintain the secure base.

Loss   For Bowlby, loss, or threatened loss, was central to much psychological distress. He also saw that the capacity to cope with loss is a key component of psychological maturity. Loss is the main theme in several chapters of this book. A paradox of coupledom, of two people being together, is that it can only be achieved if its members can negotiate a separateness in their relationship. Getting together involves giving up the uncommitted and sexually free state of being single, and being in a couple means running the risk that the loved one may be lost: for the English philosopher Francis Bacon, a wife and children were 'hostages to fortune'. Taking *this* path means that one cannot take *that* one, and having something inevitably means that one may lose it. Each member of a couple brings with them a history of separations and losses that will colour their relationship. As Chapter 9 shows so movingly, one reason why the death of a child is devastating for couples, and divorce rates are so high after such a tragedy, is that each partner is so grief-stricken that neither is able to provide secure base comfort for the other. Working with the histories of loss that partners bring to their relationship, and coming to understand how they may influence current difficulties, are essential aspects of couple work.

Internal working models   It is impossible to practise an atheoretical psychotherapy. Any attempt to help people in psychological distress will be underpinned by a set of models about the structure of the mind, the nature of thought, characteristics of intimate relationships and so on. Different approaches use different languages, and it is often hard to distinguish between points of overlap and real differences. For example, the notion of internal representation is described psychoanalytically in terms of an inner world populated with internal objects and the relationships between them. Cognitive therapy focuses on 'schemata', the fundamental and relatively immutable assumptions about the self and its relationships. Systemic therapists are interested in 'event scripts', sequences of behaviour of self in relation to others that are laid down in childhood, and which give colour and shape to subsequent relationships. Bowlby's version of this phenomenon was the 'internal working model', a term chosen deliberately as an 'action language' which would capture the Piagetian 'scientist-practitioner' process by which children construe their world (Bretherton, 1999).

Eschewing the notion of the unconscious, Bowlby wrote of 'defensive exclusion' to describe ways in which unwanted painful feelings and thoughts are kept out of awareness, and the consequent restrictions to internal working models, and therefore adaptability, that entails. Thus the internal working model is a more cognitive construct than the psychoanalytic theories which most contributors to this volume espouse. The distinction between implicit and explicit memory can perhaps help overcome this gap. Implicit, or procedural, memories are those that are laid down in the early years of life. They consist of the 'ways in which things are done', patterns of relationship, and include, for example, parental responses to infant distress that are stored within the child's mind and will influence subsequent relationships even if there is no explicit awareness of their role. Explicit, or episodic, memories are the specific events and self–other behaviours which comprise people's 'memories'. Psychotherapy works with both.

Each member of a couple brings to their relationship a complex set of working models, schemata, scripts and/or object relationships. Couples are attracted to one another if there is some kind of 'fit' between their own inner world and that of the other. Each must consciously or unconsciously know the steps of the other's dance. The more intimate they are able to be with one another, the more their own inner world will be exposed. Areas of pain and vulnerability will inevitably come into play. Thus, paradoxically, a certain maturity or self-confidence in the coherence and survivability of the self is needed for the childlike regression that is inherent in coupledom to take place successfully.

The three main variants of insecure attachment provide a useful framework for thinking about the vicissitudes of this process. Avoidant strategies sacrifice intimacy for an exaggerated form of autonomy, while ambivalent strategies give up autonomy for the sake of a dependent form of intimacy (Holmes, 1996). Individuals relying on these strategies will seek out a partner who can tolerate the pattern dictated by their own internal working models. But each will also be unhappy with the restrictions it brings, so every relationship also contains the hope that old patterns will be transcended. This hope is the starting point for successful couple therapy. Couples need to come to understand how the 'trigger' points in their relationship – for rows, or disappointment, or misery – arise at these nodal connections between one person's set of painful assumptions and those of the other. The dance between Martha and George in Albee's play *Who's Afraid of Virginia Woolf?*, so beautifully analysed in Chapter 8, is a good example of this process.

Trauma can altogether destroy part of the security regulating system (Garland, 1998), leaving partners bereft of strategies for responding to threat. Internal working models are not just restricted but also have lacunae – for example, in the area of sexual or physical violence. Disorganised attachment, typified clinically in patients suffering with borderline personality disorder, provide no consistent relationship pattern for their partners to adapt to, and, except when partners are excessively avoidant, tend to have radically unstable relationships. Couple therapy here needs to occur in parallel with individual help.

Reflective function and narrative competence A key finding in the attachment literature is the relationship between 'reflective function' as revealed in the Adult Attachment Interview (the capacity to talk cogently and coherently about oneself and one's difficulties) and security of attachment. The importance of this for psychotherapy is self-evident. Psychotherapy is essentially a narrative process in which therapist and patient together develop a dialogue about both the patient's life and the nature of the therapist–patient relationship itself (Holmes, 1999). Therapy is an *in vivo* situation in which the patient learns to become self-reflexive. This is particularly exploited by the transference-based approaches used by most of the contributors to this volume. When representations can be made explicit in language, they are then available for 'thinking about thinking', and so for modification. This is the cognitive aspect of the neo-Kleinian conceptualisation of the Oedipal situation already referred to. Simply asking couples to describe how they met, a typical row, or what they both want for the future will not only reveal their difficulties but also start them on the road of mutual self-reflexion, which is a key to successful outcome. While implicit in analytic therapies, this is made explicit in behavioural and systemic ones where couples may be asked to write letters to one another, bring family photographs to sessions, draw pictures and in general use any technique that will enhance representations of their relationship patterns.

To conclude these introductory comments, attachment theory has never aimed to become a therapy in its own right. Nevertheless, it provides a framework in which theory, research and clinical practice can meet and begin to speak a common language. Just as with individuals and couples, so it is for theories: exploration and intercourse is not possible until security has been established. A shared language and set of assumptions has to be laid down before useful thinking can begin. This book is a perfect illustration of the creativity that can be released when different disciplines begin to talk to one another within a common setting.

Dr Jeremy Holmes
Department of Psychiatry, North Devon District Hospital, Barnstaple

Acknowledgements

The idea for this book arose out of an international conference held in London in July 1998 to mark the fiftieth anniversary of the Tavistock Marital Studies Institute. Although several of the contributors were speakers at that conference, they have rewritten their material for this book. To them, and to the other contributors, I wish to express my appreciation for the friendly spirit of co-operation in which this project has been completed. I also want to thank the President, Chair and members of the Council of the Tavistock Institute of Medical Psychology who provided both moral and financial support for the originating conference.

A particular debt of gratitude is owed to the couples who have allowed us to draw on their experience to illustrate some of the themes in this book. We have taken care to ensure that no-one other than themselves will be able to recognise their identity, and we hope we have done justice to their generosity by portraying our shared experience in ways that others will find helpful.

The excerpts from *Who's Afraid of Virginia Woolf?*, by Edward Albee, are reprinted with the permission of Scribner, a Division of Simon and Schuster, and the Random House Archive and Library (for the Jonathan Cape edition), copyright © 1962 Edward Albee. I am also grateful to the Random House Archive and Library and the estate of C. Day Lewis for permission to quote from the C. Day Lewis poem, 'For Sean', which appears in *C. Day Lewis: The Complete Poems*, by C. Day Lewis, published by Sinclair-Stevenson (1992). Chapter 1 is reproduced with some revisions from *Sexual and Marital Therapy*, Vol. 12, No. 3, 1997, and thanks are extended to Taylor & Francis Ltd/Carfax (website http://www.tandf.co.uk) for permission to do this. Finally, I would like to acknowledge Kathleen Haldane, whose sculpture from her 'Held Free' series formed the inspiration for the cover design.

List of Abbreviations

AAI	Adult Attachment Interview
CABC	Child Adaptive Behavior Checklist
CAI	Couple Attachment Interview
CAJI	Couple Attachment Joint Interview
CCETSW	Central Council for Education and Training in Social Work
CRI	Current Relationship Interview
MAI	Marital Attachment Interview
PMWI	Psychological Maltreatment of Women Inventory
SBSS	Secure Base Scoring System
SST	Strange Situation Test
TMSI	Tavistock Marital Studies Institute

Introduction

Christopher Clulow

When I first heard John Bowlby talk about his theory of attachment he left me with a lasting image. A mother is seated on a park bench. In front of her plays her toddler son. As his confidence grows he ranges in ever-increasing circles away from her, investigating his new surroundings while occasionally checking on her continuing presence. The approach of a stranger, or a frightening sound, sends him running back to her for reassurance and comfort. If his retreat is blocked – for example, by a barking dog coming between him and her – he becomes distressed, and may even run into danger trying to get back to her. Touching base with mother becomes an imperative, and is the precondition for him continuing to play and explore.

The image will be instantly recognisable to anyone familiar with attachment theory. It illustrates the concept of a 'secure base', a term first coined by one of Bowlby's closest colleagues, Mary Ainsworth, and which he took for the title of his collected papers on the clinical implications of attachment theory (Bowlby, 1988). The image also hints at a relationship dilemma that is particularly apposite for adults in committed partnerships: what to do when the person who provides you with security also constitutes the threat from which you seek refuge? This conundrum surfaces repeatedly in this book because it contains a paradox that is central to human development: in the adult couple, as in the parent–child relationship, there can be no intimacy without a capacity for being apart; yet the capacity to be apart results from intimate involvement with others.

But what does 'security' mean in the context of a secure base? The word can be problematic insofar as it carries different associations. Often it is used in a constrictive sense to describe the policing or regulation of relationships and behaviour that are thought to be threatening. Sometimes it is used as a synonym for safety, describing the metaphorical burrows most of us habitually retreat to from time to time to reassure ourselves that nothing has changed and all's well with the world. For attachment theorists, however, the word has a quite specific meaning.

Bowlby conceived of individual security as the product of social relatedness. For him, security resulted from accessible and responsive caregiving. It was visibly evident in the behaviour of young children who were confident in seeking out their parents when frightened or distressed, could protest when separated from them and would use them as a base from which to explore other relationships and activities. Security was associated not with compliance or competitiveness, but with a capacity to need and value the care provided by others *and* to act autonomously. Enterprise and endearment are inextricably linked in this psychology of security, a marriage of values that has proved both creative and problematic in its working out in the private and public theatres of life.

Mary Ainsworth increased our understanding of security by closely observing how very young children and their mothers managed separation and reunion experiences in a standardised laboratory procedure that she and her colleagues described as the Strange Situation Test (see Chapter 1). Her focus of attention was not just on how infants managed the tension between attachment and exploratory behaviours, but also how their parents managed the reciprocal tension between protecting them and letting them go. What was observed was an interaction, a kind of dance, in which the behaviour of one party had to be understood in relation to that of the other. Secure infants sought out their parents when they felt threatened, protested at being separated from them and were quickly comforted upon reunion. Their parents were attentive and responsive to their needs. Insecure infants either mirrored the distance and disconnection of their parents, or clung to them in an anxious and ambivalent way that reflected the inconsistencies in the parenting they received. Security was a feature of relatedness, not a fixed personality characteristic. The same infant could behave securely with one caregiver and insecurely with another; he or she could elicit different responses from the same person. However, patterns of relatedness were not simply dictated by a succession of externally defined experiences; they reflected enduring constellations of assumptions about relationships that had become embedded within the child's inner world and persisted over time. These matrices of internalised assumptions were what Bowlby (1969, 1973, 1980) described as 'internal working models': relational templates that children unconsciously constructed from their reading of past social experience, and upon which they relied for guidance in their current dealings with others.

The persistence of these models over time has been demonstrated by subsequent study. The work of Mary Main and her colleagues (1985), resulting in the Adult Attachment Interview (see Chapters 1 and 2), was notable in shifting the focus of attention from children to adults, and from observed behaviour to representations of attachment disclosed by the different ways adults spoke about their early family experiences. The hallmarks of security were to be found in the coherence of the stories people told about their early years, and their capacity to engage simultaneously with themselves in remembering experience and with the interviewer in focusing upon the questions asked.

Attending to the interconnections between childhood and adult experience has been the province of both attachment research and psychoanalytic psychotherapy. But can *adult partnerships* in any sense be described as attachment relationships?

The first study to conceptualise romantic relationships in attachment terms recorded considerable continuity between them and previous attachments: 'The best predictors of adult attachment type were respondents' perceptions of the quality of their relationship with each parent and the parents' relationship with each other' (Hazan and Shaver, 1987: 516). The researchers in this study distinguished adult romantic from childhood attachment in terms of the activation of sexual and caregiving behavioural systems.

Following their work there has been a proliferation of research that assumes the pair bond is accurately described as an attachment relationship (see Feeney, 1999, for a review). Some continue to argue that this assumption is fallacious because adults do not need each other for protection in the same way that infants need their parents. A recent investigation of this proposition has concluded that the functions of attachment in adult life *are* essentially the same as in infancy: helping to ensure the development of an enduring bond that enhances survival and reproductive fitness in direct and indirect ways (Hazan and Zeifman, 1999). The significant differences between childhood and adult attachment are that, in the latter, attachment is reciprocal, the initial motivation for proximity-seeking is sexual attraction rather than the alleviation of distress, and that it tends to result in rather than follow from genetic relatedness. Through the physical proximity afforded by sexual behaviour there are opportunities for developing emotional closeness; emotional closeness fosters conditions in which attachment and caregiving are valued; valuing attachment and caregiving is good for the continuance of the species. It is not just a question of breeding, but of pedigree. Contemporary evolutionists, such as Cronin (1999), are clear that human behaviour is guided by qualitative as well as quantitative factors, and that a changing environment changes behaviour. From an evolutionary perspective, committed caregiving can be more adaptive than promiscuous sexuality, especially when health can be taken for granted and education bears powerfully on life opportunities.

Practitioners have thought about the couple relationship in attachment terms for longer than researchers, although their conceptualisations have been various and, by and large, not subjected to the tests of conventional research. Concurrent with Bowlby's work there evolved within the Tavistock Centre (at the Tavistock Marital Studies Institute and the Marital Unit of the Tavistock Clinic) a formulation of marriages and partnerships as transference relationships capable of collapsing boundaries of time and psychological space through their capacity to awaken and replay the dramas of early childhood (Bannister, 1955; Pincus, 1960; Dicks, 1967; Mattinson and Sinclair, 1979; Clulow, 1985; Clulow and Mattinson, 1988; Ruszczynski,

1993; Ruszczynski and Fisher, 1995; Fisher,1999). These studies are rooted in the British object relations tradition of psychoanalysis, and directed towards practitioner rather than researcher communities.

Generally speaking, practitioners and researchers have communicated very little with each other, each tending to believe the methods of the other were antithetical to their primary purpose. Bowlby himself acknowledged the communication gap in a paper that distinguished between the art of psychoanalytic therapy and the science of psychoanalytic psychology. He proposed that a principal difference lay in the mental outlooks of practitioners and researchers: 'The practitioner must deal with complexity, the scientist strives to simplify. The practitioner uses theory as a guide, the scientist challenges theory. The practitioner's modes of enquiry are inevitably limited whereas progress in science requires that data obtained by one method be cross-checked by data obtained by others' (Bowlby, 1979: 13). He espoused the discipline of direct observation as a check against clinical inference, a method that has been used to good effect in both clinical training and attachment research, along with more recent developments that permit the systematic analysis of mental representation. Happily, there is a growing rapprochement between attachment research and clinical practice which augurs well for the development of both (for example, Sinclair and McCluskey, 1996; Steele and Steele, 1998).

One aim of this book is to further the dialogue between practice and research. I want to suggest that, as well as there being differences, there are similarities between clinical and research activities that allow each discipline to learn from the other. Both clinicians and researchers operate as participant observers when it comes to studying human behaviour. Each must engage with and take account of intersubjective processes in carrying out their different tasks. Clinicians and researchers constitute part of the field of their studies; they cannot pretend they are separate from it. The truth of this proposition first presented itself to me years ago when reading an account of a sociological study of the transition to parenthood in which the researcher described how interviewing women to understand their experience of becoming mothers actually changed that experience. Research processes, I then understood, could have therapeutic effects. This understanding has been reinforced by my subsequent experience of action and clinical research. It is only a small step to reverse the proposition and assert that therapeutic processes might have research utility.

Today I tend to conceive of the psychotherapeutic process with couples as sharing some of the features of research (see Chapter 5). Psychotherapy tries to promote a collaborative endeavour between couple and therapist(s) for understanding the meaning of what happens when they meet within predefined parameters to explore problems that the partners locate within their relationship as a couple. The processes of developing theory and practice are inextricably linked – even in this context. They derive from testing hypotheses generated within the clinical situation against the couples' and therapists' experience. To be viable and credible these hypotheses must take account of different realities and viewpoints. Observation and experiment overlap. Collecting and analysing data is an ongoing and reciprocal process. Insofar as the efficacy of the endeavour relies on a collaborative relationship between couple and therapists, the process of establishing that collaboration is part of the research data. The focus of study is intersubjective and requires a reflexive approach: couples are called on to reflect on their own experience (including their experience of therapy); therapists must likewise reflect on their responses to the couple and the therapeutic situation in order to access data about unconscious processes. Much can be learned through the process of implementing change, and clinicians have privileged access to data that tend to elude conventional research procedures.

This open systems view of the therapeutic process implies an open systems view of marriage and partnership. Neither is at odds with the basic assumption underpinning attachment and object relations theories: that human behaviour can only be understood in a social context. While systems theory reminds us that the study of one system is always the study of a sub-system of a wider system, attachment and object relations theories can be relied upon to retain the complementary, and equally valid, perspective, that systems are created in the image of their sub-systems.

This brings me to the second aim of the book: to encourage dialogue between different theoretical stances – specifically, between attachment and object relations theories. Historically, these different approaches have not always been comfortable bedfellows. Although both conceive of humans as relationship-seeking rather than instinct-driven beings, this very commonality has contained the seeds of dissent that pitted Bowlby's ideas against those of the psychoanalytic community of his time. His criticism of Freud for disbelieving his patients when they told him they had been seduced and abused as children (opting instead for a theory of unconscious phantasy that placed infantile sexuality centre stage), and of Klein for the place she accorded to the role of auto-generated phantasy as a primary motivational drive in human relationships, seemed to overturn the central tenets of psychoanalyis. He was read as dismissing the significance of psychic realities in favour of accepting, as fact, the reported accounts of patients. In the polarisation that followed, psychoanalysis was represented as being preoccupied with unconscious phantasy at the expense of external realities, and attachment theory as preoccupied with biologically and environmentally programmed behavioural systems at the expense of internal realities. The connection between inner and outer worlds, central to both theoretical approaches, was sometimes lost sight of as the various protagonists took up their positions.

Because Bowlby and his theory have been regarded as the 'black sheep' of the psychoanalytic family (Fonagy, 1999a) it sometimes needs to be restated that attachment theory *is* psychoanalytic. In understanding human development and behaviour it takes account of unconscious and defensive processes, the formation and persistence of an internal world and the relationship of reciprocal influence between this and the individual's environment. But Bowlby was also influenced by other lines of thinking in constructing an empirically based theory of personality and social development (for example, evolution, ethology, control systems and cognition), and it was this, perhaps, that made him suspect. Courting different ideas can be as problematic in professional circles as it can be in marriages and partnerships; working across disciplines can be regarded as a form of infidelity.

Time has moved on. Attachment theory is providing an empirical basis for many of the clinical assertions rooted in object relations theory, and offering a conceptual bridge that allows conversations to develop between different approaches to providing psychotherapeutic help. There are satisfying convergences of meaning between terms such as 'psychic reality', 'internal world', 'internal working models' and 'mental representations', that have allowed object relations and attachment theorists to learn from rather than fight with each other. So, I hope, this book will provide opportunities to open and continue the dialogue between different ways of understanding the same phenomena – a task that is, after all, close to the hearts of couple psychotherapists given the nature of their work.

However, my experience as a couple psychotherapist alerts me to the challenges posed for the reader in engaging with the dialogue between practice and research, and with the linguistic and conceptual differences between attachment and (predominantly Kleinian) object relations paradigms contained in this book. The chapters speak in voices whose differences are not simply accounted for by the fact that there are seventeen contributors to the volume. The dialect of the practitioner is different from that of the researcher. The cadence of each reflects different emphases, assumptions and concerns. Moreover, the same is true within as well as between the disciplines. The conversations represented here are in the process of becoming rather than already formed, and there are places where the dialogue is halting and circumscribed. How could it be otherwise? Moving from hypothesis to evidence, from attribution to recognition, 'from narcissism to marriage' (Fisher, 1999), is a hard-won struggle, as every therapist, researcher and human being knows.

It needs also to be said that by focusing on heterosexual couples there is no intention by any of the contributors to exclude the concerns of gay couples. Indeed, there is every reason to believe that much of what applies to different-sex partnerships will also apply to same-sex partnerships (see Chapter 3). That these connections are not pursued here simply reflects the populations of the research and clinical studies referred to in this book.

The book is divided into three parts. Part I conceptualises security in committed adult heterosexual partnerships, drawing principally on contemporary research. Conceptualising the secure couple is not simply an academic exercise. It has real utility for clinicians as they review their assessment criteria for couples seeking help, consider the nature of the therapeutic process, review their part in effecting or obstructing change, and explore appropriate benchmarks for measuring outcome in a culture that increasingly expects practice to be evidence-based.

In Chapter 1, James Fisher and Lisa Crandell draw on clinical and research sources in proposing the capacity of each partner to move between positions of depending on and being depended upon in their relationship as the hallmark of adult attachment security (what they term 'complex' attachment). They describe a prototype research measure for capturing the security of a partnership, as contrasted to the security of the adults within it, and so prepare the ground for re-conceptualising couples in attachment terms. By offering a typology of partnerships based on different pairings of individual attachment status they suggest which kinds of partnership are likely to generate what kinds of difficulties, and speculate about the likelihood of couples seeking help on the basis of their orientation to attachment.

Their concept of 'complex attachment' is identical to the secure base phenomenon in adult partnerships that Judith Crowell and Dominique Treboux describe in Chapter 2, and for which they have created a system of assessment based on observations of how couples interact together. In examining connections between the different domains from which attachment security is measured, they provide empirical evidence that addresses questions of central importance for therapeutic work with couples: In what ways does adult attachment differ from that between children and parents? What influence has past family experience on current relationships? Do people choose partners who are alike or dissimilar? How important is gender when considering whether the attachment security of one partner affects that of the other? What are the best attachment predictors of marital stability and satisfaction?

In Chapter 3, Kim Bartholomew, Antonia Henderson and Donald Dutton explore the nature of insecure attachment. They comment on the stability of many insecure relationships, despite the dissatisfactions they can cause the partners and the recurrence of abusive behaviour that sometimes occurs within them. In exploring why partners might stay in abusive relationships they outline a four-category model of attachment. This develops the classifications of Ainsworth and colleagues (1978) and Main and Goldwyn (1994) by identifying a fearful as well as dismissing orientation to attachment that drives avoidant behaviour, and by assessing interactions between attachment security and dimensions of regard for self and others. Breaking the mould of conventional thinking about abusive relationships, they provide evidence from four studies to support the view that relationship factors (as well as environmental or individual factors) may both predispose partners towards and protect them from violence.

In Chapter 4, Philip and Carolyn Cowan consider how attachment security

is mediated across generations, and draw attention to the potential significance of fathers in this regard. They provide evidence that links the academic
performance and behaviour of children with the quality of their parents'
relationship as a couple, an original and challenging perspective that tends to
be overlooked in public debates about parenting. Providing a bridge between
Parts I and II, they bring the results of their research to bear on the design
and implementation of a preventive intervention programme designed to
help couples with young children who are on the verge of starting school.
They show how non-didactic, facilitative groups that focus on the couple's
relationship can be more effective than groups focusing on parenting in promoting the well-being of adults and children, and suggest how the groups
acted as a secure base for the couples who participated in them.

Part II considers the implications of attachment theory for responding to
distress in the couple relationship. Every change that couples experience
combines a measure of gain and loss. The weighting of their experience will
depend on the nature of the change and what it means to the partners.
Attachment theory, through the proposition that childhood experiences
influence the way losses are managed in later life, has something to say about
whether and how relationships are used to manage change. But does it have a
utility that extends beyond other conceptual frameworks, and can it guide the
thinking of practitioners as they consider what they do when they work with
couples? In considering these questions, contributors invite a dialogue
between the paradigms of attachment and object relations theories, as well as
between process aspects of research and practice.

Chapter 5 introduces this section by considering the implications of
attachment theory and research for recasting the nature of the therapeutic
frame for psychoanalytic work with couples. In it I outline some basic
assumptions underpinning the work of practitioners who are informed by
attachment and object relations theories, and consider the therapeutic process as a co-research endeavour for couples and their therapists, one that
shares some features of attachment research methods.

In Chapter 6, Jenny Riddell and Avi Shmueli join me in presenting two
contrasting perspectives of a couple in therapy. One is drawn from the results
of Adult Attachment Interviews conducted with each partner; the other
derives from data (and especially counter-transference data) generated within
the context of therapy. These perspectives are brought to bear on dilemmas
that frequently affect couples and their therapists as they consider the potential significance of separation and loss in relation to ending therapy.

The importance of counter-transference in detecting and responding to
unresolved/disorganised couple states of mind is developed by Christopher
Vincent in Chapter 7. He considers the roles therapists are unconsciously
invited to take up by couples to protect them from psychological pain, and
the sudden eruptions of feeling – and collapse of thinking – that can occur in
sessions. He argues that such eruptions bear some similarity to the 'blips' that

denote unresolved/disorganised states of mind in the Adult Attachment Interview. He compares these with responses to partners who, as a couple, jointly present features of a 'cannot classify' grading on the basis of this research interview. He considers how far one can extrapolate from the observed behaviour of children to adult attachment dilemmas and states of mind, and introduces a classification conundrum when the couple (rather than either partner) is the 'subject' or 'patient'.

In Chapter 8 I explore violence in marriage as a product of attachment insecurity (both patterned and episodic) and narcissistic object relating. The case illustration used for this purpose is Edward Albee's play, *Who's Afraid of Virginia Woolf?* The play not only provides a vivid picture of violent dynamics operating within a relationship but also suggests how easily others are drawn into the unfolding drama. Some implications for therapeutic practice are suggested on the basis of the experience of the guests in the play, who were invited to both witness and respond to what was unfolding before them.

Chapter 9 concludes this section of the book with an examination of the results of a clinical research project that looked at the impact of bereavement on the couple relationship and its capacity to act as a secure base for the partners. Drawing on this experience, Lynne Cudmore and Dorothy Judd consider the trauma of child death and its impact on parents as individuals and on their relationship as a couple. The significance of how past losses were managed is highlighted for the individuals, and for the capacity of their partnership to act as a secure base that allowed them to experience and express their grief together and apart. They conclude with some observations about the impact of trauma on the responses of therapists and researchers, and ask about the professional and personal bases that provide the necessary platforms from which to engage with painful experience.

Their observations form a natural bridge to the concluding section of the book. Part III considers the professional, organisational and wider contexts that can support and undermine couples and those who try to help them. It may surprise some readers to come across chapters that address training, institutional and social issues in a book that is primarily concerned with different ways of accessing, understanding and responding to the couple relationship. Yet a moment's reflection will show how mutually sensitive are research and practice endeavours to organisational and cultural influences. There can be no service delivery system that fails to include agency task, although there may be a more faltering commitment to the continuing professional development that equips and supports those who carry it out. There also can be no practitioner or agency that remains unaffected by the nature of the task being carried out. Processing experience, unconscious as well as conscious, requires therapists to lend themselves to being recruited into the inner as well as the outer world dramas of the couples they see *and* – and this is crucial to the therapeutic enterprise – to be able to think about that experience rather than to replicate it. In this endeavour they, too, will need the support and containment – what, in attachment terms, we have been referring to as a secure base – that professional training, ongoing supervision and agency awareness can provide.

In Chapter 10, Felicia Olney draws on her experience of managing and delivering training services for the Tavistock Marital Studies Institute to consider how training and consultation can act as both safe haven and secure base for professional practice. She outlines how environmental pressures both challenge and increase the need for practitioners to have a secure professional base, and examines some opportunities and hazards for trainers in trying to keep clients, practitioners and agencies in mind when developing training programmes. She illustrates her themes from work with individuals and organisations in the private, public and voluntary sectors.

In Chapter 11, Anton Obholzer questions how well the secure base concept travels from the field of child development to the domain of work organisations. He examines the nature of the connections between individuals and the institutions in which they work, and considers what makes for a creative enterprise. He also addresses the impact of work-related anxiety on practitioners and organisations, and extends an invitation to consider the factors that make for vulnerability and resilience at work. Some organisational themes resonate closely with dilemmas of the couple in managing a balance between personal autonomy and collective belonging, and between the formal and informal structuring of relationships.

The book concludes in Chapter 12 with some personal reflections on the interconnections that foster and develop our understanding of what makes for secure partnerships. The couple relationship is not defined exclusively by the inner worlds of the partners. They inhabit an environment that will influence their felt and actual security. That environment may be shaped by a research relationship, or by a therapeutic frame. It will also be shaped by socio-economic and cultural factors. To adapt the aphorism of child psychiatrist and psychoanalyst Donald Winnicott, there is no such thing as a couple, only a couple in a relational context – whether the relations are between internal objects or external people (and recognising the permeability of the boundary separating these two contexts). How couple problems are fashioned from the complex interpenetration of social circumstance and personal meaning is something that has continued to fascinate me (Clulow, 1993, 1995, 1996), and it seems to me self-evident that contextual factors – social and material – are as relevant as intra-psychic realities when thinking about how able the couple relationship is to function as a secure base for partners.

So what does this have to say about the institutionalisation of the couple relationship in marriage? Because partnerships are open systems that mediate between the inner worlds of the partners and the environment which supports – or fails to support – them as a couple, their capacity to operate as a secure base cannot be thought about in isolation from the broader contexts that influence how women and men relate to each other. Some argue that the institution of marriage has undermined that base and become the cause of its own demise through perpetuating patriarchal structures, demarcations and attitudes that are deeply at odds not only with contemporary socioeconomic realities but also with the aspirations of women and men today (whose assumptions about gender roles are quite different from those when marriage was at its peak). Others observe that marriage is a public symbol of, and support for, the private commitment partners make to each other, a commitment that is likely to be the most important they ever make in their lives.

Whatever position one adopts in relation to this and other questions that concern the synergy between inner and outer realities, experience and meaning result from an interplay between the two. This is the domain of both attachment theory and psychoanalysis, and the message of hope is that, for good or ill, relationships have the power to affect relationships.

Part I

Conceptualising the couple in attachment terms

Chapter 1

Patterns of relating in the couple

James Fisher and Lisa Crandell

This chapter aims to offer a description of our attempt to conceptualise attachment in couple relationships, and to provide a brief discussion of the implications this may have for the capacity for intimacy. In the past two decades, Mary Main and colleagues have conducted seminal research directed at understanding the expression of attachment in adulthood (George et al., 1985; Main et al.,1985). They have developed the Adult Attachment Interview (AAI) which assesses 'an individual's state of mind with respect to attachment' (Main and Goldwyn, 1994: 1) and have investigated how representational models of attachment are related to dyadic functioning in parent–child relationships. We asked ourselves how one might extend this approach to an examination of attachment in couple relationships. This has led us to the notion of what we are calling 'complex' attachment.

Although some researchers have begun to expand and develop the approach which underpins the AAI for the study of adult couple relationships, these studies are at an early stage, especially with clinical populations (Cohn et al., 1992; Crowell and Treboux, 1995; Hazan and Shaver, 1994; Kobak and Hazan, 1991). To our knowledge, no-one has yet attempted to connect the AAI methodology with an object relations psychoanalytic approach to the adult couple relationship. Those familiar with the problems of psychoanalytically oriented research into intersubjective psychological processes will recognise the significant difficulties inherent in this endeavour (Shapiro and Emde, 1995). However, there is a remarkably widespread interest in the AAI among therapists from a psychoanalytic perspective, strengthening the potential links between psychoanalysis and the world of empirical research (Hobson, 1995; Patrick et al., 1994; Fonagy et al., 1991a; Fonagy et al., 1993a; Main, 1993). Therefore it was also our aim to construct a conceptual model which would reflect our psychodynamic understanding of the couple, from what is generally termed an object relations approach (Ruszczynski, 1993).

With these goals in mind, we shall now turn to the ideas and research that have formed the basis of our thinking. There is a growing consensus that the quality of a person's primary attachments in childhood is intimately linked with patterns of interpersonal relatedness throughout the life-span. In the past decade, empirical evidence has emerged to support the position of Bowlby, who stated: 'On the way in which an individual's attachment behaviour becomes organised within his personality turns the pattern of affectional bonds he makes during his life' (1980: 41).

The evidence for this assertion has come from two strands of investigation. One tradition of research has been based on observations of infants and their primary caregivers. The aim has been to identify patterns of infant social behaviour that are taken to reflect an underlying attachment organisation, and to trace the developmental sequelae of these patterns. The second strand of research has involved a shift away from behavioural observations of infants and caregivers to the study of adults' mental representations of attachment relationships. Here the focus has been on the manner in which individuals mentally organise and think about their childhood attachment relationships, and how this influences the quality and nature of their relationships in adulthood. In other words, it is not the quality of primary attachments in childhood itself that shapes adult interpersonal relationships, but rather the 'mental representations' of those attachments which are critical for adult intimate relationships.

Both traditions are relevant for our focus on attachment in couples, and each has implications for thinking about a person's capacity for intimacy. Therefore, we shall address each methodological approach in turn.

BEHAVIOURAL OBSERVATIONS OF INFANTS AND CAREGIVERS

The Strange Situation Test or SST (Ainsworth et al., 1978) has become the standard measure for assessing attachment security in the infant–caregiver dyad. In the SST, a caregiver and 12–18-month-old infant are introduced to a laboratory room supplied with toys. For 20 minutes the dyad engages in a series of standardised phases. Seven brief sequences, each lasting a matter of minutes, are recorded on film:

- a caregiver and infant are introduced into an unfamiliar room with toys in it;
- they are joined by a female stranger;
- the caregiver leaves the infant with the stranger;
- the caregiver returns and the stranger leaves;
- the caregiver leaves;
- the stranger returns;
- the caregiver returns.

In response to the two separation and reunion sequences with the caregiver, infants are classified into one of three primary attachment categories.

Infants classified as 'secure' may or may not exhibit distress when separated from their caregiver. If they are distressed, they seek contact with the caregiver upon reunion. They are effectively comforted by this contact so that they become settled and return to play. Secure infants who are not distressed during the separation, typically greet their caregiver with delight upon reunion, making a bid for emotional contact with a smile and/or gesture. There is a symmetry with respect to the infant's expression of the need for either physical or emotional contact with the caregiver and the reception of that contact in such a way that the infant is content.

Infants classified as 'ambivalent' exhibit marked distress upon separation and generally seek contact with the caregiver upon reunion. However, unlike the distressed 'secure' infants, these infants are not settled by their caregiver's attempt to comfort them. They continue to fuss and cry, simultaneously seeking physical contact and resisting it. They do not settle emotionally or return to play. In this system there is asymmetry between the infant's expression of the need for contact and the reception of that contact such that the infant remains in a state of discontent.

Infants classified as 'avoidant' generally show no or minimal distress during separation. However, unlike the non-distressed secure infants, these infants typically avoid their caregivers upon reunion. In many cases, the avoidance is pronounced and present even when the caregiver makes repeated attempts to engage the infant. Also, unlike their secure counterparts, these infants generally exhibit restricted affect. This is quite striking in its own right. In addition, there are now several studies showing that avoidant infants have elevated heart rates and galvanic skin responses that indicate physiological arousal, despite their rather bland affective presentation. In this system we might say that there is a discrepancy between the infant's internal emotional state and his or her external affective presentation.

In more recent years, a fourth category, 'disorganised', has been identified (Main and Solomon, 1987; Main and Hesse, 1990). These infants exhibit a disorganised behavioural strategy for responding to the stress of the situation and demonstrate peculiar and/or competing behaviours (for example, beginning to approach the parent upon reunion but then dropping prone onto the floor). Infants who are classified as disorganised are also given an alternative classification in one of the three primary categories.

There are a number of studies tracing the sequelae of infant attachment organisation on personality functioning and the quality of interpersonal relating in later years (for example, Arend et al., 1979; Cassidy, 1988; Londerville and Main, 1981). These studies indicate that insecure attachment is associated with difficulties in social competence and impaired peer relations in childhood. The findings are consistent with the idea that the quality of the parent–infant attachment relationship lays the foundation for social development in later childhood. The question then arises, 'what about adulthood?' Is there any evidence to suggest that attachment continues to impart an influence on relationship patterns later in life? Indeed, what *is* attachment in adulthood, and how might we assess it?

ADULTS' MENTAL REPRESENTATIONS OF ATTACHMENT AND DYADIC FUNCTIONING

A fundamental assumption of attachment theory is that, from early attachment experiences, an 'internal working model' of relationships is constructed (Bowlby, 1969, 1973, 1980) and that it is this model (which is primarily unconscious) that is carried forward and re-enacted in subsequent relationships. Therefore, as the focus moves from identifying behavioural patterns of attachment in infancy to mapping the influences of attachment in adulthood, there is a shift to the level of mental representations of attachment (Main et al., 1985).

The most sophisticated and well-validated measure for assessing representational models of attachment in adulthood is the Adult Attachment Interview (AAI). On the AAI, adults are asked to describe their relationships with their parents in childhood. They are asked to provide adjectives that characterise the parent–child relationship and to provide illustrative examples of memories that support those adjectives. Similarly, they are asked to describe incidents involving being ill, hurt and separated from parents. Finally they are asked how these relationships may have influenced their personality, and for their understanding of why their parents behaved as they did. The interviews are audio-taped and transcribed verbatim. The transcripts are then rated for the coherence of the subject's discourse using the criteria of quality, quantity, relation and manner (Main and Goldwyn, 1994). Four categories have been identified that parallel the infant classifications delineated by the SST.

Individuals classified as secure (referred to as 'free to evaluate') share a common organisation of thought regarding their early parent–child relationships. They demonstrate a flexible and reflective manner of thinking and conversing about these relationships, have access to specific memories, value early attachment experiences, integrate positive and negative aspects of their parents into a coherent presentation and acknowledge the influence of those experiences on their adult personality. Individuals classified as 'dismissing' have difficulty accessing specific childhood memories, have restricted affect, devalue the importance of early attachment experiences and present an idealised or contradictory presentation of their early parent–child relationships. Individuals classified as 'preoccupied' (also referred to as 'enmeshed') have access to specific memories but are flooded by the negative content of these memories and are unable to integrate their experiences into a coherent understanding of the parent–child relationship. Their organisation of thought is typically confused, disjointed, entangled and marked by a preoccupied anger towards their parents. Like the disorganised infants in the SST, some adults on the AAI demonstrate a disorganised, disorientated organisation of thought that is specifically related to issues of death, abuse and/or other instances of trauma. They are classified 'unresolved/ disorganised' and also given an alternative classification. (Crowell and Treboux provide further details of the AAI, including its psychometric properties, in Chapter 2.)

How is attachment, as assessed by the SST in infancy, related to representational models of attachment in adulthood? There are now a number of studies reporting that parental representational models of attachment are significantly related to infant SST classifications, even when parents are given the AAI before the birth of their child (for example, Fonagy et al., 1991a). In other words, the model of attachment that an individual has at the level of mental representation predicts attachment behaviour of his or her child at one year of age. This connection between parental representations of attachment and parent–child patterns of relating has been an important and intriguing finding.

More recently, researchers and clinicians have begun asking whether these representational models of attachment might also influence and/or reflect the quality of intimate relationships in adulthood. The studies that are emerging suggest this is the case. Couples in which there are two insecure partners show more negativity and conflict, less constructive patterns of communication, poorer marital adjustment and greater difficulty regulating affect than couples where at least one of the partners is secure (Cohn et al., 1992; Kobak and Hazan, 1991; Paley et al., 1995; Pianta et al., 1995). It is a curious finding that couples with one secure partner seem to function in a similar manner to couples with two secure partners (although see Chapters 2 and 4 for data suggesting that gender can act as a differentiating variable). It has led us to question what it is about a secure state of mind in relation to attachment that affords the capacity for more adaptive forms of relating, and what attachment means in the context of adult intimate relationships.

COMPLEX ATTACHMENT

Both the SST and the AAI refer to attachment relationships in childhood. Whether we are talking about an infant responding to separations from and reunions with his or her caregiver, or the manner in which an adult recalls and describes parental relationships from childhood, the focus is on an individual's attachment experiences *vis-à-vis* the attachment figure. When distressed, the child turns to the parent for comfort and reassurance. Or again, the adult recalls the memories of the times s/he turned (or didn't turn) to the parent. In each case, one individual is in the dependent position and the other is in the depended-on position. In this sense, the attachment is unidirectional.

We are proposing, in common with other attachment researchers, that in adult couple relationships each partner functions as an attachment figure for the other. In this way, the attachment system is bidirectional. In the ideal form, each partner can tolerate the anxieties of being dependent on the other and also being depended on by the other. As the exigencies of the relationship require, the partners can move empathically and flexibly between the dependent and depended-upon positions. In this way, each partner experiences both the position of the 'infant', who is emotionally dependent upon the attachment figure, and that of the attachment figure who provides comfort and reassurance to the 'infant'. It is this dual nature of attachment in the couple that has prompted us to use the term 'complex attachment' to indicate that this system has an added dimension compared with attachment in parent–child dyads.

We anticipate that the quality of complex attachment in the couple will be strongly influenced by each partner's representational models of attachment. That is, we expect secure states of mind in relation to childhood attachment relationships to be related to this capacity for reciprocity in the couple relationship, whereas insecure states of mind will be related to fixed positions and rigid patterns of relating. For example, in couples where there is a dismissing partner, it may be that the individual functions well in the depended-on position but is unable to tolerate the dependent position. However, we note the findings reported in Chapter 2 cautioning against assuming that representations of attachment will be the same across different relational domains.

On the basis of pilot data, a research team at the Tavistock Marital Studies Institute (TMSI) has worked at developing an instrument for assessing the idea of complex attachment and exploring how it may be related to couple functioning. The Couple Attachment Joint Interview (CAJI) is a semi-structured clinical interview that is derived from the AAI and has a similar format of probing different aspects of attachment. It differs from the Current Relationship Interview described in Chapter 2, and the Couple Attachment Interview described in Chapter 4, in that it is addressed towards and conducted jointly with both partners as if they were an entity. From this standpoint it asks about attachment-related issues in the partnership. For instance, how does the couple describe their ways of responding to illness, loss and separations? Do they feel they can depend on each other, and do they provide detailed descriptions in support of those beliefs? During the interview, do they demonstrate a capacity to see and consider the partner's position? Unlike the AAI, which activates an individual's representational model of attachment with respect to a previous caregiver, the CAJI is in some ways more like the SST, or rather, like two SSTs happening simultaneously, with each partner in potentially reversible roles. The difference is that the coder's attention is directed towards joint representations of the partnership as well as observed behaviour, thus distinguishing it from the SST and the Secure Base Scoring System described in the next chapter. Another differentiating factor is that it attempts to capture the security of the relationship as a whole rather than the attachment status of each partner in relation to it – it thereby aims to be a measure of couple functioning. The resulting couple 'template' of complex attachment is like two overlapping individual attachment templates, if one pictures a 'template' as a configuration of behaviour and mental representations. The CAJI will remain a concept until the coding manual is developed into a reliable research tool.

Based on our conceptualisation of complex attachment, and drawing from the patterns of attachment delineated by the SST and AAI, we anticipate that it will be possible to identify patterns of couple attachment which correspond with variations in couple functioning that are familiar to those assessing couples clinically. These are described below. We wish to emphasise that these are patterns that we expect to be able to identify, not patterns that have already been identified.

Secure couple attachment

Secure couple attachment involves an ability to shift freely between the dependent and depended-on positions. There is a corresponding empathic appreciation of the partner's thoughts and feelings in both these positions. Like secure attachment in the infant–parent attachment, there is an open expression of the need for comfort and contact, as well as an open reception of that contact. This is true for both partners. In this way, not only is there symmetry within the individual, there is also symmetry within the system. Finally, the partners will be moderately to highly aware of the effects of these experiences on both the self and the other as they move between these two positions.

Insecure couple attachment

We expect there to be three distinct patterns of insecure couple attachment. What they share in common is the lack of flexibility, mutuality and the reversible bidirectionality characteristic of secure couple attachment. For example, in insecure couple attachment there is a marked degree of asymmetry and rigidity in the relationship, with one partner typically in one position and the other partner in the other position, with little movement between them. They will show little awareness of the nature of the other's experiences or of the effects of those experiences on either the self or the other. How disorganised attachment features in the couple attachment system has yet to be formulated (although some thoughts about this are offered in Chapter 7), so we will keep our focus on the three broad categories of insecure attachment.

Dismissing/dismissing couple attachment

The parent–child relationship histories of individuals classified as dismissing typically involve strong rejection of dependency needs. Consequently, the dismissing individual has learned to cut off from feelings of dependency and vulnerability. Typically, such individuals present as hyper-independent and self-sufficient, much like the avoidant baby in the SST who appears to be composed, competent and content to be left alone in a strange environment. But this is more of a pseudo-independence than a natural independence – a fleeing from dependency rather than a developmental acquisition of independence. Because it is a defensive posture, there is extreme sensitivity to any expressions of dependency, and experiences which trigger the denied or repressed feelings of neediness and dependency are perceived as threatening. This has implications for the couple attachment system.

The dismissing state of mind is a disavowal of dependency in the self as well as the other. If there are expressions of dependency by the other, it arouses the partner's own dependency needs that have been exiled from consciousness. Thus, the model in a mutually dismissing couple is that dependency is forbidden and the unconscious couple 'contract' is that 'I am not dependent on you and you are not dependent on me'. In essence, both partners collude in a pattern which pretends that it has eradicated both the dependent and the depended-on positions from the relationship. If both are able to comply with the implicit 'contract', there seems to be no conflict, or at least the conflict is avoided. Things may appear to function smoothly unless the system is disrupted (for example, by unemployment, birth of a baby, or illness), at which point the couple 'contract' breaks down. It is important to note that the avoidant infant shows little emotion or concern in the SST but demonstrates more crying and angry behaviour towards the caregiver in the home. Similarly, these dismissing couple relationship patterns may be marked by episodes of anger and resentment that erupt in other, seemingly unprovoked contexts.

Preoccupied/preoccupied couple attachment

Historically, preoccupied individuals were typically involved in parent–child relationships which were role-reversing and/or inconsistent. Consequently their dependency needs were responded to, but in either an inverted or a sporadic manner. In the case of role-reversal, the parent could 'allow' the child's dependency (unlike the dismissing parent) because s/he felt vulnerable and needy. In this system, the child becomes an extension of the parent as well as an object for alleviating the parent's own distress. When the parent is inconsistently responsive the child has the experience that sometimes its needs are met, whereas at other times they are either rejected or ignored. Thus the child learns to exaggerate and intensify the bid for help in order to elicit a response from the parent. The child may also become hyper-vigilant about the presence of the attachment figure and feel chronically deprived.

This state of mind in the couple attachment system translates into a perpetual feeling of deprivation, and a complementary conviction that the other can never satiate the need for comfort. Like the ambivalent infant, the preoccupied adult seeks and demands emotional contact in the couple relationship, but is unsatisfied and angry in relation to that contact, thus resisting the very emotional contact being sought. In this couple pattern there is a high level of open disagreement and conflict because each partner, while demanding that the other satisfy their chronic and insatiable dependency needs, at the same time rejects any response as inadequate. In this pairing there is the asymmetry within the individual that is characteristic of the ambivalent position, as well as asymmetry in the system, as each partner competes for the dependent position while simultaneously resisting it.

Dismissing/preoccupied couple attachment

We have reason to suppose that this is a common pattern in couples presenting for therapy, and it may be a gender-specific pattern. This system is also highly conflictual, with the preoccupied partner typically expressing most of the discontent, while the dismissing partner believes that the only problem with the relationship is the other's discontent. They both agree that the dismissing partner avoids being dependent. However, the dismissing state of mind also attacks any expression of dependency needs by the other. Thus there is an inherent conflict in this system, with the preoccupied partner feeling chronically deprived and emotionally abandoned, and the dismissing partner expressing disdain towards the other's expression of dependency needs. As the preoccupied partner escalates and intensifies the appeal to have dependency needs met, the dismissing partner's defensive response is also escalated.

Secure/insecure couple attachment

With the above categories in mind, let us return to the question about what happens when a secure partner is paired with either a dismissing or a preoccupied partner. It may be that the presence of a secure partner, by virtue of the capacity to assume both the dependent and the depended-on positions, continually challenges the tendency of the preoccupied individual to assume the dependent position, and the dismissing individual to assume neither position. Perhaps, through the creation of a corrective emotional experience, the insecure partner in a relationship with a secure partner is able to engage in a more flexible and balanced way. Perhaps it is also true that under certain circumstances the pull goes in the opposite direction and the secure individual becomes more entrenched and inflexible, in keeping with the tendency of the insecure partner. Chapters 2 and 4 provide interesting evidence about how gender can affect which way things go.

'COMPLEX ATTACHMENT' AND OBJECT RELATIONS THEORY

We are now in a position to consider the links between a psychoanalytical view of couple dynamics and the understanding of intimacy in terms of what we are calling 'complex' attachment patterns. Bretherton pointed out the roots of such an enterprise:

> The time has come when the psychoanalytical origins of attachment theory are coming into sharper focus. Thus attachment theory can now more clearly be seen as a theory of interpersonal relationship in the lineage of object relations theory, incorporating much from ethology, but also shedding new light on and reworking from a new and more rigorous perspective the issues with which Klein, Fairbairn, and Winnicott had also been wrestling.
>
> (1991: 27)

In the Kleinian view of primary object relations there is a fundamental link between Oedipal dynamics and what Melanie Klein called the depressive position. Britton has suggested that the Oedipal triangular relationship provides the basis for the development of the capacity to be an individual in an intimate relationship. He argues that the capacity to tolerate the anxieties of the recognition of the parental relationship itself creates a boundary for the internal world, making possible what he calls a 'triangular space':

> It includes . . . the possibility of being a participant in a relationship and observed by a third person as well as being an observer of a relationship between two people . . . The capacity to envisage a benign parental relationship influences the development of a space outside the self capable of being observed and thought about, which provides the basis for a belief in a secure and stable world.
>
> (1989: 86–7)

Britton goes on to make clear that the experience of ambivalence and the developing capacity for tolerating the anxieties associated with ambivalence are central to this process:

> If the link between the parents perceived in love and hate can be tolerated in the child's mind, it provides him with a prototype for an

object relationship of a third kind in which he is a witness and not a participant. A third position then comes into existence from which object relationships can be observed. Given this, we can also envisage being observed. This provides us with a capacity for seeing ourselves in interaction with others and for entertaining another point of view whilst retaining our own, for reflecting on ourselves whilst being ourselves.

(1989: 87)

It might be suggested that this could be a marker of a desired outcome in psychotherapy with couples: that is, an increased capacity to do this for each partner *vis-à-vis* the other. We suggest that this psychoanalytic understanding of development, which forms a core aspect of our psychotherapeutic work with distressed couples (Fisher, 1993), has a resonance with the research understanding of the quality of the mental representation of attachment in the individual rated as secure on the AAI. Moreover, this capacity is central to the 'complex' couple attachment pattern we have described as secure in the CAJI.

We cannot within the constraints of this chapter develop these ideas further. Our intention here is only to indicate something of how our nascent research instrument might be linked with the clinical assessment of couples who present for therapy at the TMSI. In this way, we hope to pursue an in-depth analysis of the connections between clinical judgements and couple attachment patterns.

It might be useful to end this chapter with clinical examples of one of the couple attachment patterns that we have just outlined. This may give some idea of the cross-fertilisation between our research understanding of complex attachment patterns and our clinical understanding of the disturbances in the capacity for intimacy. We have chosen to provide a few clinical descriptors of couples in therapy who were classified as preoccupied/preoccupied on the AAI. From a psychoanalytic perspective, these couples can be seen to be functioning in a way that is characterised by the excessive use of primitive defences such as splitting, projective identification, idealisation and denial.

Often in these couples, the relationship seems to have no real beginning. It typically begins inadvertently, as when one individual suddenly finds him or herself without accommodation and moves in with the other, with neither partner feeling as though they made a decision about the partnership. While they both express intense dissatisfaction with the relationship, each partner feels that ending it is tantamount to disaster. They describe being drawn in by the other irresistibly in a way that leaves each feeling defined by the other, as if the other were holding an essential part of the self which could not be recovered. One perceptive observer said of this attachment pattern that it was 'a perversion of Proust'.

Often their therapy sessions are replete with psychological jargon that creates meaningless, entangled communications. It requires great skill and presence of mind for therapists not to become lost with these couples in a caricature of therapy. In the face of this chaotic, tense environment, the experience of our clinical staff has been that therapists become more forceful and bold than is characteristic, perhaps to prevent themselves from being overwhelmed in a whirlpool of confusion.

In this context, our understanding that developed from research discussions of complex attachment patterns became therapeutically important. In these couples, each of the partners was 'preoccupied' with the relationship and with the other, either passively or angrily, but also complained of feeling trapped by the other's preoccupation. Neither could decide to let go of the relationship, being either too angrily preoccupied with it, or too passive to take any action. When the couples, in different ways and to different degrees, became dependent on the therapists and the therapy, it became possible for the therapists to give voice to the couple's desperation to leave the damaging relationship. Paradoxically, this could also mean leaving the couple therapy. 'Giving voice' was only possible when the therapists, as secure attachment figures, could also tolerate the anxieties of being depended on to hold firm to the need to work towards a thoughtful ending. In most cases this is what happened, but very slowly, in fits and starts, and with incredibly high levels of anxiety.

We could describe this anxiety as Oedipal anxiety. In our view the capacity to be an individual, to be separate and hence capable of a relationship with another, rests on mastering the anxieties of the triangle. In brief, these are anxieties of being both excluded from a couple and of being part of a couple which excludes the third. The mastering of these anxieties results in a sense of psychological space. Conversely, the failure to master these anxieties is experienced as a desperate lack of a sense of psychological or emotional space to think, to be different and to be separate: in other words, an absence of space in which to enter or leave a relationship. We believe these anxieties and their resolution are closely linked to those associated with the experience of ambivalence, the feelings of love and hate directed towards the same person. In the end, these anxieties are only ever provisionally resolved, and they are commonly, and sometimes even dramatically, revived in the intimacy of a couple relationship. For this reason they are characteristic of many presentations for help by couples having difficulties with their relationship.

Couples in which the partners have a capacity to tolerate such anxieties in themselves and in each other – in which each can express dependency needs and tolerate the other's dependency – can be described as secure. There is, of course, much more to say about a psychoanalytic understanding of these dynamics, and about the notion of complex couple attachment. All we mean to do with these introductory observations is to suggest how research and therapy can work towards a satisfying and constructive marriage between frames of reference which are often felt to be antithetical. To put it in the language of one of our collaborators on the project, Peter Hobson, we want to explore 'how non-analytic research might complement psychoanalytic investigations of inter-subjective psychological processes' (1995: 167)

Chapter 2

Attachment security in adult partnerships

Judith Crowell and Dominique Treboux

Bowlby and Ainsworth made clear statements about the importance of attachment in adult life. According to Bowlby, human attachments play 'a vital role . . . in the life of man from the cradle to the grave' (1969: 208). Ainsworth (1985, 1991) highlighted the function of the attachment behaviour system in adult relationships, emphasising the secure base phenomenon at its core. She stated that a secure attachment relationship facilitates functioning and competence outside of the relationship. She noted there is 'a seeking to obtain an experience of security and comfort in the relationship with the partner. If and when such security and comfort are available, the individual is able to move off from the secure base provided by the partner, with the confidence to engage in other activities' (Ainsworth, 1991: 38). Attachment relationships are distinguished from other adult relationships as those that provide feelings of security and a sense of belonging, without which there is loneliness and restlessness. This is in contrast to relationships that provide guidance or companionship, sexual gratification, opportunities to feel needed or to share common interests or experiences, feelings of competence, alliance and assistance (Ainsworth, 1985, 1991; Weiss, 1974, 1982).

Although Bowlby and Ainsworth identified the normative elements of the attachment system in adult life, they provided relatively few guidelines for its specific function and expression. Despite great attention to the study of adult attachment in the past ten to fifteen years, the research has emphasised and explored individual differences, the patterns of attachment and attachment representations (Crowell and Treboux, 1995; Hazan and Shaver, 1987, 1994; Main and Goldwyn, 1994), and has not focused on normative development. In this chapter, we propose to return to the ideas expressed by Bowlby and Ainsworth, and address the normative elements of the attachment system, its development, function, and manifestations in adult partnerships, from both theoretical and empirical perspectives.

ATTACHMENT THEORY AND ADULT ATTACHMENT

In the development of attachment theory, Bowlby preserved Freud's hypothesis that the infant–parent relationship is a prototype for later love relationships (Bowlby, 1958; Freud, 1949/53; Waters et al., 1991). This tenet of attachment theory can serve as a guide in the investigation of the adult attachment system.

First, and most importantly, this hypothesis suggests the attachment system is active in *both* the parent–child relationship and later love relationships, and that in infancy, childhood and adulthood, attachment relationships are powerful influences on behaviour, cognitions and emotions. Such relationships are not given up voluntarily or completely; the disruption of an attachment relationship is painful and leads to grief and mourning (Bowlby, 1969; Freud, 1949/53). Just as it is in childhood, Ainsworth (1991) described the secure base phenomenon as the core of the attachment system in adult attachment relationships. That is, a secure relationship with an attachment figure perceived as available and responsive provides a base for confident exploration (Ainsworth, 1985, 1991; Ainsworth et al., 1978; Weiss, 1982). It is important to note that in focusing on the secure base phenomenon, Ainsworth and Weiss provide a relatively narrow definition of an attachment relationship, a definition that does not include all aspects of close relationships. This definition suggests what to look for (and what not to look for) in either empirical or clinical exploration of the attachment system in adults.

Although attachment theory supports the level of understanding of the prototype hypothesis described above, Bowlby and Ainsworth did not offer more complex interpretations. The nature of later love relationships was broadly specified (Bowlby, 1969), and possible differences among close and loving relationships were not addressed: for example, a parent/adult–child relationship versus an adult partnership. Nevertheless, the prototype hypothesis suggests that the pattern or quality of attachment in the parent–infant relationship may be similar to or even influence the pattern or quality of attachment in later love relationships. An extreme view of this interpretation suggests that whatever happens in infancy is fated to be played out again in later life regardless of what happens in between. A more moderate view suggests that continuity of early and late relationship patterns can be explained in two ways. First, there is an expectation of relatively stable ongoing caregiver–child interactions (Sameroff and Chandler, 1975; Waters et al., 1991; Waters et al., in press). Second, Bowlby hypothesised the development of mental models or attachment representations that would operate outside of conscious awareness and serve as guides to behaviour, thoughts and feelings in attachment-related situations.

The secure base relationship

Ainsworth and colleagues identified specific behavioural components of secure base use by the infant and secure base support by the caregiver (see Chapter 1). These behavioural interactions occur routinely and repeatedly in the course of ordinary life, as well as operating in more emergent situations (Bretherton, 1985). In the context of repeated experiences with the caregiver, the child develops expectations of his or her availability and responsiveness. In complement to the caregiver's behaviour, the child signals his or her needs clearly and consistently, seeking proximity and contact with the caregiver. The contact is maintained until the child is comforted. The child is able to re-establish equilibrium and return to normal activity and optimal exploration.

In the most adaptive or secure relationship, the caregiver maintains an ongoing pattern of support for exploration, and responsiveness in times of stress and danger. The caregiver is available and sensitive in detecting signals, correctly understands the child's need, and gives an appropriate response in a timely fashion. The way in which the caregiver understands the child's need may not match the child's expressed wishes. The caregiver presumably has a larger frame of understanding than and a different perspective from that of the child, and hence her responsiveness may be appropriate and timely even if it does not directly match the expressed desires of the child.

In the context of repeated interactions with the parent, individual differences emerge in the expression of the child's attachment behaviour, differences that reflect expectations about the infant's own behaviour and parent's likely behaviour in various situations (Ainsworth et al., 1978; Bretherton, 1985). We have described the secure pattern above: the infant seeks and receives protection, reassurance and comfort when stressed. Confident exploration is optimised because of the support and availability of the attachment figure. Insecure patterns (avoidant, ambivalent, disorganised) develop when attachment behaviour is met by rejection, inconsistency, or even threat from the attachment figure, leaving the infant 'anxious' about the caregiver's responsiveness should problems arise. To reduce anxiety, the infant's behaviour comes to fit or complement that of the attachment figure – it is adaptive or strategic within that relationship. Nevertheless, exploration is compromised because of the child's lack of confidence in parental availability and responsiveness.

Attachment representations

Bowlby (1982) hypothesised that individuals develop an attachment representation of the functioning and significance of close relationships – that is, the sum of a person's beliefs and expectations about how attachment relationships operate and what one gains from them. With repeated experiences and interactions with the caregiver(s), certain behaviours and expectations of the young child become automatic, not requiring active or conscious reappraisal for each relevant occasion. The child abstracts a model about how close relationships operate and how they are used in daily life. They are the basis for action in attachment-related situations and, in principle, are open to revision as a function of subsequent significant attachment-related experiences. Because the caregiving environment is usually stable and mutually reinforcing (Sameroff and Chandler, 1975), the models are relatively stable constructs which operate outside awareness, guide behaviour in relationships with parents and influence expectations and strategies as well as behaviour in later relationships.

In childhood, attachment patterns and representations are subject to change only if there is a corresponding change in the quality of parent–child interactions (Bowlby, 1969). However, Bowlby hypothesised that change in attachment patterns could occur in later life through the influence of new emotional relationships (that is, another type of change in the caregiving environment) and the development of formal operational thought. This combination of events would allow the individual to reflect on and reinterpret the meaning of past and present experiences. Incorporation of mental representations within attachment theory allows for a life-span perspective of the attachment behaviour system, providing a way of understanding developmental change in the expression of attachment and its ongoing influence on development and behaviour in relationships.

The secure base phenomenon in adult partnerships

The behavioural components of the secure base phenomenon in adult partnerships can be extrapolated from Ainsworth's outline of infant and parent behaviour (Crowell et al., 1998). The 'child role' can be considered as secure base *use* and the 'parental role' is thought of as secure base *support*. In optimal secure base use, a partner signals his or her needs clearly and consistently until there is a response, approaching the other partner directly for help or support. The support received is comforting. That is, the adult is able to re-establish emotional equilibrium and return to normal activity and exploration. In providing secure base support, the other partner is interested and open to detecting signals, recognises that the partner has a need or is distressed, correctly interprets the need and gives an appropriate response in a timely fashion. One partner's responsiveness to the other's concerns need not exactly match what the partner expresses s/he wants at that moment. It is possible for a partner to give a response which is appropriate and timely even if it does not match the immediate desires of the other, as long as the response considers the well-being of the partner and the relationship as a whole.

We hypothesise that the existence and quality of such exchanges in adult relationships lead to their development as attachment relationships. Just as the attachment relationship in infancy develops out of countless interactions in the course of daily life with a particular caregiver, it seems likely that adults require repetitive interactions of the secure base type for a romantic partnership to develop into an attachment relationship.

A major difference between adult–adult attachment relationships and parent–child relationships is that, as we saw in Chapter 1, the attachment behaviour system in adults is reciprocal. In other words, adult partners are not assigned to or set in the role of 'secure base support/caregiver' or 'secure base use/care seeker'. Both secure base use and secure base support should be observable in adult individuals, and the partners must shift between the two roles. The potential for flexible reciprocity adds complexity to assessment issues in adult attachment from both empirical and clinical perspectives.

Another critical difference rests in the issue of past history. Whereas the parent–infant relationship can be considered 'new', at least from the infant's point of view, both adults in a partnership have had many attachment-related experiences. Integration of past attachment experiences and representations into a new attachment relationship is one of the great challenges for the individuals and the developing relationship. Both partners have been influenced by a history of attachment experiences in three broad domains, although the relative importance of these domains can be debated. The three domains, or sources of influence, can be roughly divided into parent–child attachment relationships, peer and romantic relationship experiences (including the experience of the parents' marriage) and the current adult attachment relationship. What are the implications for the relationship when the new caregiving environment does or does not match the one from which the partners have developed their representations of attachment?

The Stony Brook Attachment Relationship Project was started to investigate these and related issues of adult attachment. It is a longitudinal study of young couples; 157 were recruited just prior to their weddings and 101 were recruited as steadily dating couples. We have used and developed several assessments of attachment that are particularly useful in exploring adult relationships and the secure base phenomenon. In the next sections, we present a brief review of the key measures and early findings from our study.

ASSESSMENTS OF ADULT ATTACHMENT

The Adult Attachment Interview (George et al., 1985)

Exploring their interest in attachment representations, George, Kaplan and Main created the Adult Attachment Interview (AAI) 'to assess the security of the adult's overall working model of attachment, that is, the security of the self in relation to attachment in its generality rather than in relation to any particular present or past relationship' (Main et al., 1985: 78). As we saw in Chapter 1, it assesses adults' representations of attachment based on their discussions of childhood relationships with their parents and the effects of those experiences on their development as adults and as parents. The purpose of the AAI is to demonstrate that 'mental processes vary as distinctively as do behavioural processes' (ibid.) based on the idea that representational processes are reflected in language, itself a form of representational thought. Construct validity and discriminant validity of the AAI have been well established (Crowell and Treboux, 1995; Crowell et al., 1999).

The semi-structured interview elicits information about an adult's early childhood experiences and the perceived influence of those experiences upon subsequent development. Scoring is based upon the quality of parenting experiences in childhood (*in the coder's opinion, not via the expressed views of the adult*), the language used to describe past experiences and the ability to give an integrated, believable account of those experiences and their meaning (Main and Goldwyn, 1994). Hence, the scoring system goes beyond the individual's report of what s/he feels about attachment and attachment experiences by having the goal of tapping processes which are not necessarily available to direct enquiry. Coherence is the core component of the scoring system – the degree to which the narrative is believable and consistent in its content, is relevant, gives enough (but not too much) information to present a clear picture and is free of jargon and other mannerisms (see Table 2.1).

Coding yields classifications of secure-autonomous, insecure-dismissing, and insecure-preoccupied states of mind with respect to attachment. Two other insecure classifications may be given: unresolved state of mind with respect to a loss or abusive experience, and 'cannot classify' due to high insecurity and mixed discourse style. Depending on the research question, studies have used the classifications in a variety of ways (Crowell and Treboux, 1995; Crowell et al., 1999). Discriminant analyses based on the AAI scales of 364 individuals have demonstrated that a continuous score of security is correlated with discourse coherence (Fyffe, 1997). Hence the score of coherence may be effectively used as a score of security.

The Current Relationship Interview (Crowell and Owens, 1996)

The Current Relationship Interview (CRI) is one of several interviews developed to address adult attachment within close relationships. In particular, the CRI was developed as a way to examine the prototype hypothesis and to explore the process by which a new attachment relationship is either integrated into an already existing representation of attachment or a new representation develops. As a narrative assessment, it is intended to examine the influence of the partner's attachment behaviour and ideas on the individual's representation of attachment and his/her own attachment behaviour.

The interview investigates the attachment representation within the adult partnership. The scoring system parallels the AAI scoring system in that

Table 2.1 Adult Attachment Interview classifications (based on Main and Goldwyn, 1994)

	Secure	Dismissing	Preoccupied	Unresolved
Past experiences:	Loving or unloving parents.	Rejecting parents.	Role-reversing parents.	Significant loss. Abuse.
Present state of mind:	Recognises importance of early relationships in development; Balanced view of self and parents; Coherent: believable and consistent.	Minimises or denies effects of early experience; Idealises parents; Emphasis on personal strength; Incoherent: lack of evidence, poor recall.	Preoccupied with parents; Angry or passive; Incoherent: vague, irrelevant, oscillating.	Expresses disbelief; Feelings of causing loss/abuse; Incoherent: disoriented, disorganised, confused.

experiences with the partner, discourse style and believability/coherence are assessed using a number of scales. Rating scales are used to characterise (a) the individual's behaviour, (b) the partner's behaviour and (c) the individual's discourse style, including overall coherence. Scale scores are used to assign classifications that parallel those of the AAI: Secure, Dismissing, Pre-occupied and Unresolved. CRI scale scores reflecting state of mind regarding attachment, and the individual's specific attachment behaviours of secure base support and use, are given primacy in the determination of attachment security rather than the individual's reported feelings about the relationship or the behaviours of the partner (see Table 2.2). As with the AAI, the coherence score is highly correlated with a continuous security score based on discriminant function analysis with 290 individuals.

The Secure Base Scoring System for adults (Crowell et al., 1998)

Secure base behaviour is scored within the Secure Base Scoring System (SBSS) from an observation of partners interacting in a standard couple task. Each partner is asked to identify topics on which the couple disagrees and the frequency with which they disagree. The most frequently discussed topic is then selected from the lists and the couple is asked to discuss it in a 15-minute videotaped session. The disagreement is stressful for both partners and hence likely to activate the attachment system. It is a valid task with strong links to marital research.

The scoring of the interaction involves the identification of one partner, and possibly both, as having a concern, and apparently seeking help, reassurance or comfort from the other in relation to it. Not all interactions involve such issues (some arguments are more philosophical or are problem-solving), but most discussions prompt more personal material and an expression of a concern about the relationship, a personal need or desire for the partner to do something. When a partner is identified in the role of 'secure base user', s/he is scored on each of the following scales: initial clarity of the concern, continued expression of the concern when necessary, approach to the partner with the expectation that the partner will be helpful and ability to be comforted. A summary scale of secure base use is also given that is not an average of scores, but weights some scales more heavily than others and relies also on the coder's opinion.

When one partner expresses a concern and seeks a response from the other, the other partner is put in the role of 'secure base supporter'. S/he is scored on the following scales: interest in the partner's concern, recognition that the partner is distressed, interpretation of the meaning of the partner's distress, and responsiveness. Again, a summary score of secure base support is given. It is not uncommon for partners in this secure base supporter or caregiver role to raise their own concerns in response to the partner's problem. They

Table 2.2 Current Relationship Interview classifications (based on Crowell and Owens, 1996)

	Secure	Dismissing	Preoccupied	Unresolved
Experiences with partner:	Partners' behaviour does not distinguish the classifications.			Loss of or abuse by previous partner.
Present state of mind:	Acknowledges importance of partnership in personal development;	Minimises or denies effects of relationship on self;	Preoccupied with partner;	Strong emphasis on previous relationship;
	Balanced and empathic view of self and partner;	Idealises partner, self or relationship;	Active anger at partner or vague, passive speech;	Confused statements;
	Notes influence on relationship;	Emphasis on independence;	Confusion and ambivalence;	Disoriented/ disorganised speech;
	Clear and coherent;	Describes self as rejecting;	Describes self as involving or controlling;	Describes alterations in current relationship behaviour that are related to previous experiences.
	Valuing of attachment evident in own behaviour.	Incoherent: lack of evidence, remote, terse; materialistic relationship goals.	Incoherent: unclear, irrelevant, oscillating.	

are then scored in the 'secure base use role' and the original secure base user is scored in the 'secure base support' role.

The combination of measures described above can provide insight into how generalised attachment representations based on experiences with parents in childhood relate to attachment representations and attachment behaviour in couples. We have used them to investigate important questions of adult attachment.

EARLY FINDINGS

The findings presented in this chapter explore the attachment system in adults and the prototype hypothesis. Most of the results are from the study of 150 young adult couples recruited within three months of their marriages, and followed across the early years of marriage. The couples were recruited from the general population of a predominantly suburban and rural county of Long Island, New York. The participants were predominantly white, had not been married prior to the current engagement, and had no children at the time of recruitment.

Our results indicate there is modest concordance between partners for attachment status as assessed with the AAI (Owens et al., 1995; Crowell et al., 1995). This finding has been reported in other studies as well (van IJzendoorn and Bakermans-Kranenburg, 1996). The concordance is accounted for by the secure/secure pairings (50–60 per cent for three major classifications). Thus there is some evidence for assortative mating. However, attachment status based on childhood experiences does not appear to be a dominant factor in partner selection for most people. The premarital CRI concordance between partners of the three major classifications is approximately 63 per cent (k = 0.29; p = 0.05).

AAI classifications in the sample are very stable: 86 per cent over 18 months (k = 0.73). CRI classifications are also stable with 66 per cent of the men (k = 0.28; p = 0.05) and 74 per cent of the women (k = 0.49; p = 0.001) having the same classification across an 18-month period from before marriage to after marriage. These findings support the idea that attachment representations are resistant to change, although those related to the current, potentially still developing attachment relationship appear to be somewhat less stable than those based on childhood experiences.

Examining the relation between the AAI and the CRI enables us to understand the potential influence of early attachment relationships on the development of later attachment relationships. Using the coherence scores for each interview as an index of attachment security, there is a correlation between the two types of representations (r = 0.51; Crowell, 1998). Sixty-seven per cent of individuals had matching classifications – that is, they were either secure for both representations or insecure for both. This finding is consistent with the hypothesis that early experience influences later relationships, but not in a 'strong sense'. That is, it suggests that the child's interactions with an attachment figure are not the only framework by which later love relationships can be understood. Rather the findings support the hypothesis that the quality of the current attachment relationship and ongoing interactions, as well as previous experiences with romantic partnerships, influence the construction of attachment representations of the shared relationship.

Couples' security and secure base behaviour

The relations between the couples' secure base behaviour and the AAI and CRI have also been explored (Gao et al., 1996). With respect to secure base behaviour, men and women are equally good at using a secure base or providing secure base support. Engaged men and women classified as secure with the AAI or with the CRI are more likely to be effective in using secure base support, and providing support to the partner, than individuals classified as insecure. Their behaviour is also related to the AAI security of their partners and, to a lesser degree, to the CRI status of their partners. Thus a secure partner of either gender helps an individual both use and provide secure base support (see Table 2.3). No interactions of the individuals' and partners' security status were found for either the AAI or CRI, suggesting that there is no particular type of couple (e.g., insecure/secure versus secure/insecure) that significantly differs from the others.

Couples' AAI security and self-reports of feelings and behaviour in the relationship

With few exceptions, AAI security is not related to individuals' premarital or five-year anniversary reports of their feelings in the relationship (with regard to satisfaction, dedication, constraint, commitment, intimacy and passion) or the reported conflict behaviour of their partners (verbal aggression, physical aggression and threats of abandonment). The exceptions are that men who are AAI insecure were more likely to threaten to leave the relationship premaritally and to be more verbally aggressive premaritally. Their partners also tended to be more likely to threaten to leave the relationship before marriage and to be more verbally aggressive. Secure men felt more committed/ constrained to stay in the relationship before marriage, and men who reported such feelings also tended to have secure partners.

These findings (a detailed breakdown of which is contained in Appendix 1) suggest that, premaritally, individuals' representations of attachment based on childhood experiences (AAI) do relate to their secure base behaviours in interactions with their partners, and with some of the conflict tactics they employ as reported by their partners. Their partners' security status also influences their secure base behaviour. Interestingly, in contrast to their

Table 2.3 2 × 2 Analysis of variance: her security status (secure vs. insecure) and his security status (secure vs. insecure) for the AAI and the CRI with premarital secure base behaviour

Means scores and standard deviations for the AAI

Secure base behaviour	Women		Men		Her security $F(1, 109)$	His security $F(1, 109)$	Interaction $F(1, 109)$
	Secure	Insecure	Secure	Insecure			
Her secure base use	4.3 (1.7)	3.5 (1.6)	4.2 (1.6)	3.7 (1.6)	5.32*	2.80†	ns
Her secure base support	4.5 (1.9)	3.4 (1.7)	4.5 (1.8)	3.6 (1.7)	7.46**	4.72*	ns
His secure base use	4.5 (1.6)	3.6 (1.5)	4.8 (1.5)	3.5 (1.6)	4.54*	14.83***	ns
His secure base support	4.3 (1.8)	3.5 (1.7)	4.7 (1.5)	3.3 (1.8)	3.23†	15.65***	ns

Means scores and standard deviations for the CRI

Secure base behaviour	Women		Men		Her security $F(1, 86)$	His security $F(1, 86)$	Interaction $F(1, 86)$
	Secure	Insecure	Secure	Insecure			
Her secure base use	4.3 (1.7)	3.1 (1.5)	4.2 (1.8)	3.5 (1.6)	9.56**	ns	ns
Her secure base support	4.3 (1.6)	3.2 (1.9)	4.3 (1.7)	3.5 (1.9)	3.95*	3.66†	ns
His secure base use	4.3 (1.6)	3.6 (1.5)	4.8 (1.4)	3.5 (1.6)	2.78†	4.01*	ns
His secure base support	4.4 (1.9)	3.4 (1.6)	4.7 (1.5)	3.3 (1.9)	ns	5.14*	ns

†p = 0.10; *p = 0.05; **p = 0.01; ***p = 0.001

behaviour, individuals' AAI attachment security has little association with the feelings that they report about their relationships.

Couples' CRI security and self-reports of feelings and behaviour in the relationship

Premarital

In contrast to the AAI, CRI security is related to premarital reports of feelings as well as behaviour (see Appendix 1). For the women, premarital self-reports, with the exception of discord, are significantly related to their own CRI security status. In addition, men's CRI security was related to their partners' premarital feelings of satisfaction. Secure men's partners reported less discord and were less verbally aggressive. CRI insecure women married to CRI insecure men were significantly different from women in the other three groups: they were the most verbally aggressive and reported the lowest feelings of intimacy and commitment.

For the men, several of the premarital reports were related to CRI status. Men classified as CRI secure were more satisfied, less verbally aggressive and reported more feelings of dedication, passion and intimacy. Their premarital reports of satisfaction, feelings of constraint and intimacy, as well as their partners' reports of his conflict tactics, were related to the partner's premarital CRI. Men with CRI secure wives were more satisfied and felt more constrained and intimate. The CRI secure wives also reported their partners were less verbally aggressive, less physically aggressive and less likely to threaten to leave.

Five years of marriage

Women's premarital CRIs were unrelated to their self-reports at their five-year anniversaries. However, their spouses' CRI security was related to the women's verbal aggression, such that CRI insecure men reported their wives to be more verbally aggressive than secure men did, and the wives of CRI secure men reported greater feelings of dedication to the relationship. Women in couples in which both partners were insecure reported the lowest feelings of intimacy and dedication after five years.

With respect to husbands' behaviour and feelings after five years of marriage, there were few main effects of premarital CRI security of the men or women. Men with CRI secure wives were reported to be less verbally aggressive and tended to feel more satisfied and constrained. It was noteworthy that men classified premaritally as CRI insecure endorsed significantly greater depressive symptoms than CRI secure men, and CRI insecure men married to insecure wives had more depressive symptoms than men in the other groups. There were several other interaction effects, such that insecure CRI men paired with insecure women were significantly lower in feelings of dedication, constraint, commitment, passion and intimacy than insecure CRI men paired with CRI secure women.

Thus, in contrast to the AAI, CRI security status for both men and women is related to reports of their behaviours and their feelings both concurrently (premarital) and over time (five years later). Couples in which both partners were insecure premaritally stand out as more emotionally distressed, although interestingly, most of their reported behaviour was not significantly different than other pairings.

Couples' AAI and CRI status and marital break-up

Concordance and/or discordance of security status could place couples at risk of marital break-up. However, with respect to the AAI, no such risk appears: couples of all pairings (secure/secure, insecure/secure, etc.) were equally likely to have divorced or separated when marital status was examined five years after the initial assessment. The four groups each had a break-up rate of about 20 per cent (see Table 2.4).

In contrast, CRI security status of couples is related to marital break-up. Couples in which both partners are classified insecure are significantly more

Table 2.4 Couples' security status: AAI and CRI concordance and rates of marital break-up after five years

Couples' security	Still married	Separated/divorced
AAI pairings (n = 146)	n =	n =
Secure/secure	21 (78%)	6 (22%)
Secure woman/insecure man	22 (79%)	6 (21%)
Insecure woman/secure man	24 (80%)	6 (20%)
Insecure/insecure	49 (80%)	12 (20%)
CRI pairings (n = 115)	n =	n =
Secure/secure	28 (87.5%)	4 (12.5%)
Secure woman/insecure man	25 (89%)	3 (11%)
Insecure woman/secure man	13 (81%)	3 (19%)
Insecure/insecure	24 (61.5%)	15 (38.5%)

likely to break up than couples of other types. Therefore, while attachment representations based upon childhood certainly are related to secure base behaviour in the relationship, it is the representation of attachment in the current relationship that is associated with separation and divorce. When both partners were insecure in their descriptions of the attachment elements of the current relationship there was a high rate of marital break-up.

In summary, the relations between secure base behaviour and attachment representations are consistent with predictions from attachment theory. Attachment representations based upon childhood experiences are clearly linked to relationship behaviour, both observed and reported by the couples themselves. The attachment representation of the current relationship, even at the premarital stage, is linked to relationship behaviour and feelings before marriage and into the early years of marriage. These findings support the prototype hypothesis and provide the foundation for further exploration of the secure base phenomenon in adult relationships.

The work we have described can be used to explore how partnerships develop as attachment relationships over time and what benefits accrue to couples with secure attachment relationships. Early findings suggest there may be gender differences. A particularly important extension of this work is to examine the relation between the couple's attachment relationship and their parenting behaviour.

Attachment theory and the secure base phenomenon present us with an ideal: how an attachment relationship works optimally, and what its function is. Such an ideal is appealing and potentially of great value to clinicians attempting to redirect and reframe dysfunctional behaviour, as it provides both a clear rationale for change and a goal towards which to work. Attachment-based clinical work with couples is a new arena for attachment researchers and clinicians that hopefully will be beneficial to all involved.

Chapter 3

Insecure attachment and abusive intimate relationships

Kim Bartholomew, Antonia Henderson and Donald Dutton

A few years ago, we conducted a study in which partners in couple relationships were given multiple attachment interviews over a two-year period (Bartholomew, 1997; Scharfe and Bartholomew, 1994, 1995). We interviewed partners simultaneously, but in separate rooms. What became obvious, when the interviewers later compared notes, was that the most dysfunctional relationships were also the most stable. We had embarked upon this study naively expecting that the more secure individuals were, and the more security they were able to gain from their intimate relationships, the more satisfying and enduring those relationships would be. Instead, we became impressed by how particular forms of insecurity appeared to put individuals at risk of becoming involved in, and having difficulty leaving, problematic and even abusive relationships. This shift in focus led us to pursue research specifically on abusive relationships.

In this chapter we will first discuss relationship abuse (both perpetration and receipt) from an attachment perspective. We will then briefly describe Bartholomew's two-dimensional adult attachment model. Then we will present highlights of four studies that our research team has conducted in the area of attachment and domestic abuse over the past seven years. Since research in this area has tended to focus on perpetrators and victims of abuse in isolation, we will end with a discussion of the relationship context in which abusive behaviour develops.

AN ATTACHMENT PERSPECTIVE ON RELATIONSHIP ABUSE

Attachment theory was proposed by John Bowlby (1969) to explain why humans, and many other animals, seem to have an innate tendency to form strong emotional bonds or attachments to particular others. Bowlby proposed that infant attachment behaviour, such as crying, clinging and seeking contact, is regulated by the *attachment behavioural system*, an innate motivational system. The goal of this system is presumably to promote the survival of young children by ensuring that they maintain proximity to a caregiver (the *attachment figure*), especially under conditions of threat. Thus, when children feel anxious or afraid they will seek closeness and support from a caregiver; if the caregiver is successful in providing a sense of security, the attachment behaviour will be terminated. This is the *safe haven* function of attachment relationships. In addition, attachment relationships function to provide a *secure base*, an ongoing sense of emotional security that facilitates exploration of the environment. Hazan and Shaver (1987) observed that these same attachment dynamics characterise adult intimate relationships, although in adult relationships, unlike parent–child relationships, attachment is typically reciprocal; that is, as described in the previous chapters, partners function as attachment figures for one another. Research suggests that in adulthood sexual or romantic partners most often serve as the primary attachment figure for one another (Hazan and Zeifman, 1994; Trinke and Bartholomew, 1997).

Bowlby further proposed that repeated interactions with caregivers are internalised in *internal working models* or schemas about the self, close others, and the self in relation to others (1969, 1973, 1980). If caregivers have been consistently responsive and supportive, children are hypothesised to develop positive expectations of close others and confidence in their own worthiness as someone deserving of support. Such secure models then facilitate the development of secure attachment relationships in adulthood, relationships that provide a safe haven and secure base. In contrast, a family history characterised by various forms of inconsistent and rejecting caregiving would be expected to give rise to less secure models. Through an active process of construction, these insecure models would tend to lead individuals to recreate insecure patterns in their adult relationships.

Receipt of relationship abuse

Bowlby proposed that the strength of attachment bonds is unrelated to the quality of the attachment relationship. In adult intimate relationships, where partners are typically primary attachment figures, abused individuals are likely to feel strongly attached to their abusive partners. This attachment makes it difficult for them to leave these relationships, even in the absence of external constraints or obstacles, and they may even seek proximity to their abusers. Bowlby further suggested that situations of threat and fear activate the attachment system and thereby may lead to the formation of especially strong attachment bonds, even when the attachment figure is the source of threat. Thus, abused children typically show signs of being strongly (albeit insecurely) attached to their abusive caregivers. The difficulty of leaving abusive relationships will be further exacerbated if past experiences have led individuals to feel that they are not likely to receive better treatment in other relationships or may even be to blame for the abuse directed toward them.

Perpetration of relationship abuse

Bowlby (1982) viewed interpersonal anger as arising from frustrated attachment needs and functioning as a form of protest directed at regaining or maintaining contact with the attachment figure. In adults, such protest is likely to be directed at romantic partners and can take the form of verbal abuse, control of a partner's behaviour and even violence. Such abusive behaviour is most likely to be precipitated by real or imagined threats of rejection, separation or abandonment by the partner. As Bowlby stated, 'violence . . . can be understood as the distorted and exaggerated versions of behaviour that is potentially functional' (1984: 12).

Individuals whose attachment histories have made them especially susceptible to anxiety, separation and rejection may be most likely to perceive ambiguous behaviour by a partner as rejecting and unsupportive, and they may be most at risk for becoming abusive. This perspective is consistent with a large body of literature suggesting that abusive men tend to be insecure and overly dependent on their partners, and that jealousy and fears of separation are common triggers of abusive episodes (Dutton, 1995).

A two-dimensional, four-category model of attachment

In our research examining attachment in abusive relationships, we have worked with a four-category, two-dimensional model of attachment (Bartholomew, 1990; Bartholomew and Horowitz, 1991). In this model we have looked to Bowlby's conceptual analysis of the internal working models of self and other to provide a framework for exploring the potential range of adult attachment patterns (see Figure 3.1). Four prototypic attachment patterns are defined in terms of the intersection of two underlying dimensions. The *positivity of the self* dimension (on the horizontal axis) indicates the degree to which individuals have an internalised sense of their own self-worth. In terms of the attachment behavioural system, a positive self-model facilitates individuals feeling self-confident, rather than anxious, in close relationships. In contrast, a negative self-model indicates a dependency on others' ongoing approval to maintain feelings of self-worth, a dependency that fosters anxiety in close relationships. The *positivity of the other* dimension (on the vertical axis) reflects expectations of others' availability and supportiveness. In terms of the attachment system, a positive other-model facilitates the willingness to seek support from close others. In contrast, a negative other-model is associated with the tendency to withdraw and maintain a safe distance within close relationships, particularly when feeling threatened. A heuristic model of the dynamics of the attachment system (see Figure 3.2) will be used to characterise each of four attachment patterns defined in terms of the intersection of the self-model/anxiety and other-model/avoidance dimensions.

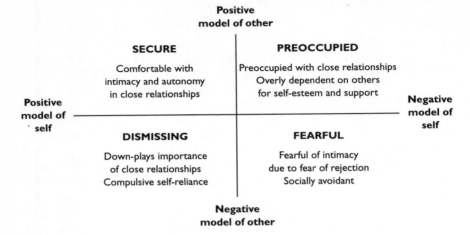

Figure 3.1 Two-dimensional, four-category model of adult attachment

Secure attachment

Experiences of consistent responsive caregiving are hypothesised to facilitate
the development of a positive image of the self and positive images of others.
Secure individuals are comfortable with autonomy and intimacy, and able to
use others as a source of support when needed. They are characterised by

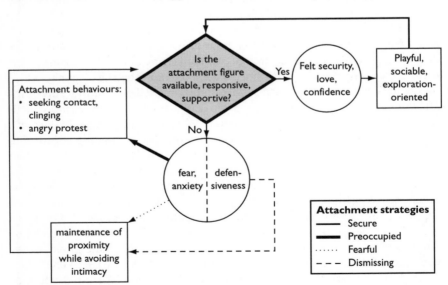

Figure 3.2 The dynamics of the attachment system

high self-esteem, and an ability to establish and maintain close intimate bonds with others without losing a sense of self. The secure pattern is represented by a solid dark line on Figure 3.2. Secure individuals expect their attachment figures to be supportive, facilitating inner security and behavioural competence. They are likely to form intimate relationships in which both partners act as safe havens and secure bases for one another.

Preoccupied attachment

Experiences of inconsistent and insensitive caregiving are thought to contribute to preoccupied attachment – defined in terms of a positive model of others, but negative model of the self. This kind of parenting may lead children to conclude that they are to blame for lack of love from the caretaker. The result is an overly-dependent style, characterised by intense feelings of unworthiness and an excessive need for others' approval. In their attempts to get attachment needs fulfilled, preoccupied individuals demonstrate an intrusive and demanding interpersonal style. A typical quote of a preoccupied individual is 'I scare away partners. I want to be so close, all the time, and they get nervous.' At the extreme, preoccupied individuals exhibit histrionic and borderline tendencies. Turning to Figure 3.2, preoccupied individuals will often question the availability of attachment figures because they do not expect consistent responsiveness and their unrealistically high demands for support are unlikely to be met. When they feel that attachment figures are not responsive, they experience anxiety and respond with high levels of attachment behaviours in an attempt to get their needs for support met (see bold arrow).

In contrast, both of the avoidant attachment patterns (fearful and dismissing) are characterised by avoidance of close contact with others. Presumably because of a history of rejecting or unresponsive attachment figures, they have learned not to turn to others as a source of security. But the two groups have arrived at very different conclusions about their own self-worth.

Fearful attachment

These individuals have concluded that others are uncaring and unavailable, and that they themselves are unlovable. Although they desire acceptance by others – in fact, they are hypersensitive to social approval – they avoid intimacy due to a fear or expectation of rejection. A typical quote of a fearful individual is 'I'm incapable of vocalising my feelings because I'm afraid I'll say something that will ruin the relationship.' Fearful individuals do not expect others to be responsive, giving rise to fear and anxiety. However, in contrast to the preoccupied, they are inhibited in expressing their anxiety and asking for support. Instead, they deal with their anxiety by maintaining a comfortable distance within their close relationships (see dotted arrow in

Figure 3.2). They can thereby avoid anticipated rejection of their attachment needs by the attachment figure, while gaining some indirect support through not alienating him or her.

Dismissing attachment

Dismissing individuals, in contrast, have managed to maintain a positive self-image by distancing themselves from attachment figures and attachment relationships. With their characteristic compulsive self-reliance and emotional control, and a defensive down-playing of the importance of intimate relationships, they become relatively invulnerable to potential rejection by others. As indicated by the broken line in Figure 3.2, dismissing individuals have learned defensively to deactivate the attachment system, reducing their tendency to experience the anxiety that typically follows from unmet attachment needs. This defensive emotional stance is complemented by an avoidant behavioural stance in which they maintain distance within close relationships.

In summary, preoccupied and fearful individuals are similar in their attachment anxiety and dependence on others' acceptance to validate their own self-worth. However, they differ in how they respond to this anxiety and their willingness to approach others for support. In contrast, the fearful and dismissing are similar in their avoidance of intimacy, but differ in their internalised self-concept and in their emotional reliance upon acceptance by others.

Each of the four attachment patterns described in this model represents a theoretical ideal or prototype. However, individuals vary in the degree to which they approximate each of these prototypical patterns. Thus, in our coding scheme, participants are rated on their correspondence with *each* of the attachment prototypes (secure, fearful, preoccupied and dismissing), resulting in an *attachment profile* for each individual. With this system, data can be analysed continuously, by examining participants' ratings on each of the attachment patterns (on 1 to 9 scales), or discretely, by identifying the best-fitting attachment category.

In our research we have used various methods to assess attachment, although in the following studies we relied primarily on in-depth, semi-structured attachment interviews which explore individuals' experiences with friends and romantic partners (the Peer Attachment Interview; Bartholomew and Horowitz, 1991). More recently, we have been using the History of Attachments Interview (Henderson, 1998), which asks participants for a chronological history of relationship experiences beginning with parents and caregivers and moving to current peer and romantic relationships. These interviews are then rated by expert coders to yield attachment profiles. Coders consider both the *content* of participants' relationship accounts and *how* participants discuss their experiences (including the coherence of their accounts, defensiveness in discussing difficult experiences and so on). Some of our research has also relied on self-report measures of attachment developed by

Bartholomew and colleagues (Bartholomew and Horowitz, 1991; Griffin and Bartholomew, 1994).

Attachment patterns and their relationship to receipt and perpetration of abuse

How can these attachment patterns be expected to relate to the receipt and perpetration of relationship abuse? In terms of *receipt*, we would not expect individuals with a positive self-concept and an internalised sense of self-worth (the secure and dismissing) to stay in abusive relationships. Secure individuals would be unlikely to tolerate aggression from a romantic partner because of an integrated sense that they deserve more respectful treatment. Dismissing individuals, characterised by high self-reliance and an avoidance of intimacy in close relationships, would be unlikely to have sufficient investment to remain with an abusive partner. Conversely, the dependency and separation anxiety characteristic of fearful and preoccupied individuals may make it especially difficult for them to leave abusive relationships. In fact, the negative self-model of the preoccupied and fearful patterns may serve to exacerbate the conditions necessary for attachment bonds to an abusive partner to be maintained or possibly enhanced. The power relationship can easily become pathologically unbalanced when the abused individual feels that he or she is unworthy of the assaulter, and the assaulter (who may also hold a negative self-model) may seize this advantage to live out the illusion of his or her own power (Dutton and Painter, 1993). Not only are preoccupied and fearful individuals more likely to believe that the violence perpetrated against them is justifiable, but they may also be more likely to respond positively to the assaulter's expressions of regret and contrition that sometimes follow abusive episodes (Walker, 1979). Without the expectation of more respectful treatment, individuals with a negative self-model may be particularly vulnerable to remaining with abusive partners.

In terms of *perpetration*, we would expect security of attachment to be inversely related to abusiveness. Secure individuals are able to establish supportive relationships and to communicate effectively their attachment needs without resorting to violence. Dismissing attachment has rather different implications for the perpetration of abuse. The stereotype of the distant and callous abuser suggests that assaulters might be likely to show dismissing orientations. As well, the frustration of attachment needs associated with this style may give rise to anger (Kobak and Sceery, 1988) and potential violence. However, research suggests that dismissing individuals are not prone to angry protest in intimate relationships, presumably due to the deactivation of their attachment systems. Rather, dismissing individuals would be more likely to leave an unsatisfying relationship than to act out in protest.

In contrast, individuals showing the two attachment patterns defined in terms of a negative self-model – the preoccupied and fearful – are chronically anxious about rejection and abandonment in their close relationships. These anxious attachment patterns are, therefore, expected to be associated with high levels of negative affect, including anger in intimate relationships. The rationale for expecting preoccupation to be associated with abusiveness is especially compelling. Preoccupied individuals have such excessive needs for support and reassurance that they are inevitably frustrated in having these needs met. Abusive behaviour is consistent with the preoccupied individual's approach orientation, and their confrontational and controlling inter-personal style. Torn between a pathological need for approval from their partner and the terror of never feeling satiated in this regard, the preoccupied individual may become increasingly more demanding and potentially aggres-sive when attachment needs are not fulfilled.

Things become somewhat more complex in considering how fearfulness may relate to the perpetration of abuse. The tendency to withdraw when anxious or threatened would seem contrary to the active protest behaviour shown in aggressive acts. However, the fearful individual's avoidant orienta-tion may lead to more chronic frustration of attachment needs than that experienced by preoccupied individuals (who would be expected to inconsis-tently gain support), and hence higher levels of frustration and anger. Whereas preoccupied individuals have some hope of having their needs met through constant effort, fearful individuals may experience these same needs but be reluctant to make them known because they are less hopeful about the responses of others.

PUTTING HYPOTHESES TO THE TEST

In each of the following four studies we explored the associations between attachment patterns as conceptualised with the four-category model and rela-tionship abuse. Where possible, we assessed both physical and psychological abuse perpetrated by both men and women. Previous work has shown that physical and psychological abuse are closely linked, and that psychological abuse can be just as harmful and hurtful as physical abuse, in many cases even more so (see, for example, Follingstad et al., 1990). Although the most severe relationship violence is probably most often perpetrated by men against their female partners (and perhaps also by men or women against same-sex part-ners), it is clear that both men and women can abuse and be the victims of abuse (Straus, 1993; Straus and Gelles, 1986). Much, if not most, relationship abuse is reciprocal or bidirectional in nature (Magdol et al., 1997; Stets and Straus, 1990). In such cases, it can be hard to distinguish the role of abuser from that of victim. For example, in the Vancouver Domestic Abuse Project (see below), individuals' reports of receipt of partner abuse were highly associated with their reports of their own perpetration of abuse (with corre-lations ranging from 0.60 to 0.72). In other words, individuals who have been the the victim of partner abuse in most cases appear to act abusively toward their partner, suggesting mutually abusive relationships.

As expected, security of attachment across our studies tended to be associated with low levels of relationship abuse, both perpetration and receipt. However, there were no consistent associations between dismissing ratings and abuse, although dismissing attachment is strongly related to relationship satisfaction and functioning (Scharfe and Bartholomew, 1995). As a result, we will focus on how the two insecure patterns defined in terms of attachment anxiety – fearfulness and preoccupation – relate to abuse. We will focus on psychological abuse because psychological abuse measures are more consistent across studies than are measures of physical abuse. Due to the potential role of gender in abusive relationships, we will present findings separately by sex.

The *Assaultive Husbands Project* was a study of 120 abusive men with 40 matched controls (Dutton et al., 1994). All of these men had been convicted of assaulting female partners and were in court-mandated treatment programmes. They were, for the most part, a group of severely abusive men. Attachment was assessed by a self-report measure, the Relationship Scales Questionnaire (Griffin and Bartholomew, 1994), which yields continuous ratings of each of the four patterns. Abuse was assessed by female partners' reports on the Psychological Maltreatment of Women Inventory, or PMWI (Tolman, 1989). The dominance and isolation sub-scale of the PMWI assesses controlling behaviour and isolation from social networks (for example, restricting access to friends, family, car, telephone and money). The emotional-verbal abuse sub-scale assesses various verbal forms of abuse such as insulting a partner and humiliating a partner in public.

The majority of abusive men in this sample described themselves as preoccupied or fearful; their ratings on these patterns were much higher than those of the comparison group. Moreover, continuous ratings of degree of both fearful and preoccupied attachment were positively associated with the severity of their perpetration of both forms of abusiveness (see Table 3.1). Even within the group of predominantly insecure abusive men, the higher their levels of fearfulness and preoccupation, the higher the levels of abusive

Table 3.1 Assaultive Husbands Project: associations between attachment ratings and partner reports of psychological abuse

	Attachment patterns	
	Fearful	Preoccupied
Partner reports of abuse		
Dominance/isolation	0.46**	0.27*
Emotional/verbal	0.52**	0.26*

N = 160; *p < 0.05; **p < 0.01

behaviour reported by their female partners. The same pattern held for partner reports of the men's violence. See Dutton et al. (1994) for further information on this study.

In the next study, *Women Leaving Abusive Partners*, we turn to women who had been abused by male partners (Henderson et al., 1997). This project studied 63 women who had recently left an abusive relationship. The women were recruited through various sources, including refuges and newspaper advertisements. The average length of their abusive relationship was eleven and a half years. All these women had experienced psychological abuse, and the vast majority had experienced physical abuse. The women were given an interview shortly after they left the relationship, which we used to assess their profile across the four attachment patterns and their overall best-fitting attachment category. Six months later they completed measures concerning how they were dealing with the separation. The women's continued emotional involvement with their partners was assessed by a scale including items such as 'Without him I have nothing to live for' and 'I spend a lot of my time thinking about him'. Women were asked whether they felt more distant or close since the separation and, surprisingly, some women said they felt closer since being separated. They were also asked to what degree they still loved their partner and wanted to get back together, and whether they had been socially or sexually involved with their partner since the separation.

The large majority of the women were predominantly fearful (35 per cent) or preoccupied (53 per cent), confirming that these attachment patterns are associated with the receipt of abuse. We also looked at how the degree of fearfulness and of preoccupation were related to how the women were coping with the separation at the six-month point (see Table 3.2). Findings indicated that the more preoccupied the women were, the more they reported difficulty in separating from their partner. Preoccupation was associated with continued

Table 3.2 Women Leaving Abusive Partners: associations between attachment ratings and separation resolution variables

| | Attachment patterns | |
	Fearful	Preoccupied
Emotional involvement		
CEI scale	−0.13†	0.27*
Emotional distance	0.26*	−0.27*
Still love	−0.12	0.42**
Partner contact		
Social	−0.32**	0.26*
Sexual	0.17†	0.39**

Note: Partial correlations controlling for physical and psychological abuse
†p < 0.10; *p < 0.05; **p < 0.01

emotional involvement, reduced emotional distance, reported continued love and increased social and sexual contact with the partner since separation. Findings were not as consistent with fearfulness; but there were indications that the more fearful the women were, the less likely they were to report continued involvement and contact with their former partner, and the more likely they were to feel distant from him. These findings suggest that the combination of attachment anxiety and approach orientation characteristic of preoccupied attachment may put such women at particular risk of returning to abusive relationships. On the other hand, the avoidant orientation characteristic of fearful attachment may help fearful women stay out of abusive relationships once they have managed to leave these relationships. See Henderson et al. (1997) for further information on this study.

These two studies looked at attachment and abuse in samples selected for high levels of male-to-female abusiveness. In the next two projects, we focused on general community samples rather than select samples. As part of the *Longitudinal Couples Project*, we assessed the associations between attachment and partner abuse in a sample of young established couples (Henderson et al., 1994). The sample consisted of 41 couples with a mean relationship length of 5.2 years and a mean age of 26. Both partners were given an attachment interview (the Peer Attachment Interview) at the first meeting. Sixteen months later they completed adapted versions (to be appropriate for both genders) of the PMWI to assess the infliction and receipt of psychological abuse within the relationship.

Somewhat different patterns of findings emerged for female and male partners (see Tables 3.3 and 3.4). The degree to which women were rated as preoccupied was associated with both their own and their partner's abusive behaviour. The associations between women's preoccupation and their tendency to be dominating and isolating toward their partners was especially strong. However, women's fearfulness did not predict abuse by either partner. Men's preoccupation was associated with their self-reports of emotional/verbal abuse, but not with any measures of their partner's abusiveness, whereas men's fearfulness was predictive of abuse by both partners (especially emotional/verbal abuse).

Finally, the *Vancouver Domestic Abuse Project* involved a large community sample of women and men living in the City of Vancouver (British Columbia, Canada) recruited through a random digit dialing procedure. Over 1,200 men and women completed a telephone survey focusing on experiences of relationship abuse, both perpetration and receipt. A sub-sample of 68 women and 60 men completed a follow-up session in which they participated in a two-hour attachment interview (the History of Attachments Interview). Contrary to previous findings with select samples, we did not find fearfulness to be associated with either perpetration or receipt of abuse. However, as indicated in Figures 3.3 and 3.4, the higher the degree of preoccupation, the higher the levels of reported perpetration and receipt of psychological abuse.

Table 3.3 Longitudinal Couples Project: women's attachment ratings and both partners' reports of psychological abuse

| | Women's attachment | |
	Fearful	Preoccupied
Women's abusive behaviour		
Dominance/isolation		
Self-report	−0.10	0.41**
Partner-report	−0.05	0.46**
Emotional/verbal		
Self-report	−0.23	0.27*
Partner-report	0.12	0.17
Men's abusive behaviour		
Dominance/isolation		
Self-report	0.04	0.24*
Partner-report	−0.01	0.17
Emotional/verbal		
Self-report	0.02	0.26*
Partner-report	−0.22	0.28*

*p < 0.05; **p < 0.01

Table 3.4 Longitudinal Couples Project: men's attachment ratings and both partners' reports of psychological abuse

| | Men's attachment | |
	Fearful	Preoccupied
Women's abusive behaviour		
Dominance/isolation		
Self	0.21*	−0.26
Partner	0.19	−0.11
Emotional/verbal		
Self	0.44**	−0.13
Partner	0.26*	0.11
Men's abusive behaviour		
Dominance/isolation		
Self	0.18	0.06
Partner	0.13	−0.21
Emotional/verbal		
Self	0.23*	0.35**
Partner	0.39**	−0.12

*p < 0.05; **p < 0.01

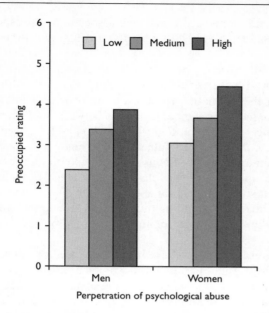

Figure 3.3 Vancouver Domestic Abuse Project: associations between preoccupation and perpetration of psychological abuse

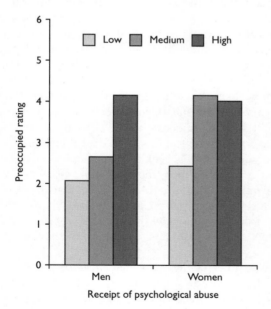

Figure 3.4 Vancouver Domestic Abuse Project: associations between preoccupation and receipt of psychological abuse

This pattern held for men and women, although the association was especially strong for men. See Henderson (1998) for more information on these findings.

Across studies, and for both genders, preoccupied attachment was quite consistently associated with both the perpetration of abuse in relationships and the receipt of abuse (or the inclination to return to an abusive relationship). For women, there were few consistent associations between fearfulness and abuse, although fearfulness was common in women who had left abusive relationships. In contrast, the degree of fearfulness was strongly associated for men with the perpetration and receipt of abuse in all the studies but one. The finding that both preoccupation and fearfulness predict abusiveness for men has been replicated in a study of male same-sex relationships (Landolt and Dutton, 1998). We are currently extending this work on attachment and abuse in same-sex relationships in a large community sample of gay men (Bartholomew et al., 1998).

One of our big surprises in looking at abuse in intimate relationships is the degree of similarity we have found in men's and women's experiences of abuse. We also have been struck by the similarity in the dynamics of abuse in heterosexual and male same-sex relationships (we have yet to study lesbian relationships). In most cases, there would be no way of identifying the sex of the partners from the stories told of histories of abusive relationships. This calls into question the sufficiency of a patriarchal model of relationship abuse in which violence is fundamentally seen in terms of men's domination of women. In contrast, from an attachment perspective, we would not necessarily expect gender differences in the psychological mechanisms underlying abusive behaviour in relationships. However, some of our findings are moderated by gender. In mutually physically abusive relationships, women are more likely to suffer injury than are men (Stets and Straus, 1990). It is our impression that this difference stems primarily from the greater size, strength and fighting competence of men. Second, we have seen a gender difference in the implications of fearful attachment for abuse. In women, fearfulness sometimes has been associated with the receipt of abuse, but never with perpetration. In men, there are indications that the most severely physically assaultive men are likely to be fearful. When pushed to the edge, when feeling overwhelmed and attacked, fearful men appear to be more likely to strike out physically than fearful women. It may be that gender roles interact with attachment dynamics to explain this finding.

We would like to emphasise that all the work described here has been carried out in a particular cultural context, and that this work cannot necessarily be generalised to any other contexts. Key features of this culture are freedom to choose relationship partners, the ability to end even long-term marital relationships and societal attitudes that male violence against women is unacceptable but female violence is relatively acceptable (if it is acknowledged to exist at all). In such cultures, attachment dynamics may play a key role in the formation of abusive relationships. However, in cultural contexts in which marriages are arranged, in which divorce is practically impossible and/or in which male violence against women is condoned, attachment theory may have less to offer in understanding domestic violence.

INDIVIDUAL VERSUS RELATIONAL CONCEPTIONS OF ABUSE

Contrary to the dominant feminist perspective, which sees domestic violence as stemming from the patriarchal structure of society, we believe that relationship abuse is best understood within a dyadic or relationship context (see Chapter 8 for an illustration of this). Both persons in an abusive relationship need to be considered in relation to one another. In two of the studies reviewed (the *Assaultive Husbands Project* and the *Longitudinal Couples Project*), we did include both members of couples. Unfortunately, we have not completed our couple-level analysis of these findings. However, in the process of conducting and listening to hundreds of attachment interviews we have formed some strong impressions of the attachment dynamics in the abusive relationships we have seen. We have also looked descriptively at the most common combinations of people in abusive relationships and identified three common patterns.

First, we have frequently observed the combination of two preoccupied partners in our select samples of assaultive men and abused women. These couples are locked in highly volatile and conflictual relationships. Such relationships tend to be mutually abusive, although, as mentioned earlier, as violence becomes more extreme the female partner is most likely to sustain injury. We have observed this same pattern in abusive male same-sex relationships and in the less severely abusive relationships found in our study of young couples.

Second, we have observed combinations of fearful women with preoccupied men, especially in our clinical samples. These couples show more unidirectional abuse from male to female, conforming to the common stereotype of the demanding and controlling abusive male and passive female victim attempting to accommodate to her partner to avert further violence.

A third pattern, that of preoccupied females with fearful males, was common in the abusive relationships in our community samples. This pattern is also characteristic of the most severely abusive relationships in our clinical samples. Such couples are likely to show mutually abusive behaviour or higher rates of female abusiveness.

Case illustration

Because this third pattern does not conform to our stereotypes of abuse relationships, we will describe a typical abusive couple with this pattern. We have chosen the couple with the highest scores on the measures of psychological abuse in our study of young couples. These partners had been together for 10 years and were engaged, but not living together. They were chosen because they appeared to be in the process of developing a severely violent relationship.

The male partner outlined a history of fearful attachment. Although he described his mother as 'okay', he continued to be afraid of his father, a highly dominating and critical man whose discipline bordered on abuse. As a child, he learned that others were not available as sources of support. When upset, he would go to his room to hide and to be by himself. His parents would occasionally try to persuade him to talk about his feelings, but this would lead him to withdraw even further. He felt that his family experiences had led him as an adult to hold his feelings in and to deal with problems on his own.

His preoccupied female partner had an histrionic mother who was psychologically and physically abusive to her and her father. She described her mother as aggressive, obnoxious and unpredictable. Her mother also frequently told her daughter that she was unwanted, contributing to her obsessive fear of being rejected and abandoned. Her father was quiet and tried to avoid conflict, choosing to appease her mother. Nonetheless, he was someone she trusted. This young woman had a long history of violent behaviour. Throughout childhood she had temper tantrums, and she frequently beat her younger brother when he would not comply with her wishes. When teased by friends as a child, she would physically fight back. Since childhood, she had continued to demonstrate a highly volatile, demanding interpersonal style.

Both members of this couple independently provided remarkably similar descriptions of their relationship in a series of attachment interviews conducted over two years. Their key sources of dissatisfaction in the relationship were complementary. He felt overwhelmed by his partner's extreme jealousy and possessiveness, and complained that he was constantly pressured to spend more time with her and was not free to see his friends. She also pressured him to share his every thought with her; but he felt that if he did so, that would only lead to conflict. He felt he could not live up to her expectations, and that he was unable to gain her approval. This made him feel stupid, insecure and rejected. He did not feel safe expressing his needs for support because she became upset when attention was diverted from her. His partner, in turn, complained that he did not spend enough time with her; she was especially angry that he insisted on doing things with other people (mostly sporting activities with male friends). She was also frustrated that he did not share enough, that he did not tell her everything right away, that he was too private and not committed enough.

Given the two individuals and the issues they were dealing with, the dynamic of the relationship was quite predictable. In fact, it sounded remarkably similar to the relationship of the female partner's parents. On a daily basis, she was dissatisfied with something that her partner had or, more often, had not done. She screamed, criticised, belittled him and sometimes became violent. Although the violence was not severe, he often suffered scratches and bruises. However, the effect of these attempts to gain his attention and make him more responsive to her needs was the opposite of what she hoped for. He backed off, shut down, tried to appease her and sometimes fled. The more he withdrew, the angrier and more desperate she became. When he tried physically to leave the relationship, she threatened suicide or made suicidal gestures 'to test him'. Alternatively, she went out with other men. On his side, he felt attacked, cornered and powerless. He experienced a mixture of fear, frustration and anger. He had tried to swallow these feelings, but found his frustration occasionally building to explosion point, resulting in him physically striking back at her. He then felt extreme shame and remorse. The relationship was slowly moving from predominantly female-to-male abuse to mutual abuse. We felt that if the violence continued to escalate, it might lead to disastrous consequences for both partners.

This couple illustrates how the particular combination of two individuals and a relationship dynamic that becomes established between them can give rise to an abusive situation. To understand fully the development of abusive behaviour, it is necessary to consider both general attachment tendencies that individuals bring to their relationships and relationship-specific patterns. In the couple described, the extremely preoccupied woman tended to repeat her abusive style across relationships and would be expected to continue doing so. However, being with a partner who tended to shy away from intimacy, especially under conditions of stress or conflict, was especially frustrating for her and would exacerbate her tendencies to strike out in anger. Moreover, male partners who were more secure than her current partner may not have been inclined to stay in relationships with her. Although we expect that her partner might not be abusive if he was with a more secure partner, he may well have difficulty sustaining a relationship with a secure partner given his degree of fearfulness. His partner's behaviour serves to confirm his negative perception of himself and his expectation that others cannot be trusted to give support, further reinforcing his fearful pattern. It is this complementary attachment dynamic of individuals within intimate relationships that we believe helps to keep couples locked in abusive relationships.

From the studies we have described we cannot determine whether attachment patterns are antecedents or consequences of abusive experiences in relationships. As is evident from the histories of the partners just described, it is likely that both are the case. Particular insecure patterns probably put individuals at risk for becoming involved in and staying in abusive relation-ships. Almost without exception, individuals in severely abusive relationships describe relationship histories in their families of origin that indicate insecure attachment orientations. But once in an abusive relationship, individuals are likely to become more insecure over time. Long-term longitudinal work is needed to disentangle these effects.

FINAL THOUGHTS

Looking at relationship violence from an attachment perspective allows us to come to a rich understanding of the mechanisms involved in both the receipt and the perpetration of abuse. It is noteworthy that individuals with attach-ment patterns associated with a negative self-model and tendency to experi-ence anxiety in close relationships (preoccupied and fearful) appear to be at greatest risk for both receipt and perpetration of relationship violence. Receipt of relationship abuse can best be understood with Bowlby's propo-sition that the strength of an attachment bond is not related to the quality of the attachment relationship. Simply because one's attachment figure is not a kind person, attachment bonds are no less intense, anxiety when separated from an attachment figure is no less urgent and the inconsolable grief upon loss of an attachment partner is no less debilitating.

Attachment theory offers an equally compelling rationale for the perpetra-tion of relationship violence when one reflects upon an infant's angry protest when separated from an attachment figure. Crying, reaching out and even tantrums are all typical attachment behaviours exhibited by an infant in order to regain proximity to an attachment figure. An assaulter's abusive episodes can be seen as an adult version of protest when attachment needs are not satisfied.

Although attachment theory offers a promising framework for understand-ing both sides of the abusive relationship dynamic, we need ultimately to consider abuse within the context of adult attachment relationships. Child-hood experiences may serve to shape and guide future relationship experi-ences. But the development of these internal representations and associated attachment strategies is an ongoing process, with each subsequent relation-ship serving to maintain, enhance or change established patterns. We have seen cases in our research where repeated and severe psychological or physical abuse has undermined even reasonably secure models of self and other, especially when individuals face abuse in their initial romantic relationships as young adults.

We have also seen the positive impact that a loving and supportive partner can have in changing very negative internal models. Consider, for example, the following excerpt from a woman in our Vancouver study who had lived her childhood in terror of her father's unpredictable and increasingly violent rages. As an adult, her ceaselessly loving partner was able to provide her with the proverbial 'secure base' that was so lacking in her childhood.

> [My father] could turn just like that, so you never really felt safe with him . . . I had nightmares for years . . . recurring nightmares. And this lion would be in the house chasing me. I had that dream right up until I married [John] . . . I used to have it over and over. After [John] I stopped having those nightmares. Like I could trust him, but I couldn't trust before that.

In the field of domestic violence, it has sometimes been argued that looking at psychological factors associated with the receipt and perpetration of abuse implicitly blames victims and excuses perpetrators. We believe this position is misguided. By looking at abuse from an attachment perspective, our goal is not to blame or excuse the individuals involved, but rather to further our understanding of relationship abuse. The ultimate hope is that such understanding will inform programmes to prevent relationship violence and inform therapeutic intervention with individuals and couples experiencing abuse. Working from an attachment-based perspective, Johnson (1986) suggests that the perception of a partner as emotionally unresponsive underlies much marital conflict, with the conflict further compromising the capacity of the relationship to serve as a secure base for either partner. Individuals who lack confidence in the availability and responsiveness of their partners will be prone to high levels of attachment anxiety, leading them (in some cases) to act in aggressive, seemingly counterproductive ways in an attempt to gain proximity to their partners. Couple therapy may help partners to understand their mutual needs for security and closeness, and to find ways for them to function more effectively as a source of security for one another.

Chapter 4

A couple perspective on the transmission of attachment patterns

Philip Cowan and Carolyn Pape Cowan

William and Sarah, exhausted parents of a six-year-old, are having a heated conversation late at night.

Sarah: I don't think we can let Kevin act that way in school.

William: He's just defending himself against some tough kids.

Sarah: You're just trying to get him to do what *you* could never do. What your parents nagged you to do.

William: Well, at least my parents tried to help me cope with the bullies in life. What did yours do? They were sweet and proper, but they never stood up for you when you needed them.

Sarah: I don't have to defend my parents here. The issue is *you* and your son's behaviour.

William: The issue isn't me. It's *your* overprotection. You're smothering him. Not letting him be a man. It's too threatening to you.

Sarah: William this isn't the time to start up with this issue. I'm still tired from our last fight.

William: Well, I can't tolerate you trying to change something that's very important to me about my relationship with my son.

In the United States, as in Great Britain, there are many different theoretical approaches to understanding what causes problems in couple relationships. Perhaps the most popular current American perspective comes from researchers and couples therapists who focus on communication from a behavioural or cognitive-behavioural point of view. A therapist from one of these theoretical orientations would be concerned that William and Sarah are not using effective communication rules. They tend to blame each other, they 'read each other's mind', and they are not giving each other positive reinforcements. Therapists from this point of view would point out that each partner is thinking negative thoughts about the other or making negative attributions about the other's motivations and questioning his or her good intentions. While it is certainly true that William and Sarah are not being very effective communicators, many tired couples fail to communicate effectively at the end of a demanding and frustrating day. How can we think about this tension between them?

We take the view that positive relationships between partners are not simply a matter of having an effective communication repertoire. How partners attempt to resolve differences between them is shaped in part by each one's earlier experiences in his or her formative relationships. Each partner develops a working model or template concerning intimate relationships that colours his or her expectations and reactions to stressful interactions. We adopt the view from attachment theory that this template plays an important role in how we behave with our adult partners, our children and our close friends, especially when our relationships feel precarious or threatened.

In this chapter, we describe results from our recent longitudinal, preventive intervention study of couples with young children. The findings provide support for the hypothesis that parents' attachment patterns from their families of origin tend to be replicated in the family relationships they create in the next generation. First, consistent with the findings reported in earlier chapters, our results reveal significant links between partners' working models of attachment with their parents, as assessed from their narrative recollections, the attachment patterns they describe as a couple and the quality of relationship we observe between them.

Attachment to parents → Attachment to partner

Second, with data gathered from families over time, we show that partners' attachment patterns – with their parents and with each other as a couple – are associated with the quality of relationship we observe between them and their young child.

Attachment to parents → Attachment to partner → Parent–child relationship quality

We then go on to describe how parents' working models of these two key relationships in the family, assessed before the children enter school, function as powerful predictors of the children's academic, social and emotional adjustment in their first year of elementary school (which American children enter when they are approximately five years old).

Attachment to parents → Attachment to partner → Parent–child relationship quality → Child's early adaptation

We are interested in adults' attachment patterns with parents and partners not only because we believe that they play a role in couple relationship quality but also because we expect the quality of parents' attachment as a couple to play a significant role in amplifying or reducing the tendency for positive or negative family relationships to be repeated across generations. Our research examines the hypothesis that unsatisfying relationships in the parents' families of origin are more likely to be recreated in their current families when their relationship as a couple is mired in unresolved conflict. On the other hand, a well-functioning, satisfying couple relationship may serve as a buffer that protects parents with insecure attachment patterns from simply repeating old unproductive and unsatisfying ways of relating with their partners and children.

In telling the story of attachment from one generation to another, we emphasise the fact that, despite considerable consistency across relationships, the attachment template is by no means rigid and monolithic. Fortunately, this allows considerable potential for breaking the cycle in which negative family relationships in one generation are replicated in the next. To further test this idea, we briefly describe a preventive intervention in which mental health professionals offered help to couples as their children set out to make the transition from the family to more formal schooling. We offered a randomly chosen set of couples entering our *Schoolchildren and Their Families Project* a chance to participate in a couples group led by mental health professionals. By following couples with and without this intervention, throughout the transition period, we were able to evaluate whether helping parents with couple, parent–child and three-generational problems led men and women to find more effective ways of relating as partners and as parents. Finally, we tested the hypothesis that children of couples who moved toward more satisfying couple and parent–child relationships had more successful adaptation to school – academically, socially and emotionally.

Our discussion of the results from this project focuses on two central issues in extending Bowlby's (1988) parent–child-based attachment theory to an understanding of couple attachment. First, we show how an intervention based on earlier research findings provides a powerful test of our theoretical notions about the central role of couple attachments in the family system. Second, we use attachment theory in a speculative attempt to account for the results of our intervention.

HOW WE STUDY FAMILIES

Rationale

We began studying and working with partners becoming parents in the 1970s based on our own early personal and professional experiences. We and our contemporaries found ourselves struggling with the unexpected strain of trying to be responsive parents while maintaining viable work outside the family and relationships inside the family. We have described that first study and its intervention extensively in a number of sources (for example, Cowan and Cowan, 2000, 1997; Cowan, 1988). Here we simply summarise its essence in order to show the line of argument in our current study. As others before us had suggested (see Rapoport et al., 1977), we argued that coping with major family transitions demands new skills and adjustments that leave parents and children feeling anxious and unsure of themselves at times. Everything that we knew from developmental research and from work with distressed families suggested that the psychological resources of a family make a significant difference at these transition times, not only to how adults and children cope with a major life shift but also to how they ultimately feel about themselves and their ability to manage the challenges that life throws in their path. Because we conceptualised our interventions as preventive of potential stress and distress, we set out to work with couples who were about to become parents and had not already sought help for troubling family relationships. When we followed those couples and their children through their children's first year of formal schooling, we found that the quality of the parents' relationships as couples, *and* with their children, made substantial contributions to the children's adaptation to school (Cowan et al., 1994). Because these results suggested that working with couples whose first children were making the transition to formal schooling might have an impact on the children's adaptation, we designed a second study of families whose first child was about to enter kindergarten at age five. We describe the couples group intervention in more detail below.

The families

The couples who responded to both projects were remarkably similar, coming from 28 cities and towns in northern California. Spanning a range from working class to upper middle class, 85 per cent were Caucasian and 15 per cent were African-American, Asian-American or Hispanic. They were well-educated, all having completed high school, and many having additional speciality training or college and postgraduate degrees. Despite their advanced educational levels, the parents represented a broad range of background, attitudes, jobs, couple relationships and parenting styles. They were between the ages of 20 and 40 when they had their first babies. At that time, they had been together an average of four years, although some had been together as few as eight months and some for as many as twelve years when the first pregnancy began. Almost all the partners in both studies were married, although a few were living together and planning to raise this first child together – our only criteria for a couple's inclusion in the two studies.

Our model of the family as a system

The conceptual model of development that underlies our work is derived from clinical family systems theory (e.g. Minuchin and Fishman, 1981; Wagner and Reiss, 1995). We set out to learn about five key aspects of the couples' lives in order to evaluate how well the family was coping: that is, how the parents were managing (1) as individuals, (2) as couples and (3) as parents; (4) the parents' models of relationships based on experiences in their families of origin; and (5) the balance of life stress and social support outside the family. In terms of attachment patterns, we set out to learn whether the partners felt that they could rely on others to 'be there' in times of stress, and whether each felt worthy of being cared for.

Assessing individual, couple, parent–child and family functioning

In a family visit to our project playroom, we presented children and parents with challenging tasks and games to see how they managed in mildly stressful situations. Families visited before the children entered school when they were four years old, again when they were in kindergarten at age five, and in our current project, when they were in first grade at age six. Two members of our research staff observed each parent working individually with the child, and then together as the whole family worked and played together. The observers focused on how much the parents showed warmth, responsiveness, humour or anger, how much they helped the child by structuring difficult tasks or setting limits when their child was upset, getting off task, or out of control, and how much they encouraged the child's autonomy at a level appropriate to his or her age. Other observers rated the children's reactions to the parents in these situations.

On another day, parents visited as a couple to talk in some detail about their key family relationships. In the first year of the study, we asked about their relationships with their own parents using the Adult Attachment Interview (see Chapters 1 and 2) to get a sense of each parent's working model of attachment relationships with their parents. In the second year, we asked in detail about their relationship as a couple, using a Couple Attachment Interview (CAI) that we developed to get a sense of their working model of attachment as a couple (Silver et al., 1990 – see below).

At the end of each of these in-depth interviews with each parent individually, we invited the partners to come together for one half-hour. There we asked them to select two real problems that they had not resolved – one to do with parenting their child, the other having to do with their relationship as a couple. We asked them to spend ten minutes trying to make some headway on each of these problems. We used these videotaped snapshots from two different years to characterise the tone of their interaction as a couple: how much warmth, humour, co-operativeness, argumentativeness, anger, conflict or threatening behaviour they show when working together without their children present.

Other members of our research team made home visits to all the children in our study, every summer, during which they assessed their academic achievement and asked them what they worried about or had difficulty doing, and what they felt they were good at – at home and at school. Once the children entered school, in approximately 90 different public, private or parochial schools, we asked their teachers to work with us by completing a Child Adaptive Behaviour Checklist, or CABC (Cowan et al., 1996), that included typical positive and negative behaviours. Each fall and spring, teachers completed the CABC for every child in their classrooms, without knowing which child in the class was participating in our study. This gave us an estimate of each child's academic competence, social adjustment and behaviour problems, *relative to the other children in his or her class*.

In sum, we have a wealth of information about each of the families, from the adult and child participants' perspectives as elicited in questionnaires and interviews, from our observations of interaction in different family relationships, from teachers' reports about the children's behaviours, skills and difficulties, and from achievement tests administered yearly to each individual child. One of the advantages of complex projects like this is that when we find correlations between qualities in different family relationships, we know that they are the result of different types of information from many sources and various methods of measurement.

Parent–child and couple attachment: evidence for a 'template theory'?

Bowlby made a major contribution to our understanding of intimate relationships. His central question was: What happens when a relationship is threatened by an actual loss or separation, or by psychological loss or distance from a loved one? What do people do to cope? As we have seen in earlier chapters, researchers have observed four main strategies of reacting when an intimate relationship is threatened by separation or loss. People who have insecure models of attachment become upset, but take action in order to get back in touch with the loved one through behaviour or fantasy. In general, research has shown that approximately two-thirds of the children and adults studied are characterised as having secure working models of attachment.

People who have insecure attachment patterns have three quite different types of reactions. The first is a 'dismissing' response in which they try to reduce their anxiety about a threat to a key relationship by denying the importance of the relationship or by claiming that the relationship is ideal. They may say that they don't really care about the relationships, or that the relationship is perfect. In either case, they deny the fact that they sometimes get upset because a loved one is not available to provide comfort in times of distress. A second insecure style is one in which individuals are fearful of attachments and spend a good deal of energy trying to avoid them. That is, they do not dismiss the importance of close relationships but find that they cannot trust them enough to enter into them. A third insecure strategy involves ambivalence or preoccupation with the relationship. When a relationship with a loved one seems threatened, these individuals become obsessive, thinking about the other all the time, and becoming more and more anxious or angry. In sum, one insecure strategy is dismissing, another is avoidant and withdrawn, and a third involves the amplification of anxiety and sometimes anger.

According to Bowlby, people form working models based on experiences in their families of origin. These models are construed as cognitive/emotional/behavioural systems that are carried into new relationships. Particularly when their close relationships are threatened, the working models become activated and act as prototypes to filter perceptions and shape interpretations of what is happening in the current relationship. Owens et al. (1995) wrote about a strong form of a prototype hypothesis in which every current romantic relationship is guided by the same template of working models based on early family experiences. In Chapter 2, Crowell and Treboux write about their scepticism about such a strong form of model – based on evidence that individuals do not react to every important intimate relationship in adulthood in the same way – and we concur with this.

In our current project, we measured adults' working models of attachment with reference to their earliest relationships in four ways, two drawn from the social psychology tradition of using questionnaires (Bartholomew and Horowitz, 1991; Collins and Read, 1994; Hazan and Shaver, 1994) and two drawn from the developmental psychology tradition of using individual, structured interviews (Hesse, 1999; Crowell and Owens, 1996).

First, we administered a questionnaire taken directly from Bartholomew and Horowitz (1991). The questionnaire presents people with a description of four different types of attachment styles and says, in effect, 'which one most resembles you?' (see Appendix 2). We used the seventeen sentences from the four paragraphs as separate statements. All of these measures from the social psychology tradition of assessing attachment style refer to current models of adult relationships. Daniel Silver, a member of our research team, noticed that in the social psychology approach, most or all of the statements were presented in a general form, such as 'I am comfortable without close relationships'; few or no statements referred specifically to a romantic partner, as in 'I often find that my partner is reluctant to get as close as I would like.' To see whether the general or specific context made a difference, we asked men and women to respond to two versions of the statements, one with the sentences referring to relationships in general and the other with the same statements referring specifically to the current partner.

Then, in a qualitatively different approach to measuring adult attachment, we used the Adult Attachment Interview (AAI) with each parent in our study. From transcripts of these narratives about adults' descriptions of their relationships with their parents, raters used Main and Goldwyn's coding scheme (see Hesse, 1999) to characterise adults as having secure or insecure working models of attachment.

In order to obtain a sense of each parent's working model of their couple relationship, we developed, with Daniel Silver and Deborah Cohn, members of our research team at the time, the CAI referred to earlier. With this interview, modelled on the AAI approach, we ask each parent to: (1) describe the relationship with the partner, using five adjectives to characterise it; (2) give examples that illustrate each of the adjectives chosen; (3) consider whether the partner has been available in times of trouble; (4) talk about why they think their partner has acted as he or she has; and (5) describe his or her *own* tendency to be available when the partner is vulnerable or in distress.

One of our central questions in this part of our study was: do the various questionnaire and interview methods of measuring adult attachment yield the same information or the same type of working models of attachment? The strong version of template theory would suggest that, whether the focus is on parents, partners or relationships in general, people will have similar working models across all three types of relationship. Perhaps it is not surprising that our study results suggest a more complex answer.

General versus partner forms of attachment questionnaires

We found that attachment style category (insecure, preoccupied, dismissing, fearful) on the general and partner forms of the questionnaire were related at a statistically significant level, but the correlations between the two were not high. Although a person who responded to the statements using a secure characterisation with regard to relationships was, in general, more likely to describe his relationship with his partner in the same general style, there were many exceptions.

We found that people who described positive attachments on the form that was specific to partners tended to say that they were happy with their couple relationship on a relationship-adjustment questionnaire, but adults' descriptions of positive attachments on the general form were less likely to be systematically related to their level of satisfaction with their overall couple relationship. In other words, the results we obtained depended, in part, on which form of the questionnaire we used.

After completing these interviews with the parents in our study, we discovered that both Judith Crowell and her colleagues, and Susan Dickson and her colleagues, in other parts of the United States, had developed similar interviews in which they asked adults to describe their relationships as couples.

Connections between questionnaires and interviews regarding adult attachment

Several investigators have found little or no connection between adult attachment measured by questionnaire and by the AAI (for example, Crowell and Treboux, 1995). We found a significant but low association between the two. It is important to remember that not only do these measures of attachment differ in method (interview versus questionnaire) but they also differ in focus. Since the questionnaire asked about adult relationships that were current, and the interview asked about relationships with parents in the past, it is not clear how much agreement should be expected.

Adult Attachment and Couple Attachment Interviews: continuity across relationships?

Using an interview similar to our CAI, Dickstein and her colleagues (1996) found 90 per cent agreement in a preliminary study of the relation between adults' security of attachment (*vis-à-vis* their parents) based on the AAI and security of attachment with a partner based on her Marital Attachment Interview (MAI). Crowell and her colleagues (1997) found about 65 per cent agreement between security of attachment on the AAI and the CRI (see Chapter 2). At this point in our longitudinal work, we have analysed the data from only fifteen of the couples in our longitudinal study who completed both the AAI and the CAI. Because of the large number of hours required to code the AAI, we were eager to find a more global way of coding our CAIs. We asked colleagues at the University of California in Berkeley, California, and at the Tavistock Marital Studies Institute in London, to read the verbatim transcripts of the CAI interviews and use a more global scoring procedure to place the adults in one of the three main attachment categories – insecure, dismissing or preoccupied. This method of coding couple attachment style yielded an agreement of 12 out of 15 (80 per cent) between AAI and CAI using the three categorical scores. What these preliminary results suggest is that, when measured by in-depth interviews, security of working models with reference to parents and partners is fairly consistent, although the correlation is not perfect. That is, despite a general trend for consistency of working models across relationships, a meaningful number of people who are insecure with reference to parent–child relationships are not insecure with reference to couple relationships. This leaves room to speculate on how those inconsistencies can be understood.

Let us describe one couple as an example.

Mona described a very difficult early childhood and cried throughout the AAI interview. Nevertheless, she had been able to come to grips with her early experiences with her parents, which she showed by talking about her understanding of why her parents had reacted as they did. She related that she had worked on these painful issues through sporadic periods of psychotherapy over a number of years. Using the standard coding scheme, coders characterised Mona as having a secure model of attachment of relationships based on her responses to the AAI.

Coding of her partner Donald's AAI suggests that he was highly dismissing of relationships overall. Separate coders of his CAI characterised his working models of relationships as insecure. We know from other interviews with him that Donald had had a serious work-related accident early in their marriage, which apparently affected his functioning. Donald and Mona both said that he was temperamentally irascible or remote. Just as she had during the AAI, Mona cried throughout the CAI, but she did not describe her relationship with Donald in a coherent manner, which led the coders of her CAI to characterise her attachment *vis-à-vis* her partner as insecure. This is just one example of two adults in one couple, in which he appeared to have a similar attachment style in discussing two of his major family relationships, whereas she gave the impression of having qualitatively different working models for these two key attachment relationships.

Links between adults' responses to the AAI and behaviour with a partner

So far, we have described relationships from the perspectives of men and women who have completed questionnaires or lengthy interviews. In using both types of materials, researchers or clinicians focused on what adults reported and their manner of reporting it. With the additional rich information from observing the parents and children in our longitudinal study, we were able to ask several other questions about how qualities of key attachment relationships played out in what we observed *between the partners* when they were in moderately stressful situations. That is, our observations allowed us to examine how adults characterised as securely or insecurely attached (a) behaved together when they were working with their children on tasks that challenged them, and (b) behaved with their partners when they were working on a troubling problem in their relationship – situations in which one or both partners might feel some anxiety about the relationship.

Pairing of partners' attachment style and couple relationships

Cohn and her colleagues (1992) found that couples in which both partners had insecure working models of attachment on the AAI showed more conflict when they were working and playing together with their children in our laboratory playroom than couples in which only one partner was classified as having an insecure working model of attachment. In a new study, Bradburn (1997) found links between spouses' attachment pattern and the way they discussed a problem when their child was not present. Men classified by AAI coders as having secure working models of attachment were coded by Bradburn's observers as having fewer negative interactions with their partners; they were less avoidant, rejecting, blaming, ruminating or controlling than men classified as having insecure working models. Women classified as having secure working models of attachment on the AAI were more supportive, constructive and collaborative with their partners than women classified as insecure.

Since *both* partners come to a couple relationship with models based on their family-of-origin relationships, Bradburn examined the links between the two attachment patterns, taking the *pairing* of partners' working models into consideration. Not surprisingly, men with secure working models, and in relationships with women with secure working models, had the least negative interaction as they worked on their couple problem. However, we were surprised to find that there were no statistically significant differences between the quality of discussion in the secure–secure pairs and those of men with secure working models whose partners had insecure working models: these relationships between partners with different working models were also characterised as quite positive overall. By contrast, couples in which both partners were categorised as insecurely attached were *very* negative toward each other. Thus, if the man had a secure working model of attachment based on his description of relationships with his parents, his interaction with his partner tended to be productive regardless of her attachment pattern, and even when they were working on a 'hot issue'.

The most dramatic contrast was in the interactions of men with insecure models of attachment whose partners had secure working models. Not at all similar to the secure–secure pairs, these couples represented the most negative and volatile combination. The men in these couples expressed more anger toward their partners than any other men in the study. What was it that was so difficult about this combination? Perhaps something about her sense of security allowed her to freely express her angry feelings. From a more dynamic perspective, it may be that insecure men sought women whom they hoped would be qualitatively different from their mothers – that is, more nurturing, responsive and accepting, qualities typical of women with secure models of relationships. But, when their partners failed to be as nurturant as the men had fantasised, the men became angry. It is conceivable that the women may have chosen vulnerable, insecure men, in hopes of being able to help them feel more loved and secure, but our observations suggested that if this central task proved too difficult to achieve, the long-term relationship was very difficult to manage.

Another possible explanation of the outcomes for these 'mis-matched' couples focuses on societally influenced gender role stereotypes. The combination of a man who is securely attached and a woman who is vulnerable when the relationship feels threatened, fits the gender stereotypic pattern of men playing a more protective role when their partners are vulnerable. The reverse-stereotype pattern, of men who feel vulnerable or threatened and women who feel more secure in their expectations about relationships, is discrepant from societal expectations for men and women. It is our observation that many men who experience vulnerability, or a sense of threat, especially if their partners do not simply coddle them when they are fearful, feel so uneasy that they become angry at their feelings of impotence and direct that anger at their wives.

Pairing of partners' attachment style and parenting

We have described our observations of partners as they discussed a troubling problem in their relationship. In our most recent analyses, replicating earlier findings from Cohn and colleagues (1992), we found similar trends between the parents' models of attachment and their style of interacting as a couple while helping their child solve challenging tasks. We saw the most negative interaction *between the parents* in front of the child in couples in which his model of attachment on the AAI was coded as insecure and hers was coded as secure. That is, in the whole family situation too, the insecure men with secure partners were the most volatile when parenting their child together.

Attachment patterns, couple relationship quality and children's adaptation

We have been painting a portrait in which the quality of the relationship between parents and children in one generation – referred to here as adult attachment – was associated with the quality of both the couple and parent–child relationships in the next generation. Our information about the quality of family relationships over time helps us understand how these key family relationships shape children's early adaptation to the challenges of school.

The attachment data from our current longitudinal study (Cowan et al., 1999) provided a replication of the results from our first study of families (Cowan et al., 1996). When parents had insecure working models of attachment based on descriptions of relationships with their parents, they fought more when they were alone as a couple *and* when they were parenting their child. In turn, when parents' responses to their child were more negative before the child entered school, the child had lower achievement scores and was more aggressive or shy and withdrawn in the first and second years of school according to their kindergarten and first grade teachers. In other words, the state of the key relationships in the family (the couple and parent–child relationships) when the children were pre-schoolers foretold a good deal about the success of their adaptation to kindergarten two years later, particularly in terms of the quality of their relationships with other children at school.

When we looked more specifically at the parents' attachment patterns, we found that information from the fathers' attachment interviews was more useful in predicting the children's aggression, whereas information from the mothers' attachment interviews was more helpful in predicting the children's tendency to be depressed, shy or withdrawn when they were five and six years old. We can summarise these findings by saying that adults' insecure patterns with their parents and partners were associated with less positive parenting styles (referred to here as adult attachment, couple relationship quality and parenting quality) and all three constituted risk factors for the child's adaptation in the first two years of school.

INTERVENING TO BREAK THE CYCLE

Let us return for a moment to William and Sarah's argument at the beginning of the chapter. If we want to help them improve the quality of their relationship as a couple, it seems clear that enhancing their communication skills will address only part of the problem between them. We would also need to help them modify some of the attachment patterns that they refer to in their argument. Our studies suggest that the ability to regulate or deal with positive and negative emotion in the parents' families of origin is related to their ability to regulate negative emotions in their new family – in their relationships as a couple and with their children. As we have seen, the tone of these family relationship patterns is related to their children's ability to manage their relationships with other children at school, and to their general style of responding to the academic and emotional challenges in their lives. The results suggest that if we could help William and Sarah to shift to a more responsive and rewarding way of working on their problems together, that could have positive consequences for them as individuals, as a couple and as parents.

In our earlier *Becoming a Family Project*, some couples expecting a first child, randomly chosen from all those entering the study, participated in a couples group with mental health professionals as leaders. The groups met weekly for six months, from late pregnancy to three months after the birth of their first child. The results of following all couples over time showed that partners who had taken part in the couples group intervention showed fewer disappointments in their mutual role arrangements and less decline in satisfaction with their overall relationship as a couple than partners in a randomly chosen control group. Furthermore, all the intervention parents remained together as couples for the first three years of parenthood, compared to the new parents without intervention, 15 per cent of whom separated or divorced by the time their first child was three years old. The more satisfied partners were more responsive and effective when they worked and played with their children in the pre-school period, and their children were less likely to have troubling behaviour problems and more likely to be academically competent in their first year of elementary school two years later when they were five (Cowan and Cowan, 2000; Cowan, 1988).

Based on those findings, we offered two-thirds of the couples entering the *Schoolchildren and their Families Project* an opportunity to participate in similar professionally led couples groups when their first children were pre-schoolers. We offered the remaining one-third a brief consultation with a staff couple once a year in each of the first three years of the study, when the children were four, five and six years old. Because these couples also had a first child making the transition to kindergarten, our two studies provided overlapping information about this family transition. In the second project, we followed the couples from the time the children were four years old until they completed fourth grade, when they were ten.

The results of our intervention in the more recent *Schoolchildren and their Families Project* suggested that working with parents on their couple and parenting problems during this family transition helped couples make more positive and satisfying shifts in their relationships as partners and parents than those in comparable couples who were not offered the group intervention. When parents who participated in a couples group for the four months surrounding their child's transition to school changed in a positive direction, their children also made more successful adjustments to the first two years of elementary school. Before we speculate on how the intervention may account for these results, let us describe the couples groups in more detail.

Couples group intervention

The main goal of the couples group intervention in both studies was to bolster the strengths in the parents' couple relationships *and* to support them in developing effective and rewarding relationships with their children. As we have said, the results of our *Becoming a Family Project* revealed that the quality of the parents' relationships as couples and with their children during the pre-school years was an excellent predictor of the children's adjustment to school (Cowan and Cowan, 2000). Based on these findings, we asked our staff couples in the newer *Schoolchildren and their Families Project* to emphasise couple relationship issues during the open discussions in half of the couples groups and to focus more on parent–child issues during the open-ended part in the other half of the couples groups. These distinctions in focus were randomly assigned and known only to us and the staff couples, not to the parents.

The couples group format

Four or five couples with a child about to enter kindergarten met for two hours every week for four months – sixteen sessions altogether. The staff couples were psychologists, social workers or marriage and family counsellors that we trained and consulted with regularly. Almost all of the couples who agreed to be in a group met with the leaders weekly throughout the four months, but most couples offered the brief consultation did not take advantage of the offer. This means that when we compared the shifts of couples from the groups with those of couples offered the brief consultation, we were really comparing the effects of a more intensive intervention with little or no intervention.

The groups were semi-structured in format, in the sense that they combined (1) an ongoing, somewhat structured agenda formed collaboratively by the leaders and participants from week to week, and (2) an open-ended 'check in' each week, during which couples were free to raise any issue or problem for the group to discuss. We worked to make the groups a safe setting in which men and women could share personal and troubling issues. We tried to help parents elaborate on their own personal ideas and experiences, in part by referring to the study questionnaires that they had completed before the groups began, and in part by asking more about the fresh issues they raised each week. We hoped to help parents recognise some of the links between these different parts of their lives – for example, how their conflicts as a couple might be affecting their relationships with their child, or how their experiences of being parented by their parents might be colouring their ideas, feelings and parenting practices with their own children. Based on findings from our earlier studies and those of colleagues, we tried to help make these parts of parents' lives conscious so that they could have more control than before over patterns that felt unsatisfying or destructive.

The problems and worries that men and women brought to the groups were many and varied. Some raised dilemmas about whether to send their child to a private school that cost as much as sending them to college, or to risk keeping them in a neighbourhood school where they might get 'lost' in large classrooms with disruptive problems. Others wanted help with how to handle a child's tantrums when they set a limit about going to bed but found it painful to follow through when their child became extremely upset. Some partners talked of serious disagreements about how to manage relationship problems, or about crises that led to painful fights between them as partners, or between them and their parents.

Whatever the content, it was common for couples to find it challenging to manage passionate differences between them. Whose attitudes would guide the family, how that was to be decided, and how to keep track of everyone's needs were common dilemmas that most parents faced as couples. When they considered their current patterns in relation to those in each partner's families of origin – some of which they wanted to repeat and some of which they hoped to change – most couples found it difficult to know how to conduct their key family relationships in ways that felt satisfying to all family members. By using leaders who were clinically skilled at making the groups a safe and supportive environment in which to work on these complex issues, we found that we could help men and women at the same family life stage discover more about what goes on in real-life families across a broad spectrum of background and attitude.

The goals of the staff

We listened very carefully and drew partners out about what happened when they reached an impasse as a couple or as parents. Besides providing a sympathetic ear, we tried to help partners clarify their own points of view and get them heard, especially by their spouses. We encouraged partners to be more tolerant of their differences in point of view, behaviour and individual needs – one of the most difficult things for partners to do without getting upset or worried about who is 'right' or 'wrong'. We also attempted to help couples develop more satisfying and less aggressive ways to solve the problems they had, since it is clear that aggression in the family puts children and adults at risk for troubled relationships (see Cummings and Davies, 1994).

A more unusual approach in a relatively brief group situation for couples was our explicit encouragement to explore how experiences in each partner's family of origin might be playing a role in their reactions to one another and to their children, particularly when they were upset and feeling vulnerable or threatened. This is where our work drew quite directly on attachment theory. We assumed that 'forgotten' or unexamined painful relationship experiences would keep partners from being able to engage fully in the troubling aspects of their relationships as couples and with their children. We found that as men and women became able to discuss and reflect on some of these issues in a supportive environment, they developed more coherent narratives about the past, and, we think, an increased ability to cope with difficult emotions in times of stress.

The leaders in the groups were not in the business of giving advice to parents but of trying to help them uncover what kind of parents and partners they were hoping to be, and supporting them in moving closer to their ideals. The couples found it refreshing to have a setting in which they were encouraged to work toward these goals when they were not upset. Partners could come back together in subsequent weeks, with the support of the staff and the other parents, to assess how successful their 'experiments' in shifting mind-sets and tactics had been. What we are trying to convey is that these groups were not just a short course on couple communication, but a safe place for spouses to begin the kinds of discussions about three-generational and other family issues that most of them did not have in the ordinary course of events.

Impact of the variations of the intervention: focus on couple or parenting issues

The couple-focused and parenting-focused groups seemed to have rather specific effects, and overall, the couple-focused groups seemed to have the most positive effects on the families. For example, we found that fathers from the groups emphasising parenting were warmer and more responsive to their children one year after the groups ended than they had been before the groups began, whereas fathers in the control group showed no significant changes over the same period. Mothers who had been in a group emphasising parenting issues were more helpful in structuring difficult tasks for their children than they had been the year before, meaning that they helped break down the difficult tasks into solvable parts and set more limits on misbehaviour than they had before the groups began. By contrast, we saw no significant changes in the mothers without the intervention over the same period.

When we looked at what was happening between the parents during their visits with the children one year after the couples groups ended, we saw no change in parents from the groups emphasising parenting, but couples from the couple-focused groups were showing less conflict than they had before the groups began; they were less argumentative and hostile with one another when they worked and played with their child. By contrast, the couples with no intervention were showing more conflict as a couple in front of their children. Then, almost two years after the couples groups ended, men from the couple-focused groups told us that they were experiencing less conflict with their partners – mirroring what we had observed a year before – and both the men and their partners reported less volatile, violent behaviour during arguments. By contrast, couples who were in the parenting-focused groups, or in the control group with no intervention, reported no significant changes in their conflict and disagreement or in their strategies for resolving problems as a couple.

As we described, our intervention was based on our concern for the wellbeing of the couples *and* of their children. We were gratified to find that children of parents who shifted in a more positive direction as a couple or as parents after attending a transition-to-school group made greater gains in academic achievement scores, were more successful in negotiating relationships with their classmates and had fewer acting-out, aggressive or shy, withdrawn, depressed problem behaviours at school.

When we looked at the intervention results from an attachment perspective, we found hints that the work in the groups seemed to help break some of the unrewarding relationship patterns from the parents' families of origin. For example, *without intervention*, parents classified as having insecure models of relationships were not likely to show positive shifts in their relationships as couples or in their parenting style over the next few years. On the other hand, if parents classified as having insecure models took part in one of our couples groups, they were *as likely as parents classified as secure* to shift in positive directions in their relationships with their partners or their children.

Despite results about the different impact of the two variations on our couples group, we would not choose a couple-focused group over a parenting-focused group in our next intervention for couples. Some parents are more amenable to talking about their parenting problems first, after which they can more easily move to discussing their difficulties as a couple. This may be particularly true for parents with a dismissing style of thinking about relationship issues. In any intervention we plan in the future, we will continue to work with both parents as a couple. We cannot emphasise enough how important the fathers are to the success of family relationships and to their children's development. We also recommend incorporating a focus on each of the major aspects of couples' lives that we have mentioned, being certain to focus on the parents' relationship as a couple. We found that the parents in the groups emphasising couple issues tended to show positive shifts as a couple *and* with their children, but the reverse was not true. In other words, to focus only on parenting risks is missing an important opportunity to strengthen the relationship between the parents, one of the key ingredients in young children's adaptation. We believe that together, these relationships provide a secure family base to minimise anxiety about needs when members are vulnerable, and to maximise parents' and children's freedom to explore and learn new things.

Because there are stringent limitations on funds for family services on both sides of the Atlantic, let us comment briefly on our strategy of working with couples in apparently low or moderate risk circumstances. According to their initial reports, the couples in our study would not be considered at high or even moderate risk for distress or dysfunctional relationships. As we have written elsewhere (Cowan and Cowan, 1997), these well-educated, non-divorced, middle-to-high-income parents appeared to be an advantaged group. Nevertheless, between 5 and 35 per cent of them entered our projects showing clinically significant levels of distress on questionnaire measures of depression and marital adjustment; 20 per cent also described themselves as 'adult children of alcoholics'. By the time their children entered formal schooling at age five, 10 per cent were diagnosed by their teachers as having significant emotional, behavioural or learning problems. These figures make clear that low-risk does not mean problem-free. Even in these samples of fairly well-functioning families, men's and women's effectiveness as couples and as parents is significantly linked with their children's early academic, social and emotional competence. Since in contrast to no intervention, a modest intervention with couples is followed by a majority of the parents moving toward more satisfying couple and parent–child relationships, the more appropriate question may be whether we can afford *not* to offer such help to the families of young children. If we are interested in *preventive* intervention, this may be the most important population to reach.

How do these interventions work to produce these effects?

It is our view that these interventions worked in four ways to produce these effects. First, they provided social support that normalised the couples' experience of the particular transition they were making. Second, they strengthened the family as a secure base. Third, the couples group itself may have constituted a secure base for the parents when they were anxious and unsure of themselves. Finally, we think that the mental health professionals were helping the parents to regulate their emotions when they were upset.

Social support and normalisation

First, we know from what the parents told us following their completion that the groups provided a powerful and socially supportive group of couples for parents to identify with. The refrain we heard most often from parents in both of these projects was, 'Thank God, I'm not the only one who has trouble with that!' They felt less alone, less extreme in their awkward handling of tricky issues, which led them to conclude that they were not 'crazy' as they sometimes feared when their middle-of-the-night exchanges left them feeling more like petulant children than adults. Slowly, many of them began to attribute some of their stress to the demands of the transition they were facing, not to a partner who suddenly seemed like an enemy.

Strengthening the family as a secure base

Byng-Hall (1999) writes about the family as a potential secure base for its members. He suggests that when the family is able to provide a reliable and readily available network of attachment relationships and appropriate caregivers, the members feel sufficiently secure to explore their potential. Our results are quite consistent with this way of viewing attachment in the family. When the couple and parent–child relationships were less conflictful and more nurturing, the children felt less anxious and depressed, were less likely to use aggressive strategies in their relationships with others, and their higher academic scores suggested that they were freer to explore and learn new things.

The couples group as a secure base

We might think of the couples groups as providing a secure base for adult couples to turn to when they were under stress. When we provided settings in which partners could talk about their hurt and angry feelings as well as their dreams, many said that they felt less like adversaries and more like partners working on problems that they were mutually invested in. By becoming more conscious about the patterns they were trying to change, some men and women began to consider why their parents behaved as they did, which is one of the marks of a secure working model of attachment. With the staff's empathetic way of drawing them out, some parents began to show a little more understanding and empathy – often for their own partners, sometimes for other parents in the group and occasionally for themselves.

Security and emotional regulation

Researchers at the University of Washington in Seattle have studied parents' abilities to be 'emotion coaches' for their children when the children are upset (Gottman et al., 1997). They found that when mothers or fathers of young school-age children were able to help them talk about their sad or angry feelings rather than sweep them under the proverbial carpet, the children were more successful in their academic work and developed more sophisticated social skills with other children at school. We think that our couples group leaders did this kind of emotional coaching by drawing parents out when they were upset. This ability of the leaders to stay calm and supportive while one or more of the group participants is distressed is another function of a secure base. Perhaps this explains why we found more systematic links between positive shifts in parents' emotionally troubled conversations and their children's increasing success at school, but only for parents who took part in the groups.

Keeping the couple in mind

What have we learned about attachment in couple relationships? The concept of attachment has often been conceptualised as a characteristic of an individual in a relationship. Our longitudinal data on families suggest that adults' working models of attachment regarding their relationship as a couple is only modestly related to their attachment patterns regarding their relationships with parents. Characteristics of both these working models are related to *observable* qualities of the relationship between the parents, and between each parent and their child. We showed that the quality of each of these central attachment relationships plays a part in explaining how the children in the next generation manage academic, social and emotional challenges in their lives.

These findings suggest that attachment issues play out dynamically across the generations of a family. In the ordinary course of events, all things being equal, patterns tend to get repeated – from parent–child relationships in the families of origin, to the relationships parents establish with their partners and children, and ultimately to the relationships their children establish with important people in their lives. But all things are rarely equal. None of these templates is fixed. Some individuals with insecure working models of attachment are fortunate or skilled enough to establish a satisfying relationship with an adult partner that buffers them and their children from the automatic repetition of negative or destructive patterns in the new generation. In some cases it seems that individuals or couples find therapeutic help that changes not what occurred in their past, but how they think and feel about and make sense of those relationships. The data suggest that, as expectations shift, loved ones reap the benefits of more nurturant relationships. In other words, the influence or absence of a secure base helps us explain how parents' models of attachment, as individuals *and as couples*, affect their children's adaptation to the challenges of their lives, and suggests the potential of preventive intervention programmes as agents of change with regard to them.

Part II

Applications to couple psychotherapy

Chapter 5

Attachment theory and the therapeutic frame

Christopher Clulow

Bowlby (1969) proposed that secure attachment in infants resulted from three social experiences: frequent and sustained physical contact with a primary caregiver, the sensitivity of that caregiver to the infant's signals, and an interpersonal environment that supports the infant in sensing and learning from the consequences of his or her actions. For him, parents, as caregivers, provided both a safe haven and a secure base from which children might explore and learn about their world and themselves in it. Rutter (1981) developed Bowlby's position by asserting that the key to secure attachment was active, reciprocal interaction, the quality of that interaction being more important than the quantity provided or the gender of the provider. So, proximity, responsiveness (what Stern, 1985, described as 'attunement') and a facilitating environment combine, from an attachment perspective, to form the building blocks of human growth and development.

As well as recognising the significance of environmental influences, Bowlby was also aware of the power of the inner world to replicate itself in the outer world of relationships through the operations of those relatively stable structures that he described as 'internal working models'. A confident outlook on life can prompt a positive response from others, confirming and consolidating the initial sense of confidence. A mistrustful or hostile outlook is capable of evoking responses that fulfil negative prophecies about human nature. A cycle of reciprocal influence blurs the boundary between internal and external realities, acting to confirm or confound the assumptions of both. This is not to deny that there are other influences upon relationships – the genetic and psychological predisposition of a child is relevant to the kind of response a parent makes, and vice versa – but it does locate individual experience in a relational context. Even those considering the nature of mind from a neurological perspective highlight the role of the *pathways* connecting the myriads of cells in the human brain in fashioning individual identity, and the relevance of social experience to determining which connections are, and are not, made (Greenfield, 1999).

If attachment security in childhood is a product of social relatedness, and the quality of social relatedness reflects attachment security, is the same true for adult couples? Thompson asserted the prototype hypothesis, described in Chapters 2 and 4, when he described marriage as the 'most direct heir of the intense primary relationships of childhood' (1960: 3). 'Marriage' provided continuing opportunities for development through combining physical proximity, emotional attunement and a holding environment. Taken on their own, any one of these conditions is insufficient to foster security. Physical proximity may be increased as a result of the emotional engagement between two people, but there is no guarantee that the process will work in reverse: those who believe that social (and thereby personal) cohesion depends on maintaining the married state at all costs miss the point that the cost of maintaining the married state can sometimes be the breakdown of personal (and thereby social) cohesion. It is the quality of the environment that couples create together, whether linked or not with the married state, that is likely to be the key to security for both adults and any children they may have. Evidence for this is contained in previous chapters and substantiated elsewhere (see, for example, Berlin and Cassidy, 1999). Partnering affects parenting affects partnering – and so the cycle goes across the generations.

When couples seek help it is because their jointly constructed environment is no longer proving adequate to the tasks they are facing as a couple. In a culture promoting companionate values in marriage and partnership (Richards, 1995) these tasks are likely to be of an emotional and relational nature, although they are clearly very relevant to society's investment in regulating sexuality and bringing up children. Colman (1993) accounts for couple insecurity in terms of the partnership no longer being able to *contain* the tensions associated with the needs of the partners to develop both within and outside their relationship. In attachment terms, the couple relationship is no longer serving as a safe haven or secure base for the partners. Help may then be sought to establish, or re-establish, a containing function in the partnership that can facilitate the work the partners want or need to do together.

What kind of response does psychoanalytic psychotherapy offer in these circumstances? I want to suggest that it contains some of the elements of a research enterprise. When in crisis, couples often lack the means of identifying and addressing key questions that trouble them in their partnership. Their questions may be very clearly defined: 'Why doesn't he show more affection?' 'What should I do about her affair?' 'Should we separate?' Or they may be hard to articulate, like knowing something is wrong but being unable to locate what it is. Their questions may take the form of a statement or an accusation: 'My partner is depressed/violent/has a sexual problem/needs help.' Whatever form the questions or statements may take, they often contain implicit hypotheses for which evidence is being sought. Psychotherapy is one means of addressing them, so that there are opportunities for arriving at, if not evidence and answers, at least better questions.

One might say that when partners are in this state they are like investigators in search of a methodology. For them, the questions are likely to carry a powerful emotional charge; the search for answers is neither academic nor remote. It is fearfulness rather than intellectual constraint that inhibits their quest. In these circumstances the task of the therapist is not to come up with answers, but to provide a framework that facilitates their research. Partners may then discover they have their own means of working out answers, or of identifying what they need to supplement their resources to work through the 'fieldwork' stage of this joint enterprise. Helping couples to think about the questions they define, and focusing on the feelings generated by them (as well as those generated by the questions they don't ask), are part of the therapeutic process.

If psychotherapists were empirical researchers they might well describe the therapeutic frame as their methodology, the session as their laboratory, the analytic process as data and the couple as co-researchers. I want to comment on each of these dimensions as a prelude to the succeeding chapters in this section of the book.

THE THERAPEUTIC FRAME AS A RESEARCH METHOD

The therapeutic frame is made up of many elements, all of which stem from a theoretical stance that defines the nature and purpose of the therapist–patient relationship, and prescribes certain boundaries or 'rules of engagement'. Because this stance is contextually important for succeeding chapters I will summarise some key assumptions that attachment and object relations theories hold in common.

Theoretical assumptions

Attachment theory, like object relations theories, draws attention to the potential significance of childhood insecurity in understanding troubled adult relationships. Each offers an approach to understanding child development, and attends to mechanisms that act both to block and to connect inner and outer realities. Social learning is understood to result from testing the relationship between these realities. It is inhibited to the extent that anxiety-inducing ways of relating are repressed and split off from consciousness because of the threat they are believed to represent to personal security. The greater the sense of threat, the more reliance there is on defensive processes, and, consequentially, the poorer the emotional and relational repertoire of the individual concerned is likely to be.

Within these frameworks, repressed, wished-for relationships are understood to be constantly seeking expression and recognition through symptom formation, neurosis and 'acting out' behaviours. Spatial confusions – what's me and what's not me – and temporal confusions – what belongs to the past and what to the present – are external signs of unconscious mental activity. Psychoanalytic psychotherapy relies on the assumption that both 'required' (defensive) and 'avoided' (repressed) relationships, to use Ezriel's (1956) reformulation in relational terms of the classical Freudian defence-impulse paradigm, will be activated and enacted in the therapy relationship because of its attachment-related associations and purposes. An important function of the therapist is to be open to taking on the mantle of the patient's objects, and to gather in their associated affects, through the process of transference. Such enactments and re-enactments provide access to unconscious data about the inner world, as well as offering opportunities for development through the therapist containing what the patient finds uncontainable.

These assumptions are particularly useful in understanding adult hetero-sexual (and, indeed, same-sex) partnerships. The physical and emotional proximity such partnerships afford will resonate closely with early family experience. They are therefore particularly well-placed to become transferen-tial as well as actual relationships, incorporating parental, sibling and peer imagoes (Scharff and Savege Scharff, 1991). In consequence, they have the capacity not only to activate destructive patterns of relating but also to con-tain and change them. Development occurs through the support partners are able to afford each other, and the degree to which they are in touch with and able to process (and reprocess) each other's conscious and unconscious experiences. Here, partnering is closely allied with parent–infant interactions: the 'infant's' unprocessed thoughts, feelings and experiences are contained by the 'parent' in ways that allow them to be recognised and owned. One way of defining the aim of couple psychotherapy is as the endeavour to enhance the capacity of the couple relationship to assist the partners in performing this processing function for each other.

This formulation shifts the focus of attention from the security of the individuals within a partnership to the security of the partnership. It implies that a partnership can, in itself, function as a secure base by providing a social and psychological 'skin' of accrued experience, unconscious assumption and external support that holds the partners through testing times. When the pressures are such that the skin cannot hold, a surrogate may be needed. The role of therapists can be envisaged in such terms. In his last collection of papers, Bowlby outlined this very specific surrogate task in the following terms:

> A therapist applying attachment theory sees his role as being one of providing the conditions in which his patient can explore his represen-tational models of himself and his attachment figures with a view to reappraising and restructuring them in the light of the new understand-ing he acquires and the new experiences he has in the therapeutic rela-tionship. . . . The therapeutic alliance appears as a secure base, an internal object as a working, or representational, model of an attachment

figure, reconstruction as exploring memories of the past, resistance as a deep reluctance to disobey the past orders of parents not to tell or not to remember.

(1988: 138, 151)

In his view, the central task for therapists was to establish a secure base from which patients would feel safe enough to explore unknown and potentially threatening aspects of their experience. In the context of therapeutic work with individuals he defined five tasks:

- providing a secure base from which a person might explore, think about and reconsider painful aspects of experience;
- encouraging the patient to consider how s/he engages in significant relationships, and the expectations and unconscious biases s/he brings to them;
- examining the patient–therapist relationship as a means of gaining access to the working models operating in relation to attachment figures;
- considering how current perceptions and expectations might be linked to relationship experiences and parental messages during childhood and adolescence;
- unshackling the patient from the legacy of past traumatic experience by supporting the review of historically dominated internal working models and encouraging new, autonomous models to emerge.

Bowlby was explicit in seeing the therapist's role as analogous to that of a mother who encourages the child to explore the world from the secure base she creates. He was therefore concerned to emphasise the role of the therapist, as well as that of the patient, in accounting for whatever happened in their relationship together. Aware of the huge literature on counter-transference, he simply flagged up the reminder that therapists bring their own histories, lacunae and insecure strategies to the therapeutic process, and indicated the place of personal therapy and supervision for promoting self-awareness in therapists as well as patients.

For couple work, the move from a dyadic to a multi-relational stance is imperative. While Bowlby focused his attention on the dyadic relationship between child and parent, the couple therapist is also interested in the relationship between the parents (and between other key attachment figures) that partners internalise from their childhood experience. Moving from a two- to three-person constellation of relationships has classical significance for psychoanalysis: Freud's theory of personality development drew heavily on the myth of Oedipus. It is here that object relations thinking has more to say than attachment theory.

Contemporary thinking about the Oedipal situation highlights the significance of the parental couple (or, at least, of one parent's capacity to reflect on her or his experience sufficiently for there to be the resource of an internalised couple to draw upon) for healthy child development. While, at the beginning, there is only 'mother' (the quotation mark being used to signify that the parenting role might be taken by a man as well as a woman), later on there must be room for 'father'. The process of individuation begins with the infant's recognition of 'mother' as *other*, not as an extension of him or herself. This follows from her capacity to hold him in mind as a separate intentional being. So the first stage of developing a 'reflective self' (Fonagy et al., 1995) comes through the infant imagining himself or herself being observed through the eyes of 'mother'. There is a metaphorical swapping of places with her to allow this new dimension to appear.

'Father', in the form of a separate third person (that is, not simply as a substitute or support for 'mother') is more obviously other from the outset. He represents the world outside the direct confines of the primary dyad, bringing excitement and disturbance into it. The infant will develop an attachment to 'him' as well as to 'mother', and he will exert a positive push away from the regressive pull of maternal symbiosis. Wright (1991) uses the image of Homer's Odysseus to illustrate the point. Odysseus ordered his men to strap him to the mast (phallus?) of their boat, and to plug their ears, so that he and his crew were not lured on to the rocks by the seductive pull of sweet siren voices. This wrenching away of the boy from the pull of his mother has been described by Hudson and Jacot (1991) as the 'male wound', and used by them to account for gender differences in which men are more predisposed than women to turn away from relationships and towards objects. In their view, this 'dismissing' resolution of the conflict between a simultaneous longing for and fear of the mother is something that women experience less painfully than men because, for them, the social culture does not require such a painful differentiation to establish a satisfactory gender identity. Wright adds that 'fathers' can be absent not only by being physically and emotionally removed, but also by being undifferentiated from 'mother'. In other words, if the parental partnership cannot tolerate difference, the couple environment does not encourage differentiation for the child.

Occupying a third position outside the primary pair, 'fathers' create the conditions for a second stage in the child's development. The child now has an experience of there being a couple from which s/he is excluded, and takes up a position as observer, watching what goes on between the parents. To be able to recognise the parental relationship, never mind the possibility of its exclusivity in certain areas (like sex), involves the child in giving up the illusion of having sole and permanent rights over 'mother' (Johns, 1996). This is both a profound loss and a substantial psychological achievement.

When the loss cannot be tolerated, as will often be the case with very young children, it must be defended against. In the polarised world of infancy – populated as it often is by fairies and witches, beasts and beauties, angels and devils – the psychologically threatened child may split his relational world into different compartments, preserving an idea of goodness against destructive realities (idealisation) or the idea of badness against the fear of loving and losing (denigration). The ability of the parent to remain connected within him or herself in the face of such pressures from the child, and of the parents to remain connected with each other in their partnership, not only reduces the child's anxiety that to wish a parent dead is tantamount to murder (children have very omnipotent fantasies), but also allows for integrating loving and hateful feelings towards the same person. When things go well, within and between parents, children can own and feel safe with powerful and contradictory feelings towards those most important to them. When they do not, anxiety may continue unchecked, or go underground to reappear in later life.

The parental partnership does something more. Being able to tolerate the link between parents provides children with a completely different perspective. They then occupy a third position, on the outside but not overwhelmed by the fear of exclusion. They can observe and absorb the workings of the parental couple, and they can imagine themselves as the objects of observation by the couple. As observers, they learn how partnerships operate, how intimacy is handled and how differences are managed without being central to the drama (which is not to say they won't try and join in!); they can enjoy the liveliness of the partnership without feeling diminished, threatened, excluded or impelled to intrude. As the ones observed, they develop a capacity for self-observation, for entertaining another point of view, and for independent thought and activity. In short, they develop a capacity to reflect on situations, to entertain differences without fearing annihilation, and to adopt a meta-perspective – critically reviewing their own thinking and experience. The Oedipal situation then becomes the crucible in which the capacity to be alone and intimately involved with others – a central ingredient of successful partnerships – is prepared.

The Adult Attachment Interview, described in Chapters 1 and 2, captures the triangular dimension of secure relating by requiring subjects to collaborate with the interviewer in responding appropriately to the questions asked *and* to access memories and emotional states that are aspects of the subject's internal relatedness. In other words, to demonstrate the coherence that is the hallmark of secure attachment the subject must simultaneously maintain a relationship with him or herself as well as with an actual other person. Collaborating with another but limiting access to the self is a feature of dismissing patterns of attachment; becoming lost in oneself at the expense of keeping to the interview task is a feature of preoccupied patterns of attachment. Operating on a dyadic rather than triadic basis can therefore be read as one indication of insecure attachment.

This triangular dynamic has implications for psychoanalytic couple therapists. It implies not only the need for therapists to *engage with* the couple and their counter-transference experience of the therapeutic relationship, but also to *observe* the couple and the engagement of the partners with each other. Exploring working models within the partnership requires focusing on transference elements enacted in that context as well as in relation to the therapist(s). When there are two therapists, the partnership between them provides an additional resource for managing the tension between involvement and observation. With or without this partnership, couple therapists must have a capacity to manage the Oedipal tensions that are inherent in the work. The risks of intrusiveness (as contrasted with engagement) and detachment (as contrasted with an observing presence) are ever present.

Broadly speaking, the aim of couple psychotherapy can be construed as facilitating the exploration of representational models of self and other as they become manifest in one of the most powerful of adult transference relationships – the committed couple. Ultimately, the aim is to improve the capacity of the couple's relationship to act as a secure base for the partners. Outcomes can be thought about in terms of the capacity of each partner to reflect upon and reappraise the adequacy of their mental representations of themselves and their partnership, and the capacity of the partnership to facilitate this exploratory, reality-testing process.

Rules of engagement

The frame implies not only the nature and purpose of the enterprise but also the rules of engagement: the boundaries that define who participates and how. These boundaries include the therapist's definition of the patient. Couple psychotherapists are clear that their patient is the partnership rather than either of the individuals within it. They work towards helping that partnership operate as a secure base for the partners. However, they also recognise that the matter is complicated by the fact that secure partnerships depend on what Kahlil Gibran poetically described as the 'spaces in your togetherness . . . for the pillars of the temple stand apart, and the oak tree and the cypress grow not in each other's shadow' (1926: 16–19). So therapists have to manage the tensions associated with relating not only to 'them' but also to 'him' and to 'her'. An assumption that everything is shared denies individual differences just as much as the assumption of individuality disregards the essential relatedness of experience.

The frame also includes a sense of place (continuity with regard to rooms, the arrangement of furniture, the use of reception facilities and so on) and time (when appointments are offered, with what frequency, and for how long). In structural terms, regular meetings in the same place and at the same time constitute the kind of predictable proximity that is part of the secure base phenomenon. For chaotic, mistrustful and manipulative couples, these elements may initially be as important as any factor in terms of therapeutic influence. The frame also defines a sense of reciprocity in the therapeutic relationship, signalled in practical terms by the trading of time and experience for money, but also, and more fundamentally, by the interdependent nature of the therapeutic process.

The different boundaries that constitute the therapeutic frame contribute towards constructing a predictable and consistent environment that encourages exploration. This research-cum-therapy 'laboratory' also puts in place the necessary conditions for meaning to be distilled from experience. Because, as I have already indicated, couple problems so often result from the elision of space (you–me) and time (now–then), attending to what happens on the boundary of the therapeutic relationship with respect to space and time is a potentially fruitful approach to learning.

In the language of attachment theory, processes that establish the therapeutic frame for couple work might then be expressed in the following terms:

- focusing on the couple's relationship as the 'patient' in order to develop its secure-base function for each partner;
- establishing a secure therapeutic base – involving the predictability of setting and time, and establishing a therapeutic alliance through working at becoming attuned and responding appropriately to the couple's signals;
- elucidating the nature of the predominant and shared working models that hamper the development of the couple by exploring patterns in their partnership and other current relationships, and through being open to capture by the internal worlds of the partners while retaining a capacity to think about what this involvement means – the stance of participant-observer;
- encouraging play and exploration within the session so that what is feared as unsafe becomes less frightening;
- recovering and reliving trauma to facilitate a joint mourning process by addressing unresolved aspects of past experience;
- providing opportunities for accessing and reprocessing feelings, and offering a sufficiently secure base for this emotionally taxing work to become possible.

This last point is perhaps the most important of all. The experience of breaking a negative interactional cycle through accessing and reprocessing feelings and fears is likely to be profound. This assumption lies at the heart of Johnson's (1996) systemically oriented work with couples, which focuses on the emotions underlying negative patterns of interaction, reframes problems in terms of underlying attachment needs, and encourages new patterns of relating to be tried and tested.

THE SESSION AS A 'STRANGE SITUATION' LABORATORY

The therapeutic frame defines rules of engagement for couples and therapists that are very different from those associated with ordinary social discourse. Structured meeting times, an open agenda, one-sided disclosure and the close attention paid to relationship process differentiates this encounter from others: there are few relationships that exist primarily to foster a person's relationship with themselves as well as with other people. In consequence, the encounter is likely to be experienced as unfamiliar and potentially unnerving.

Moreover, the relationship is punctuated by a series of planned and unplanned breaks. Psychoanalytically oriented therapists have long been alive to their patients' sensitivity to holiday breaks, and to the termination of therapy, both of which introduce separations from the attachment figure of the therapist and have a potential for activating anxiety, affect and their related defences. But what of the breaks between sessions? For therapists seeing couples on a weekly basis, the frame has a built-in cycle of separation and reunion, both in the partners' relationships with their therapist(s) and, indeed, in the nature of the encounter they have with each other in the socially strange situation of therapy.

In this respect, therapy sessions parallel the laboratory situation devised by Mary Ainsworth and her colleagues for the Strange Situation Test (SST) described in Chapter 1. To recapitulate, the SST is designed to capture the responses of very young children to a sequence of separations from and reunions with their mothers. Trained observers distinguish secure from insecure patterns of attachment from the infant's responses to these sequences. It is important to note that while individual behaviour provides the basis of classification, what is being observed is a relationship. The filmed sequences show not only whether the infant uses the caregiver as a secure base but also how able the caregiver is to provide such a base.

What the SST highlights are strategies for managing threats that not only activate the attachment system but also result from the activation of that system. The link between this instrument and the Secure Base Scoring System (SBSS) used with adult couples for assessing the attachment security of partners (see Chapter 2) will be apparent. Both measures rely on observation to assess attachment security. While the SST assesses the uni-directional attachment between infant and mother, the SBSS aims to capture bidirectional patterns in which each partner acts as a secure base for the other.

Might the sequence of separations and reunions contained in weekly therapeutic sessions provide similar opportunities for therapists to detect and work with attachment-related anxieties? In structural terms, regular meetings at the same time and in the same place constitute the kind of predictable proximity that is part of the secure-base phenomenon. However, in Bowlby's illustration of the mother on the park bench, with which I introduced the concept of the secure base at the start of this book, the mother is not simply a presence, she also responds to her child. What are the implications for a therapist who is aspiring to be responsive to the needs of not just one person but a couple? How, for example, might the therapeutic frame help in deciding what to do when one partner turns up on time for a session and the other is late?

An illustration

Let me invite you to play an imaginary game. Consider yourself as a couple therapist faced with deciding what to do when a woman turns up for her session early but her male partner is late. One useful line of enquiry is to ask what is going on for you. What are you thinking and feeling when faced with only 'half' of your patient? Is her earliness and his lateness an indication of anxiety about the session, or of different levels of motivation about coming? What meaning will your actions have for each of them once you decide what to do? On the basis of proximity you may think it preferable to see one partner than neither, and start the session with whoever is on time. That might also alleviate feelings of guilt about being paid for 'doing nothing'. It might also impact on other feelings about the couple: for example, a sense of exasperation with the husband for being late and identification with the waiting wife; or a fear of being identified with a rejecting husband by refusing to see the wife until he arrives. If they are a difficult couple, you may feel relieved about their lateness, or you may feel anxious that they will slip away from therapy before they have become properly engaged in it. Whatever you do is going to have significance for both partners, and the significance for you may feel like being in a position where you have been manoeuvred into taking sides.

In addition to knowing about your own feelings and motives for acting, or not acting, you may try to put yourself in your patient's shoes, remembering that your patient is the couple. If you take the initiative by starting the session, you may be behaving like the over-protective parent who calls her children in before they can have the experience of being alone out there in the 'park'. Acting precipitately may rob one partner of the experience of waiting, exploring what it feels like to be waiting and initiating her own action. It may also represent a rejection to the absent partner, suggesting he is not needed, or play into his belief that she is getting the individual treatment he thinks she needs to put things right between them. While it may relieve his feelings of guilt about preventing things going ahead, it may also create or confirm a sense that he counts for little and everyone can manage very well without him. On the other hand if you don't start the session, both partners might feel neglected or rejected by you – as if you were sitting on the bench and had shooed them away because you couldn't be bothered, or were immersed in something more interesting, or hadn't even noticed they were there.

Providing this thinking and feeling is going on, the session has started. You are engaged in processing an experience that the couple has, consciously or not, invited you to share. You are involved in trying to contain the anxieties and feelings that the dilemma raises without acting precipitately to export your discomfort on to them, or protecting them unduly by making their dilemma your own. You have moved from the world of structures to considering meanings, and are struggling with attuning yourself to the couple so that their 'gesture' is 'recognised' (Colman, 1995). The agenda now moves from proximity to the issue of responsiveness.

The following case vignette suggests the therapeutic potential of working with this time boundary of a session in distilling meaning from experience.

Lateness as rejection

Anne and Anthony travelled to their therapy from different places. On one occasion she arrived on time and he was late. Given the option by their therapist of waiting for her husband or starting the session without him she chose to wait. After half-an-hour she decided to start the session without him. While she knew there was a real problem with public transport, she said her decision not to wait any longer was to do with her fear that he would arrive angry, and she preferred to face him with their therapist present rather than on her own. Within minutes of her starting, Anthony joined the session. He apologised for being late, sat down and acknowledged that he would have interrupted whatever was being discussed. His expression betrayed no indication of what he was feeling. Anne waited for him to continue, looking at him in a way that could be read as either interrogation or concern. Nothing was said for a while. He then broke the uncomfortable silence by explaining, with some exasperation, that there had been a problem with transport. He said that he had tried to get to the appointment on time but had been prevented by circumstances beyond his control. She then recapitulated in a tentative and apparently concerned way what she had been saying before he came in. He said he was not feeling angry, repeated that he had had a very frustrating journey, and suggested she get on with the session.

While this was going on their therapist had in mind the fact that

For reasons of confidentiality the illustrative vignettes in this chapter are based on composites of actual clinical experience.

Anne knew Anthony might be late because she had heard about the travel problems, but she was making no concession to her husband by saying so. He was also aware that Anne had said nothing about her own feelings concerning the lateness, and that she was directing her attention to her perception of how she thought Anthony would be feeling. To the therapist, it was as if she was keeping Anthony dangling in his discomfort. She was inviting him to be angry rather than expressing her own annoyance. He reflected that, as a couple, they were behaving on reunion rather like the avoidant infant and mother, depressing visible signs of affect and talking in a polite but strained way. However, there was a palpable undercurrent of tension that, while not open to observation, was experienced strongly by the therapist: to speak about it felt like walking in a minefield.

The therapist commented on how tense the discussion about lateness had become, and asked Anne how she felt about Anthony's delay. At first she maintained that her main concern was for him, and with coping with his anger. When it was suggested that she, too, might be feeling angry, but her preoccupation with how he might respond diverted her from attending to this, she paused to consider. She then made an interesting observation. She thought she had behaved just as she tended to do at home. When Anthony was late home from work she involved herself with their children, and for the same reason. Expecting him to be angry, she busied herself with them rather than face the blast that she expected upon his arrival. Anthony remarked that this *could* make him angry, because it compounded his sense of being an outsider in his own home. He then acknowledged that, although he could understand it, he had been irritated that she had started the session without him because the time belonged to them both.

Their therapist observed that not only had their session been cut short by lateness, but also both partners had stayed away the previous week. He reminded them that on that occasion Anne had been talking about her distress concerning a decision to turn off a close relative's life support system some years earlier. She had wept about the loss, and talked about continuing to feel guilty at having been involved in ending this person's life, as she saw it. The therapist wondered if, for her, anger had become confused with destructiveness, and so she preferred to locate this in others like her husband and construe herself as the victim of their hostility. He also wondered if, for both of them, a preoccupation with angry feelings masked distress about experiences of loss and exclusion. How was this being managed in attachment terms?

Were Anthony and Anne to have undergone an AAI it is likely that his attachment status would have inclined towards the dismissing end of the continuum while hers would have been more preoccupied. He tended to answer questions in a succinct and economical way rather than volunteer information. He could be denigrating of therapy 'chats', impatient with his wife for 'wallowing in feelings', and was not at all at ease in talking about his own feelings. When he described the competitive family in which he grew up, it was others – his wife and the therapist – who experienced the impact of what he said; he dismissed it as history and of very little importance. Anne, on the other hand, was emotionally labile, easily dislodged from pursuing a thought, and frequently struggling to find an autonomous perspective on her past and present family situations. If her husband or therapist made an observation, they were sometimes left feeling as if they had intruded upon her experience.

While each partner displayed different strategies for managing their feelings, these strategies also acted upon the other and influenced their behaviour together. The more Anthony held back, the more Anne pressed him to talk. The more difficulty Anne had in organising her experience, the greater the temptation was for Anthony to shape it for her. The positive potential in this was that Anthony was given space to explore his feelings and Anne was provided with a shape for her experience. The negative potential was in the reinforcement this provided for their respective defensive systems, resulting in the fear of attack or intrusion. These patterns were played out in relation to the time boundary of the therapy session, which provided a point of access to dynamics affecting the partnership as a whole.

THE ANALYTIC PROCESS AND REPRESENTATIONAL DATA

As we saw in Part I, Mary Main and colleagues devised a method for detecting the attachment security of the parents of children observed in the SST. The 'frame' they used was the Adult Attachment Interview (AAI), a semi-structured interview that invited adults to talk about their early family relationships (George et al., 1985).

To recapitulate, the AAI captures a person's ability to relate their own experience in a coherent and autonomous way, while simultaneously collaborating with the interview task. Secure adults give coherent accounts, have good recall and show appropriate feelings in relation to a fresh, credible narrative of early experience. Insecure patterns reveal difficulties in several of these areas. Dismissing strategies are characterised by people minimising their relational and emotional experiences, while preoccupied strategies often result in the reverse – the difference often showing in the length and weight of interview transcripts. Insecurity may also be evident in disorganised responses to the recounting of specific incidents of loss or abuse, or in the absence of a coherent overall strategy for managing the interview task. Chapters 2 and 4 describe how the methods of the AAI have been adapted and applied to capture representations of current partnerships as well as past family relationships.

For psychoanalytic psychotherapists, the notion that people reveal their strategies for managing attachment-related anxieties through the way they talk is partly familiar. They may not know about or work with linguistics, but the significance of the content of a session for conveying dynamic process is well-appreciated. This is the data to be analysed, the material to be interpreted. Once again, the boundaries of the therapeutic relationship can generate information that provides access to important relational processes in the couple. In the following illustration, exploring the representational significance of money – a currency that has practical and symbolic value in the relationships of both psychotherapy and marriage – proved to be useful in assessing attachment problems for which a couple sought help.

Money and attachment

Brian and Belinda were seen for a consultation as a result of a succession of arguments they had had over whether and when to have children. They both worked in jobs that they said were not well-remunerated, so there were financial anxieties attached to the prospect of becoming parents. As a couple, they valued their independence highly, maintained their own bank accounts and had separate as well as shared circles of friends. There was no automatic assumption that Belinda would be the primary parent if they had children, and one recurring argument revolved around how they would balance their lives at work and at home if such a change were to occur.

When the fee for the consultation was discussed, the therapist was aware of feeling less comfortable than usual in asking for the full cost of the initial consultation. The couple had conveyed a sense of their limited resources in different ways, and she felt hesitant about attending to the Institute's need for income. To do so felt as if she would be signalling that she had not heard their message about limited resources, or that she was disregarding it. In order to counter the discomfort that she would be exploiting them by asking for the full consultation cost, she made much of there being provision for negotiating a lower fee.

Brian said they needed the help and would find the money to meet the full cost. Belinda asked him how he would do this, saying she was not in a position to pay her share. He said he would pay for both of them, but in the short term that would mean borrowing money from elsewhere. She would not have that, and was insistent that she pay an equal amount of whatever was agreed. She also wanted to ensure that they paid 'not a penny more' than they had to, and said that if the price was too high they would be unable to consider therapy.

Not knowing their actual circumstances, the therapist asked at what point their combined income would place them on the fee scale for ongoing therapy. This elicited the surprising response that neither knew exactly how much the other earned. Belinda explained that Brian was very sensitive to her enquiring how much money he had, fearing she was only interested in curbing his freedom to spend his money as he wished. Brian thought Belinda wouldn't tell him, and would assume that his interest was in spending what belonged to her. When they did pool information about their financial circumstances it was clear that they were in a position to meet the full cost, but only if savings were made on some individual items of expenditure and re-routed into the marriage. This involved a discussion of who should give up what.

The therapist linked this discussion with the issue of whether or not they should start a family. She also made connections with fragments of family histories they had described earlier in the consultation. Brian had talked about being sent away to boarding school at a young age and his sense of never being able to get back into his family. Petty episodes of delinquency had branded him as the 'black sheep' of the family, and he nursed a sense of aggrievement about his isolation. Yet there was also a part of him that continued to long to be accepted by his family 'at any price'. Belinda came from a large family in which she was the eldest child. She had supported her mother in bringing up her younger brothers, and was desolated when she left home for another man during her teenage years. She had felt short-changed by her experiences and cautious about making commitments. Their therapist suggested that they shared a fear of becoming dependent on each other, and upon therapy. The 'not a penny more' defence was contending with an 'at any price' need, and detachment and equality were being used to protect them from the anxiety of depending on and being depended upon by each other.

For Brian and Belinda, making sure things were absolutely equal between them appeared to be a means of protecting themselves and each other from feelings and expectations arising from any asymmetry in their relationship. If you like, a symmetrical idea about their *relationship* was being used to prevent work going on about exploring asymmetrical aspects of *relatedness* between them as a couple and with their therapist. Much as a preoccupation with 'fair shares' can act as a substitute for 'mutual concern' (Balint, 1993), their pursuit of symmetry can be understood as an attempt to avoid asymmetrical aspects of their relationship that were negatively encoded in their principal patterns of object relating. However, attempts to avoid these patterns had the anomalous effect of precipitating them. The shared unconscious assumption was that whoever expressed need, or was encouraged to believe in the hope of that need being met, was ultimately disappointed and rejected. The assumption was particularly hard to give up because it was shared and unconscious. It can be understood as the engine driving their more conscious concern for equal shares in their partnership, devised to protect against the pain of longing and loss.

The therapist learned about and worked with this dynamic through trying to understand the representational significance of money, and attempting to stay with a symmetrical aspect of the therapeutic frame – that she had needs to be attended to (financial remuneration) as well as being there to attend to the needs of the couple. Had she imposed a fee (whether in a hard-nosed, formulaic way, or by being charitably generous) she would not only have acted asymmetrically (as parents to children who could not be expected to take some responsibility for their relationships) but would also have missed an opportunity to think about a critically important aspect of the problem for which they, as a couple, were seeking help. If the frame is only a formula for defining the structure of a therapeutic relationship, it has much less potential for promoting the work of exploring representations of relatedness than if it is regarded as a boundary across which that work can be carried out. Working on the boundary elicits representations of attachment and provides opportunities for making them accessible to consciousness.

SYMMETRY IN THE THERAPEUTIC PROCESS

I suggested earlier in this chapter that, in drawing an analogy between research and practice, couples in therapy might be considered by their therapists as co-researchers. This implies a symmetry in the therapeutic relationship. Is this a defensive notion, as was the case in the illustration of Brian and Belinda's marriage described above, or a realistic proposition?

Psychoanalytic psychotherapy, while not based on a medical model of intervention, is sometimes represented as an asymmetrical relationship, in which the power of knowledge is vested in the therapist who passes this on to the patient through the medium of interpretation. I do not think this is an accurate picture of contemporary practice, and it is certainly not one that sits comfortably with attachment thinking. Bowlby described his own position in relation to patients as being 'you know, you tell me', rather than 'I know, I'll tell you' (1988: 151). As we have seen, from an attachment perspective the principal task of the therapeutic relationship is to provide a secure base from which exploration becomes possible. Observations and interpretations made by therapists do not have to be true in any absolute sense – indeed they cannot be, because they are particular and of the moment. They need only to relate to anxiety that inhibits the process of exploration. The place of interpretation is then to encourage exploration rather than to provide explanation.

Security in the parenting relationship depends upon asymmetry: attachment behaviour is displayed by the child towards a parent; caregiving behaviour is displayed by a parent towards the child. If the relationship operates symmetrically, with parent and child seeking both to care and be cared for by each other, it is likely to be insecure. Role reversal and parentification are not features of healthy child development. In contrast, the notion of symmetry is central to the concept of adult attachment security. Partners are involved with each other as both receivers and providers of care. As we have seen from Part I, secure partnerships are those in which the conditions prevail to support partners in moving flexibly and responsively between these different positions.

Psychotherapy with couples is one approach to creating conditions within which secure partnerships can be fostered. If such partnerships provide a base from which partners are supported in engaging with themselves, with each other and with people and activities outside the partnership, couple psychotherapy temporarily stands in for the partnership when it is not secure enough to carry out this function. This 'secure base' function of marriage/partnership and marital/couple psychotherapy then resonates with both Winnicott's and Bion's concept of containment (Brookes, 1991), creating the necessary support and 'thinking' space for experience to be processed. But how far do these formulations imply a symmetrical relationship between therapist(s) and couple?

The therapeutic frame is an invention of therapists. Therapists, like couples, have their own ways of organising and interpreting experience, and particular strategies for responding to what they think is going on. There is no single psychotherapy narrative. Secure, reflective, self-monitoring therapists are free to review the models that organise their behaviour. They are likely to be flexible in their approaches to couples, capable of engaging withdrawn partners and withstanding intrusive ones, activating or de-activating levels of emotional engagement in the service of making connections, and having the robustness to resist being drawn into collusive alliances (Dozier and Tyrell, 1998). Their evaluation of how they behave in the therapeutic relationship will be fashioned by the mental representations of relationships that they have constructed from personal experience and professional training. As with couples, these models can provide a secure base that encourages exploration and play. They can also provide a safe haven to retreat to when the going gets rough. They may even equip therapists with strategies that protect them from really knowing what is going on when they feel threatened, and propel them unthinkingly into perpetuating destructive patterns of relating. Marrone reviews some origins of these dysfunctional therapeutic styles, and the possible iatrogenic effects they can have on therapeutic process and outcomes (1998: 155–65).

So, the therapist's stance is as important as that of the couple in contributing to the kind of experience they jointly create in their relationship. Because therapeutic outcomes are the product of social relatedness, we can assume the 'fit' between the attachment status of the therapist and that of the couple is a highly significant variable. Therapists can be as attuned, intrusive or dismissing as those who consult them, but how is their style to be understood? Attachment theory provides both intergenerational and contextual answers to that question, and in that respect matches contemporary psychoanalytic thinking about the interactive nature of counter-transference. Counter-transference is a relational concept that juxtaposes the therapist's transference to the couple and the couple's transference to the therapist: each needs to be understood in relation to the other.

If, as researchers seem to agree, the quality of the relationship between therapist and patient is as important to outcome as the particular form of psychotherapy practised, the question of therapeutic fit deserves more study. Interest has been growing in applying and measuring the concept of 'affective attunement' (Stern, 1985; Murray and Trevarthen, 1986) in clinical practice (Rayner, 1992; Davis and Hadiks, 1994; McCluskey et al., 1997). McCluskey and colleagues (1999) place psychotherapy within the framework of the care-giving/care-seeking attachment dynamic described by Heard and Lake (1997), and see the process of creating conditions conducive to exploration within the session as 'goal-corrected empathic attunement'.

It may be, for example, that some therapists are better at supporting than challenging the couples they see, and that this reflects their own attachment status. Holmes (1996, 1997) suggests that patients displaying dismissing patterns of insecurity will be sensitive to anything they construe as abandonment and so respond better to support than confrontation. The reverse may be true for those displaying preoccupied patterns where intrusiveness dissolves interpersonal boundaries. This might suggest a simple basis for matching therapist and patient. However, attachment patterns are not static, and therapists need to be able to operate in different ways at different times. Hardy et al. (1999) have observed therapists working at different moments of psychotherapy with their patients. They see therapist responsiveness as clustering around three main areas. Early on, the primary need of the patient was for the therapist to be present and available as an attachment figure. In the course of therapy, therapists moved between helping patients to feel understood and challenging them through interpretation. The deciding factor in making these choices was the level of anxiety operating in the therapeutic relationship. Therapists worked at what they described as the level of 'proximal development', where emotions were manageable, but arousal was sufficient to enable change and development to take place.

To summarise, the therapeutic frame reflects the theories of attachment that guide therapists in their relationships with patients. From an attachment perspective, the 'strange situation' constructed by the therapeutic frame, and the opportunities it affords to access representations of attachment, aims to help couples in their joint endeavour to be more in touch with themselves and each other. It is expected that this will be reflected in their developing capacity to give coherent and autonomous accounts of how they come to be where they are. Such narrative competence (Holmes, 1999; McCleod, 1997) does not have a learned performance feel to it, but is expressed in the freshness of the story and the teller's openness to critical evaluation and review. The role of the couple therapist is to facilitate a review of representational models of the partnership, and sometimes to suggest a metanarrative that connects the different stories told by each partner. In this process, couples and therapists have an essentially symmetrical, co-researching relationship, in the sense that each depends upon the other for the exploration to be fruitful. However, the fact that each has different roles and responsibilities also means there is an essential asymmetry in the relationship. Symmetry should not be confused with sameness. The therapeutic frame provides a boundary distinguishing the role and identity of therapists from those they are there to assist. Without this distinction there can be no relationship. But through applying the frame there are unusual possibilities for learning about relatedness.

Chapter 6

Working with intangible loss

Christopher Clulow, Jenny Riddell and Avi Shmueli

Loss is ubiquitous in the consulting room. The experience of having lost something vital in a relationship prompts many couples into therapy. The nature of that loss is sometimes specific – a sense of a lost past or future precipitated by infirmity, infidelity or unfulfilled aspirations – but often it is intangible. Even when the loss is tangible the experience may be hard to locate, as if the present acts simply to overlay histories of past trauma that remain unresolved.

The fear of loss can spur people into seeking help. While some will subscribe to Tennyson's maxim that 'it is better to have loved and lost than never to have loved at all', others will understand that there is more safety in longing for what is desired than owning it: a sense of deprivation is sometimes to be preferred to the fear of loss. We can, then, be powerfully wedded to our deprivations and dissatisfactions because they appear to protect us against future loss.

It is therefore something of a triumph for those who fear the pain associated with loss (and who of us does not?) to engage in the psychotherapeutic process at all – as, indeed, it is to become part of a partnership. Neither relationship carries a blue chip guarantee of change; partnerships and psychotherapy will be used protectively as well as developmentally – there is a 'safe haven' as well as 'secure base' aspect to each. With luck the balance will be on the side of development, but we need to appreciate the fears of those for whom a conservative outcome is the preferred option. Simply being there takes courage. It is not only that engagement with therapy encourages people to talk about their feelings and fears, the structure of the relationship is peppered with separations and reunions, and the spectre of ending is omnipresent – even from the outset. Insofar as the psychotherapeutic process encourages people to explore the ways they represent themselves and their relationships with others, and to test those representations against experience, it is, in essence, a process of disillusionment. The loss of illusion can be every bit as painful as more tangible losses – all therapists are cautioned by their patients to 'tread softly' when they are dealing in dreams.

So establishing a secure base, be it within a partnership or in a therapeutic relationship, relies upon successfully managing anxieties associated with experiences and expectations of loss. A balance must be struck between the need for and the fear of the other. If either dimension is disregarded, and if there is a failure to engage the feelings that each can generate, the project will be hampered. A confident and trusting outlook on relationships will simplify the task of engaging with others. A history that builds the assumption of future loss into relationship prospects will make that process more difficult. The threshold of engagement may then offer particular opportunities for learning and development.

In this chapter we shall be illustrating two approaches to accessing and engaging experiences of intangible loss – experiences that may or may not be known about, and which provide a contextual background against which current events can stand out in relief. One comes from the tradition of attachment research, the other from clinical practice. Both are methods of locating unconscious process in couple relationships. We shall illustrate these approaches in relation to a couple who had five months of psychotherapy at the Tavistock Marital Studies Institute (TMSI), and who also participated in a feasibility exercise for a research project investigating possible links between attachment patterns and conflict management tactics in couples seeking help. In this context we shall look at strategies for managing anxiety associated with loss, consider how they were worked with by the therapists in the illustration, and conclude with a conundrum that we believe most couples and therapists will recognise in relation to the process of ending therapy.

We will begin with an attachment profile of a couple whom we shall call Sasha and Simon, and then move on to the more detailed account of their therapy. We do not attempt to synthesise the two perspectives – that is beyond the scope of this chapter – but hope that correspondences between the accounts will act as a spur to further thinking.

A VIEW FROM OUTSIDE THE THERAPY

Alongside their initial consultation at the TMSI, Sasha and Simon agreed to complete a number of investigative procedures. Among these was the Adult Attachment Interview (described in Chapters 1 and 2). As we saw there, the narrative produced by the subject is rated on a number of 'inferred experience' and 'state of mind' scales, resulting in a 'secure' or 'insecure' classification. Insecure strategies for managing attachment-related anxieties are classified under three broad headings: *dismissing* (diminishing the significance of past experiences and closing down of affect and memory in relation to them), *preoccupied* (overwhelmed by or still emotionally caught up in the past) and *unresolved* (the collapse of coherence in relation to a specific event of loss or abuse). A fourth category, *cannot classify*, indicates a global breakdown of, or contradiction in, the organisation of defences to manage anxiety. These categories, in effect, tell a story of affect regulation within the

individual. They denote which experiences have been allowed into consciousness and the meaning made of them, and which have seemingly been lost. It is
these latter with which we are principally concerned in this chapter.

Simon's classification from the AAI was 'dismissing'. In other words, his
response to the threat constituted by the interview task was to 'shut down'.
His response can be compared to infants in the Strange Situation Test (see
Chapter 1) who appear to take very little notice when their caregivers leave
them on their own, or when they come back to join them. Their seemingly
detached, 'mother doesn't matter', response to this threat to their emotional
equilibrium belies the underlying anxiety they feel about the experience of
separation. Repeated responses of this kind can become patterned into an
individual's defensive repertoire. Having an experience, but missing some of
the meaning and emotional texture surrounding it, then becomes habitual. It
is rather like seeing a film in black and white rather than in colour.

The evidence for this state of mind is signalled by a discrepancy between
semantic and episodic memories. One task of the interview is to ask for
adjectives that describe the subject's relationship with each parent, and then
to ask for an illustration that demonstrates what the subject is getting at.
Simon described his relationship with his mother as 'concerned'. This is what
followed after the interviewer asked him to provide a memory that would
show what he meant – Simon's response followed an initial eleven-second
silence and some encouragement by the interviewer:

Simon: I still keep coming back to the same images, it's the same few
                 images.
Interviewer: Of?
Simon: Oh yeah. It's sort of summers around the kitchen . . . I, I must
                 have played out a lot when I was young – not when I was five or
                 six, I suppose I did actually, yeah, we used to play out the front
                 a lot . . . (6 seconds) . . . So no, not really, no. I'm finding this
                 rather difficult.

Simon genuinely believed his relationship with his mother was characterised
by concern but he was unable to provide evidence to support this. He found
the interview task unfamiliar and difficult and, while he revised his view
about whether he played outside from a young age or not, this illustration
provided no evidence of maternal concern. If anything, it provided the
opposite. The idea was promoted in place of remembered actuality. Idealising
(or denigrating) semantic representations of relationships are one indication
of dismissing states of mind.

Sasha's classification from the AAI was 'secure', with an alternate
'unresolved/disorganised' coding for her state of mind with regard to loss.
Her secure classification denotes a capacity to provide a coherent account of
early family relationships, one that contains spontaneity, appropriate feeling

and an autonomous position in the recounting of it. This is the adult equivalent of the infant who is distressed and protests on being separated from the parent, but who makes immediate contact when s/he returns, and is quickly comforted by the attachment being restored. However, when talking about the death of her father, which had occurred four years previously, there was a slippage in her reasoning of sufficient strength to suggest the loss remained active and influential within her mind at an unconscious level. An excerpt from her transcript:

Sasha: . . . I kind of, you know, realised that there was a lot I needed to say to dada before he died, um, and so I did, I said it, but I don't know if I did the right thing, um, because the next day he died.

Interviewer: Did you think your talk with him upset him?

Sasha: I think, I think he probably misunderstood that I wanted to be set free. And I didn't . . . [4 seconds] . . . I just wanted him to know how much there was to live for, that we could face the pain together, that I could be there, and that I still needed him.

Interviewer: Are you saying you fear he might have taken another message?

Sasha: Free of him . . . that he was a burden to me, um, because I did say that, you know. I couldn't think about my own life because I was too worried about him and mum and that, you know. There was a way forward, but maybe I said the wrong things at the wrong time.

Interviewer: Did you somehow feel you might have caused his death, when you're talking to yourself about this?

Sasha: Yeah, yeah, I do.

While the interviewer might be criticised for asking a leading question, the idea that Sasha might have caused her father's death, an idea that persisted despite her knowledge that he was already terminally ill, provides a basis for classifying her state of mind as disorganised with regard to loss. We shall see in the next chapter how such states of mind can lead to unexpected eruptions of feeling in clinical encounters, when a present occurrence appears to transport the person back in time to a prior trauma. It is at these moments that the therapist may be able to say 'as if' but the patient cannot. We shall see one example of this in Sasha and Simon's therapy.

A VIEW FROM INSIDE THE THERAPY

The presenting issue

Sasha and Simon had known each other for five years before they came to therapy, and had been married for three of these. Sasha initiated their application for help at a time when she was seriously considering leaving her husband. She felt that it was difficult to engage him emotionally, that he kept her at a distance, and that she was unsure whether he wanted to be married to her or she to him. He listened quietly while she spoke, and acknowledged, rather disarmingly, that he did like to retreat to the bottom of the garden when Sasha wanted 'one of her discussions'. His dissatisfactions were more difficult to locate than hers, other than a feeling that she could be intrusive, but he was clear that he did not want the marriage to end. They both seemed to agree that he wasn't very good at talking about his feelings, or sustaining intimacy in their relationship, and that as a couple they could become frozen in an angry stand-off with each other. Just occasionally he would explode with rage, but more usually he would withdraw. They were both exhausted by work and found it impossible to resolve their different views about whether or not to start a family – something that was becoming pressing for Sasha as she was 42.

Over recent years, Sasha had received a lot of help from a co-counselling arrangement. The first of her co-counsellors was a man with whom she had become very emotionally involved, but before Simon had come on the scene. While she was now seeing a different co-counsellor, she had kept in touch with this man on a friendly basis. She thought co-counselling would help Simon, and wanted to encourage him to take it up. He was reluctant to do so, and had only come to the TMSI because their marriage was at risk. There were occasions when Simon described feeling excluded by Sasha, but he did not associate these with her co-counselling. He was more likely to feel shut out when she had long phone calls with her friends. As she talked about how much she had been helped by the co-counselling process her two couple therapists were also aware of their own feelings of exclusion and rivalry in relation to her past and present co-counsellors. Yet she was attentive to what they had to say, and there appeared to be no conscious provocation of these feelings in them. The message was rather that she had found a way of attending to her own needs, that she would need them less than would Simon, and that he certainly did need help to know about his own feelings and needs if their marriage was to be more rewarding.

In this context her therapists were interested in what Sasha had to say about the research procedures which had provided their point of entry. She had liked the sense of reciprocity she had encountered when they had come for the research meetings, and she was glad to have been able to help us as well as to receive help from us. Simon said less about this, and it was difficult to gauge his reaction to the research. Sasha's valuing of the reciprocal nature of the research relationship suggests a secure orientation towards her potential attachment to the institution. But her therapists wondered if the reciprocity that featured in both the co-counselling and research relationships might also conceal anxiety about depending on others. In other words, they wondered if *both* partners might be asking for help with their concerns about depending upon each other, and not just Simon. This would then indicate the seat of insecurity in the marriage for which they were seeking help (Chapters 1 and 2 define secure attachment in partnerships in terms of the capacity of *both* partners to move between dependent and depended-upon positions in relation to each other).

Family and relationship backgrounds

Sasha came from a large family. She was the eldest daughter, and had responsibilities for looking after her younger brothers. She described her father as emotionally inaccessible, but someone who wanted the best for her. He had died of an illness four years previously, and Sasha was still a little tearful when talking about this. When she had been very young her father had encouraged her mother to leave her with a female relative for several months. The reasons she had been given for this (when she had asked later on in life) were that the relative had been very fond of her, and that her father had been very concerned that the relationship between her and her mother was over-close. Sasha experienced her mother as emotionally accessible but demanding and vulnerable. Their relationship was complex. She had helped her mother at home, and had gained her father's confidence in exchange. Ten years earlier her mother had been admitted to hospital with a diagnosis of schizophrenia. Only since her father died did she feel she had been able to recover a better relationship with her.

Simon similarly came from a large family, although he was the next to youngest member with a series of older brothers. He described his father as a quiet and undemonstrative man, rather like himself. His mother stayed at home to bring up the children, and seemed to be chronically tired and inclined to take to her bed with 'nervous strain'. Simon could feel both special and the odd one out at home. He recalled an incident when his brothers had locked him out of the house they were staying in on holiday. Any distress this might have caused him was left to the therapists to infer. He had done better than his brothers academically, and been the only member of his family to enter a profession. While this had satisfied him and his parents, it had also set him apart in terms of how he felt, and how he felt they felt.

The couple met at their place of work. As well as the physical attraction that had drawn them together, Sasha liked Simon's quiet strength and integrity. He enjoyed her interest in him, and was ambivalently attracted to her capacity to engage him. He recalled one of their early meetings in a public house in which he had opted to talk with her at the bar rather than risk the intimacy of being on their own in a snug corner. They had reflected on their relationship sufficiently to know that, right from the out-set, he had relied on her to claim him as she had relied on him not to crowd her.

The therapy

A central experience for their therapists throughout the time they saw Sasha and Simon was an uncertainty about whether or not the therapy relationship would continue. From the outset there were practical difficulties that they – and particularly Simon – raised which looked potentially terminal for the therapy. Yet they both seemed engaged in the work and aware that these difficulties, real as they were, also masked an anxiety about what they were getting into with their therapists and with each other. In the early stages of the work much went on around this boundary. We describe the process of a session one month into the work to illustrate the different contexts in which anxiety about commitment was evident, as well as the experience of the therapists and what they did with it. The session followed one in which the female therapist had been absent, and there had been talk of ending because of the couple's practical constraints.

Sasha preceded Simon into the room. She was smiling and they both greeted their therapists. They sat down and simultaneously removed their glasses, placing them on the table between them. They looked at each other expectantly, as if to decide who would begin. Simon offered the opportunity to Sasha, which she politely offered back. There was a pause, and then Sasha began whilst Simon watched her attentively.

She said they had done some 'good talking' that week, and had taken time out of their busy schedules on two occasions. She spoke of these occasions as 'sessions', and they appeared to have been quite structured and formal in their purpose. She said how helpful they had been, and looked to Simon to continue. He said that he had also found them useful. There was a pause, and then he added that he'd also felt 'quite intruded on . . . trapped by them . . . not very comfortable, really'. They then talked about the way it tended to go. The more she felt he was avoiding talking, the more she needed to persuade him to do so. Her urgency to air her concerns was then matched by his urgency to escape, 'to get out of the house . . . a need for fresh air'. He made a joke about the weather, and how this meant he was unable to escape to the allotment so easily. He described looking out of the living room window one dark evening, and wishing he could be outside. Sasha listened carefully to him, but made no comment until there was another silence. She said how shut out from him this made her feel. Both spoke gently and were respectful of each other throughout.

Sasha then went on to describe how they had met and become close through talking about her co-counselling. He had seemed interested in what she was doing and she had practised what she had learned in relation to him, integrating it into their relationship as a particular kind of talking. She had been delighted by his initial interest in co-counselling, and disappointed that it had not continued. What had been different about the talking that week was that Simon had initiated it. Sasha wondered if this had been connected with her being angry with him for being distant during the previous week's couple therapy session. What had surprised her was that she had not been sure she had wanted to stop what she was doing to talk to Simon, as his request had intruded on something she was doing for herself.

Both therapists were surprised by this reversal, having believed that Sasha was the one to have initiated their talk time. They noticed the direct eye contact the couple had with each other and with them, but how little they seemed to expect in terms of a response from their therapists. The female therapist was struck by a particular attention in the way Simon watched her male colleague when he spoke, seeming to focus with intensity on him in a way that she saw as a longing regard. She felt excluded by this. Her colleague had not noticed because he had been addressing Sasha; on other occasions, when he had noticed Simon's eye contact, he had thought this to be more watchful than longing in nature.

Simon spoke about his discomfort with the intensity of their talk sessions. He found it difficult because he wasn't used to it. The male therapist acknowledged how difficult the therapy sessions must be for him, with the intensity of the talk, and wondered about the talk culture within his own family when he was growing up. Simon said that he had had to entertain himself as a child because his two elder brothers tended to play together, and his sister was younger than him. He thought his mother was 'too tired' for the last two children, and specu-lated that she might not have wanted them. His father had opted out, working long hours, and was rarely around. Simon had been thinking about this the previous weekend while he was decorating, an activity that he and his father still sometimes shared. All this was said in a low-key way, without evidence of any feelings on his part – which the therapists commented upon. Simon said he found it difficult to get close to people in case he lost them. Because of his own experience as a child he had never really wanted to have children of his own, 'but now it's on the agenda again as we're getting on better'.

He then changed tack quite suddenly, and spoke of his difficulty attending that week's session. He'd had to 'drop everything at work', and he agreed that he had felt quite resentful about doing so. But he spoke in polite and measured tones that belied his resentment. The male therapist linked this with a theme from the previous session: that they both were unsure about continuing in couple therapy. Simon said they had been looking at their budget . . . and left the sentence unfinished. Sasha joined him, saying she needed to nurture herself now she was no longer working, a step she had taken to recuperate from stress. She talked about her conflicting feelings between needing not to work in order to take care of herself yet finding the prospect of financial dependence on Simon very difficult. She described physical symptoms she was having: nausea, tiredness, feeling emotional and weak. The female therapist commented on the possibility that these symptoms were related to her increased dependence on Simon, and observed how similar they were to those of pregnancy. Sasha replied that she needed to feel well if she was thinking of having a baby.

She then talked about her own ambivalence towards having children. Her long-standing fear was that she would be left as a single parent, adding that 'I've always promised myself I wouldn't let that happen to me.' Simon said that he responded to the prospect of parenthood as he had to the prospect of marriage: 'say no first, and then reconsider'. They then talked about their shared apprehensions about having children, with Sasha concluding that 'we'll just have to tackle problems as they come up'.

She then went on to speak about the unavailability of her mother, despite her being the one member of the family who was demonstrative and seemed to understand about feelings. She wanted things to be different if she had children. She said she still found her mother 'difficult and draining', a woman who needed to be kept at arm's length because she sucked people in. The therapists asked what would happen if she resisted. Sasha replied 'there would be temper tantrums and accusations'. The implication was that this needed to be avoided at all costs. She had found her mother easier to manage as she took over the care of her following her father's death, but added, paradoxically, that 'the only time I was looked after by mum was following dad's death'.

Towards the end of the session the therapists returned to the couple's indecision about whether or not to continue in therapy. This was done with some trepidation since they liked the pair very much, felt very engaged with them and thought the prospects for working together were good. Sasha was concerned that if they asked to reduce their fee this would be unacceptable to their therapists. Simon wanted to know for how long they would need to come. He later commented that he expected to be told they had to come, and was all ready to rebel against this. The female therapist sensed Sasha's concern that they would have to manage the dilemma without any help from their therapists, and linked this with what she had been saying about her unavailable mother. Perhaps, she said, they feared being abandoned if they made an unacceptable offer. Sasha replied quickly and with passion: 'Don't tell me about being abandoned. I really was abandoned when I was two.' She then added more calmly: 'I don't think there'll be that sort of problem. We're in a professional relationship . . . you wouldn't behave like that.' She looked at Simon and added, 'We need to be realistic. The question is will what we can afford be acceptable to you? You need the money . . . as an institution, I mean . . . and there's our pride. We must pay our way.' Simon stuck with the unanswered question about how long therapy would go on for, although he recognised that this was a difficult question to answer. The therapists observed Sasha's need to take care of them rather than herself, and Simon's concern about becoming trapped in an unending commitment. As the session ended, the couple picked up their glasses, smiled at the therapists and left.

Loss in the counter-transference

How was Sasha and Simon's dilemma to be understood? The therapists had a hypothesis that informed their work. Put very simply it was this. Despite all that their respective families had provided for them, both partners sensed something had been missing at home which they were hard-pressed to put into words. They felt either that love was conditional upon looking after others (Sasha), or measuring up in some other way (Simon). They also shared experiences of rejection that were hard to name as such. Together they enacted a drama in which a needy child pressed an absent parent for a response. The response received was a turning away. While Sasha was most likely to pursue and Simon to withdraw, we learned that it was not always that way around. Moreover, the partner who was pressed for a response could feel controlled by the demands of the one who was doing the pressing, and this created anger. Anger was dangerous. Their shared phantasy (Bannister and Pincus, 1971) might be expressed as the unconscious belief that they were both needy children, that their needs were too much for the adults to bear and that to express their feelings about the frustration of their needs would either destroy the vulnerable parents or drive them mad.

So the pact in the marriage and the therapy was to maintain an ambivalent engagement, encapsulating their mixed feelings about having and not having something good in these relationships. This strategy might be understood in terms of trying to have something good (with the attendant risk of losing it or having it taken away) while avoiding the fear of it turning bad (which would be frightening and isolating). Enacting their ambivalence in a therapeutic context created the conditions in which the therapists could experience something of their dilemma and so be enabled to think with them about it.

The evidence for the clinical hypothesis came from what the therapists *observed*, what they *heard* told to them and what they *experienced*. For example, they *observed* the taking off and putting down of glasses at the beginnings and ends of sessions, and felt that a barrier was removed with the glasses (there were occasions when the glasses stayed on). What was striking was how their appearance changed when they were not wearing glasses. Sasha, already attractive, became beautiful and charmed the therapists. Simon appeared younger and more vulnerable, eliciting a warm response from them. Between them the therapists oscillated between thinking the gaze to which they were sometimes subjected was one of longing or wariness. It was a gaze that could include and exclude in its focus, and alerted the therapists to the importance of noticing the couple. The sense of being excluded from the gaze was experienced as well as observed, and alerted the therapist pair to the potential significance of this discomfiting experience in the sessions as well as in the marriage. In contrast, the female therapist was rewarded towards the end of the therapy with warm appreciation from Sasha when she accepted and included her by commenting on the attractive ethnic costume she was wearing, something that denoted difference in the relationship.

The therapists also *heard* the stories and histories that each partner recounted. Hearing how these were told was as important as attending to their content. Although the therapists heard about eruptions of anger between them at home, these never entered the session – either between the partners or in relation to their therapists. The talking in the sessions was done politely and considerately. It led the therapists to wonder whether feelings of anger were being avoided, and to question how far they had engaged with the negative transference in the work despite a major part of the early work being on the boundary of their engagement with therapy. They knew Sasha and Simon were cautious about placing themselves in the care of others. Part of that caution appeared to be associated with a fear of rejection and exclusion – or so it was assumed from their interactions with each other and with them. So they used what opportunities they could to elicit the feelings that accompanied what was said, and to give them due importance, as well as to think with them about the triangles that seemed so often to leave one of them out in the cold.

Perhaps most crucially, the therapists *experienced* something of the dilemma for which help was being sought. The therapy was to last another four months from the session recounted above, but the uncertainty of the therapists about whether or not they would lose Sasha and Simon continued throughout. This counter-transference experience – of constantly feeling on the verge of losing the couple while simultaneously feeling very engaged with them – was a core experience in the work. It was the principal clinical means of accessing unconscious communications about an intangible sense of loss that was associated for both partners with past experiences of rejection.

As well as reflecting the dilemma about commitment in the marriage (in part symbolised by their discussion about starting a family) the therapists' counter-transference also reflected something pervasive and less defined than might be accounted for by the very real practical costs and inconveniences of engaging in therapy. Their experience of impending loss, something that could move between them, posed some difficult technical questions. They felt very engaged with Sasha and Simon, and wanted to hold them into the relationship. But they feared they would lose them if they claimed them. They wondered if the need for the relationship to continue was being lodged by the couple with them, and thought that if this was the case the need was better managed by keeping the matter of ending open for discussion (it providing such a useful focus for considering the wider questions of commitment they were struggling with) than by discouraging them from leaving. They also feared that in claiming them they would become the needy or controlling objects in the transference that the partners were having such difficulty managing in their marriage. While they wondered if they were avoiding engaging with the couple's anger by refusing to 'trap' them into therapy (perhaps joining the 'polite talking' rather than 'talking up a storm'?), they paid less attention to the possibility that Sasha and Simon might actively have wanted to be claimed in this way. In other words, they might have replicated the non-committal response that was bedevilling the couple rather than taking the risk with them that they were finding it difficult to take with each other.

The quality of this experience, and their dilemma about whether there was more that could have been done to hold them in a therapy that might have ended too soon, put us in mind of a concept described as the 'absent sustaining object' by O'Shaugnessy (1964). From her observations as a child psychotherapist she distinguished between the nature of a benign present object (which a needy child experiences as nurturing, sustaining, good and, in phantasy, under the infant's control) and a malign absent object (experienced as rejecting, attacking and bad through frustrating the need). Because the experience of absence is unavoidable the infant must learn to come to terms with it. So as well as constituting a difficulty for the child, the absent object also acts as a spur to development: it 'breaks the hold of phantasies which protect him from the realisation of his vulnerability and dependence' (1964: 34). Pursuing Bion's (1962b) formulation in *Learning from Experience*, O'Shaugnessy observes that the absence of the object is a precondition for the development of thought and knowledge. The critical developmental advance is when the infant can manage to retain a benign conception of the object when needed but absent and not turn it bad. This conception stems from tolerating an acknowledgement of need in the self, and perceiving the absence of response as something other than either an attack, or evidence of the object having been destroyed by the infant's rage. Tolerating absence when in need involves surrendering the omnipotent phantasy of the object being in the child's control.

This developmental achievement might be described in attachment terms as the child having internalised a secure base through a sensitive and responsive caregiver gradually relinquishing that function. The experience of absence, as we have seen in preceding chapters, can also result in the development of relationship strategies that are not conducive to healthy development. Either way, the ending of a relationship tests not only the care-receiver's but also the *caregiver's* capacity to tolerate loss, as the following lines from a poem of C. Day Lewis illustrate so succinctly. Entitled 'Walking Away', it is dedicated to the poet's son, Sean, and describes a father's experience of letting his son go, observing 'the pathos of a half-fledged thing set free . . . like a winged seed loosened from its parent stem,' but concluding:

> . . . selfhood begins with a walking away,
> And love is proved in the letting go.

In the context of therapy, the 'letting go' can be a complex matter. Attachment patterns may predispose one or other partner, or both, to close down prematurely to avoid engaging with difficult feelings, or they can act to resist the reality of there needing to be an ending at all. There was an image towards the end of the therapy with Simon and Sasha which engaged them and their therapists, and which spoke to the sense of intangible loss with which this chapter is concerned. The couple had visited Simon's parents one weekend and had observed his mother attending to his baby nephew for whom she was caring. The baby was crying. Simon's mother picked the baby up but held him away from her, facing outwards, as she tried to quieten him. The couple had been struck by this. The normally unemotional Simon had felt distressed, but did not know why. He spoke of 'recognising something' in the experience, which was to do with his own unmet need. Whether this recognition stemmed from an identification with the unmet need of a distressed baby held at arm's length, or an unconscious twinge of pain at being excluded from the primary pair, was unclear. It was an image that also had meaning for Sasha: her link with her parents seemed to be conditional upon facing away from them – looking after her siblings for her mother and not pushing her father too hard in her wish to make emotional contact with him, something that had preoccupied her when he was dying.

The image also had meaning for their therapists. The paradox they faced throughout the therapy was that they felt it was only through letting Sasha and Simon go that they had any hope of engaging with them. So they did not close in on them through the many discussions about whether they could afford to continue the relationship, despite their feeling very engaged with them. Instead, they tried to work with the process of the shared experience about whether there could be a 'marriage' in the therapy as well as between them. They did not fight the decision to end when it finally came. But did they hold them at arm's length in order to keep their distress at bay? Did they avoid becoming and working with the needy, controlling internal objects that they could encounter in themselves and each other? Or did they provide them with a positive, developmental experience by letting them go (with the omnipotent implication that it is therapists and not couples who finally decide when to end)? The answers to these questions are unlikely to settle unequivocally on one side of the equation or the other, and readers will make their own judgement. Suffice it to say that the questions are important ones for therapists to keep in mind when working with therapeutic engagement and closure, especially when the couple's experience of loss is pervasive and intangible.

Chapter 7

Clinical reflections on unresolved and unclassifiable states of mind

Christopher Vincent

Conflict is an inevitable feature of all adult relationships as partners seek to balance separate interests alongside shared concerns. There is now a substantial body of research and clinical knowledge to show that it is the way conflict is managed, rather than its presence or absence, which is a crucial determinant in shaping the well-being of adults and children. Where conflict is characterised by anger, and, at its most extreme, by violent anger, couples and their children do badly (Elliott et al., 1993; McAllister, 1995; Rodgers and Pryor, 1998). It follows that therapists and counsellors need to consider how patterns of angry interaction might be transformed so destructive and damaging behaviour might be avoided.

In this chapter I shall explore how conflict can express itself in two broad categories of clinical encounter, both of which are technically challenging. I shall consider the possibility that our knowledge about the psycho-dynamics of each situation might be helped by recent developments within attachment theory. The two areas are, first, those encounters where couples experience sudden eruptions of disturbing anger which may or may not turn into physical violence. The second area concerns couples where there is a sense of non-relating. In these chronic situations, conflict is associated with feelings of frustration and betrayal in response to an absent or emotionally abandoning partner. Both types of couple interaction recreate themselves in the relationship with the therapist, producing distinctive counter-transference experiences which, it seems to me, are illuminated by the attachment theory classifications of 'unresolved/disorganised' attachment and the 'cannot classify' group. Both classifications are likely to be well-represented in clinical populations. They offer ways in which patterns of inconsistent and unpredictable relationships may be conceptualised.

Before describing these two types of couple interaction in detail, I will trace some characteristics of counter-transference and illustrate why this dimension of the therapist's experience informs an understanding of a couple's difficulties.

COUNTER-TRANSFERENCE AND THE COUPLE

Third parties inevitably become caught up in the dynamic processes of others, and this is certainly true of therapists and counsellors working with conflicted couples. Indeed, therapists working within a psychoanalytic frame seek to turn to advantage their involvement with the dynamic processes they are attempting to change by working with the phenomena of transference and counter-transference. Central to these 'here and now' experiences are the processes of projection and projective identification which help explain how clients' disowned unconscious feelings are experienced, and sometimes acted out, by those to whom they turn for help (Ogden, 1979; Sandler, 1988).

Typically, a therapist attempting to help angrily conflicted couples will be drawn into their difficulties in a variety of ways. For therapists working within a psychoanalytic frame, the paranoid-schizoid position, originally formulated by Klein (1946), provides one important explanatory framework. This position is one on an axis of relatedness (the other being the 'depressive position') and results in two contrasting states of mind: in one the subject idealises the person with whom he is relating; in the other, the object is denigrated. Both ways of relating to another involve degrees of omnipotent thinking because there is a marked dissonance between the perception and the reality of the other person.

In a study of consultations offered to couples with divorce-related problems (Vincent, 1995), clients presented two common omnipotent patterns of thinking which had a direct bearing on how they viewed their therapist and how the therapist was made to think and feel. One group placed a pressure on the therapist to be a 'magician', in the sense that there seemed to be a hope that the therapist could provide a solution that would take away the unavoidable psychological pain resulting from separation and divorce. For example, a woman client came to a first consultation seeking endorsement from the therapist for the plan she had devised to leave her husband. This plan involved purchasing a flat in secret, and moving herself and her children into it without giving warning to either them or her husband. There was no violence between the couple that might justify this secretiveness. It became apparent in the consultation that the woman could not bear the emotional prospect of facing her family with her intention to break away, and hoped that a pain-free, and hence magical, solution could be found. She invited her therapist to collude with and endorse this omnipotent thinking.

A second omnipotent phantasy was a feature of those clients who imbued their therapist with immense power and authority, creating the thought in the therapist that he was being set up as a 'judge'. His role was to come down in favour of one party at the expense of the other. These hopes were particularly prevalent when couples had an intractable childcare problem which the legal system, despite its authority, had failed to resolve. This omnipotent expectation could be replaced very quickly by its opposite when, as inevitably happened, the therapist did not pass judgement on the other spouse, and so was seen as a failure. At these moments he could be treated as a 'servant', exposed to the demands and sometimes the scorn of his clients.

Whereas in the examples of the therapist being treated as magician or judge, clients projected their authority and power into the therapist and knew only of their relative impotence, the reverse was true when the therapist was treated as a servant. Helplessness and impotence were now located in the professional helper, and one or the other of the partners would act in an excitedly triumphant, all-knowing way. It is important to stress that these frequently encountered projective processes are interpersonal, as well as being intra-psychic: the therapist is made to feel what the client cannot bear to know about at a conscious level. The challenge for the therapist is to reflect on these uncomfortable affective states and use his or her knowledge to inform interpretive comments. The intention is to help the client know more about the feelings that are disowned so that impulsive and destructive enactments are reduced and the client's ego functioning is expanded.

This processing is difficult to achieve when the paranoid-schizoid position dominates relationship dynamics. In particular, the reversal from being related to as a 'potent' therapist to being related to as 'impotent' is extremely uncomfortable to endure, and it may be scant consolation for the therapist to know that the client's core dynamic difficulty of switching between idealisation and denigration is now fully 'gathered in the transference' (Meltzer, 1990).

ERUPTIVE ANGER: 'A WALKING ON EGGSHELLS' IN THE COUNTER-TRANSFERENCE

In this first part of the chapter, I want to draw attention to those clinical situations where, even at times when the work appears to be going well, the therapist knows from reflecting on his feelings that there is an uneasy sense of calm about the work and that at any time some eruption of anger might occur, whether between the couple or, more directly, involving the therapist. It is this apprehensive state that I refer to as 'walking on eggshells'.

Case illustration

James and Patti applied for therapy following the revelation of Patti's affair. She explained that married and family life felt to her like a

---

For reasons of confidentiality the case illustrations used in this chapter are based on composites of clinical experience rather than actual case examples. The dynamics they illustrate are nevertheless authentic to the author's experience.

stultifying, claustrophobic trap from which she had escaped, in secret, by forming a clandestine relationship. James had been shocked and devastated by the infidelity, but his anger with Patti was held in constant check because he was anxious that she would retaliate in terms that would leave him even worse off than before. His concerns were linked to her capacity to belittle with words, but they both agreed that there had been earlier incidents of domestic violence which they did not wish repeated.

The beginnings of therapy felt like 'walking on eggshells'. Patti and James had a keen desire to recommit themselves to the marriage and both made serious attempts to listen to each other's perspective on events. However, it seemed to me that they did this at great cost, having to check at frequent moments the instinct to fly into angry and quite often irrational rebuttals of what they heard the other say. They were not always successful in holding their anger in check and there were regular flash points between them. In working with them I came to recognise this pattern, and commented upon it using military metaphors. While I would attempt to listen to and comment upon the detail of what they might be saying, when an angry flurry of conversation had subsided I would at times refer, as a sort of familiar shorthand, to 'another bomb having gone off', or I would suggest that either one of them had coped with 'another grenade attack'. In parallel with this commentary upon their communication with each other, I grew increasingly anxious about the potential consequences of things I might say.

Patti and James came with an explicit expectation that the purpose of therapy was to establish a safe place where they might talk with one another. From this point of view I was cast in their minds as an independent, unaligned mediator in their domestic war. In one way this assigned role felt restrictive, in that I felt my freedom to operate as I thought fit was being subtly but significantly limited. On the other hand, and from a rational perspective, it seemed utterly reasonable to me that they wished for a safe place to talk and that I should not prejudice this opportunity by becoming partisan. Initially, I was careful to respect these explicitly voiced expectations and thought that I was doing useful work in addressing their different experiences in an even-handed way. In addition to helping them process the events from the day-to-day experience of their current lives, I made a series of connections between patterns of behaviour in their marriage and their earlier family experiences.

They both had very difficult childhoods from which they wished to escape. Patti had been the conciliator between two warring parents and had longed, as an adolescent, to be released from this pressure. I was constantly reminded by her of how much normal childhood she felt she had lost, and of how a later self-confessed delinquency was one means of angrily trying to make good her losses through the self-indulgences of undergraduate life. James had been sexually abused within his family and had a series of failed adult partnerships. It was possible to see that the marriage had been created (or re-created) into a forum which echoed images and experiences from both unhappy childhoods. Patti unquestionably saw family life as pressurising, and as a trap from which she had to escape in order to 'breathe'. James, largely through his characteristic passivity and marriage to a persistently critical wife, relived some of his earlier experiences of abuse.

The problem about this even-handed way of taking up the material was that it overlooked differences between them and significant elements of the 'here and now' experience. There was a sense that linking the past with the present was safe territory, and that this was what constituted therapy. It began to occur to me that it would be much more risky, yet potentially more productive, to challenge some of the more obvious differences between them, including my growing conviction that Patti was the more overtly confrontational and powerful of the two. This showed itself in a tendency to browbeat and override views that James put forward. To a lesser extent she treated me in the same emasculating way.

This was evident in a session following a holiday they had taken together. To their surprise the holiday had gone well. Just as they acknowledged how good it had been Patti began to say that this had only been the case because they had each stifled their differences, making her feel that all they ever had from their marriage was 'second best'. After another brief passage of conversation I repeated back to Patti what I thought she had said earlier, namely, that in staying with James she had settled for second best. She replied that it was not true. Momentarily I was outraged at her denial of what I had believed her to have said earlier and insisted that I was right. Again she denied it, and this time I affirmed that my comment had 'hit the nail on the head'. The use of this term utterly infuriated Patti who turned the full force of her wrath on me. She told me that I was behaving unprofessionally, that therapists were not allowed to say such things and that she knew enough about the world of psychoanalysis to justify her position. A

description of what she said does not do justice to the repetitive, abra-
sive and unpleasant way in which it was said, nor to the very painful
experience of being on the receiving end of her criticisms. This wither-
ing attack remained with me as an agitated physical state for hours
afterwards. When the physical agitation had abated, the memory of the
interchange remained etched on my memory. As I reflected on this
interchange, and other similar clinical situations, I was helped by my
growing understanding of what it means for someone to be classified as
'unresolved' in attachment terms.

An attachment commentary

Recent studies in the field of attachment research show the significance of
unresolved states of mind in parents for disorganised behaviour observed in
their children (Lyons-Ruth and Jacobvitz, 1999). The unresolved category is
ascribed to subjects who, in completing the Adult Attachment Interview
(AAI) described in Chapters 1 and 2, show a momentary lapse in the way
they represent past trauma or significant loss. These past events have an
ongoing but unconscious psychological reality for the subject, as evidenced,
for example, by describing a long-dead parent in the present tense, or referring to a belief that a lost relative is simultaneously dead and alive, or becoming momentarily absorbed in the event as if it has just happened. This state of
mind can co-exist with secure, dismissing and preoccupied attachment patterns, suggesting that the unresolved subject has an encapsulated area of
psychological disturbance which erupts from time to time, and which may be
at odds with the predominant manner in which he or she characteristically
relates to others.

The key characteristic of unresolved states of mind is that they can result
in unpredictable behaviour. Studies have suggested that research subjects
classified as 'unresolved/disorganised' from the AAI may exhibit behaviour
which is frightening to a child, or indicative of being frightened by a child
(Main and Hesse, 1990). These behaviours are confusing to a child: frightening behaviour will motivate the child to seek reassurance from a parent who is
unable to give it; fearful behaviour from a parent will present a child in need
of reassurance with a retreating or unavailable attachment figure. Thus a
child's approach to a parent might suddenly be reversed to avoidance by a
feeling that the parent or caregiver is not to be trusted. This paradox results in
the collapse of the child's strategies for finding reassurance when levels of
anxiety are raised. Disturbed and contradictory behaviour can then reflect a
response to experiences of fright without solution (Main, 1995).

An interesting question for therapists is to wonder whether a watchful,
guarded, 'walking on eggshells' counter-transference, followed by an eruption
of anger of the sort illustrated in Patti and James's therapy, can be compared

with the approach/avoiding behaviour that characterises unresolved states of mind. This speculation makes clinical sense. In the case of Patti and James, a hitherto unknown-about and encapsulated pocket of angry pathology emerged in the context of a mutually consistent strategy of avoiding feelings associated with difference. Patti's response found a resonance in me with the result that a 'skirmish' of the sort I had previously identified as erupting between Patti and James now involved me directly.

The trigger to this flash-point, which disturbed the prevailing patterns of relating in the session, would probably have been explained quite differently by Patti and me. My view was that it was initiated by what I heard as a clear misrepresentation of the truth. While my first reaction was to be moderate but firm, I think there is little doubt that her denial made me angry and wishing to 'nail the lie'. Hence, my deliberate use of the phrase of having 'hit the nail on the head' was evidence of my retaliatory and angry impulse to pin her down. If approach/avoiding terms are applied to this interaction, my intervention was an approach response attempting to put right an injustice. Her subsequent angry response, fuelled by what she correctly perceived as my angry insistence that I was right, drove me into an avoiding position, not daring to take up the unresolved dynamic between us until some weeks later. In the sessions between the outburst and talking about it, I was conscious of avoiding the truth of what had happened, anxious that had I not done so I would have provoked yet another painful skirmish.

In making comparisons between child and adult experiences there are a number of conceptual problems. The first is that attachment research with children has tended to depend on the measurement of observed behaviours, whereas clinical work with adults involves the utilisation of subjective experience. As a result, concepts used in a behavioural domain do not necessarily track on to concepts used in the domain of clinical subjectivity. The experience Patti and I had of betrayal – she feeling that I had betrayed the rules of therapeutic engagement and I feeling that a version of the truth was being misrepresented – may or may not echo the subjective experiences of children who find their trust in an attachment figure broken.

A second problem is that the behaviour of children in relation to parents may be very different to the behaviour between adults. This is an interesting and challenging thought, because most of psychoanalytic theory rests on the assumption that child–parent interactions leave their unconscious residues in the adult mind, and can be repeatedly observed in transferential behaviour. One obvious difference between the reactions of children and adults may lie in the power of the latter when confronted by threat. Whereas children are likely to back away from adults whose behaviour is seen as threatening, adults need not adopt a flight response and can stand their ground. They might employ a fight reaction but they can also try to understand the process in the way that good therapy requires. It was telling that I was unable to pursue the therapeutic goal of advancing the understanding of what had happened in the therapy until some time after the event and, meanwhile, employed a 'child-like', avoiding response. I would say that this was the vulnerable position that Patti avoided by reconstituting it in my counter-transference.

A third problem stems from considering how thinking applied to one partner in the couple relates to the other, and to the unconscious preoccupations which both might share. In the clinical example, both Patti and James had troubled childhood backgrounds which featured significant losses and trauma. It is not unreasonable to speculate that, in an unconscious way, James's overt passivity at the time the outburst took place masked an identification with Patti's overt aggression. At the time I lacked the internal thinking space to consider this possibility, something that may have been possible had I had a co-therapist to work with. One of the advantages of co-therapy working is that one therapist can hold onto the reflective role while the other is caught up in a more intense exchange.

It is, of course, possible that states of mind other than the unresolved category may account for the phenomenon I have sought to highlight. Studies of violent relationships are relatively few. Some, like those that Bartholomew describes in Chapter 3, indicate the potentially abusive consequences that can follow from the pairing of fearful and preoccupied states of mind in partners. Others suggest that violence-prone men may be likely to display the states of mind associated with the 'cannot classify' category while abused women may be more likely to display both unresolved and preoccupied states of mind (Lyons-Ruth and Jacobvitz, 1999). This possibility brings us to think about a second phenomenon related to ruptures in the couple attachment system.

NON-RELATING: DEATH IN THE COUNTER-TRANSFERENCE

While becoming caught up in projective processes associated with the paranoid-schizoid position is uncomfortable, and sometimes frightening, the experience is, at least, part of being connected emotionally to the people one attempts to help. Possibly more disconcerting are those clinical situations where there is a strong sense of there being no real relationship operating between the couple, and a correspondingly absent relationship between at least one of the partners and the therapist. The couple may live together, have a family and come for therapy, as if relationships are active in their lives, but there is a sense of a void and of missing one another at an emotional level.

In these situations it is common to encounter one partner complaining that the partnership has gone dead and that there is little understanding between the pair. Frustrated anger often alternates with resigned hopelessness as the partners explore whether sufficient emotional glue remains to hold them together. The background circumstances to these loveless partnerships vary considerably, but they have in common a dynamic pattern that results in alienation rather than coming together. As one partner's anxiety at the thought of what is missing in the relationship drives her or him to seek understanding from the other, the other partner, who either doesn't understand what is being referred to or is alarmed by the experience of having something demanded of them, actively retreats. The consequence for the relationship is one of heightened alarm and anxiety rather than reassurance. Empathic understanding being absent, neither partner offers emotional containment or connectedness for the other.

In psychoanalytic theory, Bion (1959, 1962a) described the developmental equivalent of this adult experience in the mother who could not allow herself to know about her infant's emotional turbulence and thus help the infant give shape to his experiential world. Bion argued that containment in this context meant helping the infant to bear powerful emotional states, to 'detoxify' them and to give them symbolic expression. The mother who could do this was a containing mother, in contrast to the mother 'who could not tolerate the experience of such feelings and reacted by denying them ingress, or alternatively by becoming prey to the anxiety which resulted from introjection of the infant's feelings' (Bion, 1959: 104). Bion hypothesised that the infant faced by a mother who is emotionally absent will experience an emotional void, which he captured in the phrase 'nameless dread'. This is a state of psychological terror which can result in children becoming emotionally cut-off and lifeless.

It does not stretch the concept too far to ascribe this condition to the state of mind of individuals who have no real emotional contact with their partner and are faced by the fear of the emotional and practical consequences of permanent separation. In these circumstances, life together will be an emotionally cold experience, particularly once the stage of protest is relinquished and hope for recovery is passed. In my clinical experience, this sort of interactive pattern features in couples where one partner, for whatever reason, has already left the relationship in emotional terms and remains inaccessible. Secret affairs are common in this group.

The therapist (or therapists, if the work is undertaken conjointly) will have to contend with feelings which resonate with the emotional void experienced by the couple. Initial enthusiasm at the beginning of therapy will, in time, be overtaken by the hopelessness and emptiness that the couple experience. Often the therapist will be bemused that an apparent bid for containment from one client is so consistently rebuffed. A persisting disconnection between bid and response is a marker of a lack of basic relating, which almost inevitably begins to permeate the therapy and produces a quality of being stuck in a deadly way.

Case illustration

Lysette and Greg were seen in therapy over eighteen months by myself and a female colleague. The complaint, most forcibly articulated by Greg, was that Lysette was an unavailable, absent mother and partner. She was either involved in long hours at the office or was spending her spare time organising and helping out at a local sports club. They had two small children who were both at primary school. The couple met in Paris, where Lysette and her first husband had been posted through her work. The marriage began to go downhill very quickly, and they separated and divorced within a year. Reflecting on this failure, Lysette said that the difficulty had been that her husband had become too dependent on her in a city where his command of the language was poor, where he had few friends and little social life. She could not bear his emotional reliance on her.

She met Greg through work. He appeared to Lysette to be an independent, outgoing businessman, and they developed a full and enjoyable social life. Greg, reflecting on this time, said he had been attracted by Lysette's upper-class reserve, which he believed represented an emotional solidity and dependability. These qualities were extremely important to Greg, whom we learnt had an early childhood peppered with experiences of rejection, disappointment and abandonment. His mother had been psychiatrically ill as far back as he could remember, and had a drug problem. His parents divorced when he was four, and his father left Greg and his two brothers in his mother's care. Greg took on the role of substitute mother to his brothers, always hoping that his father would make contact and offer the care he felt he was capable of giving. In fact, he was constantly disappointed that his father remained remote from him, and very distressed when he remarried.

Behind Greg's ability to live an independent life lay a deep need to be looked after. He misread Lysette's upper-class reserve as strength and dependability. In fact, Lysette's reserve represented emotional retreat. Moreover, her capacity to think about her emotional life and development was extremely limited, so that the picture both she and we formed of her background was vague and indeterminate. However, we did suspect that her background was shaped by a very dominating father and a somewhat shadowy mother – whom Lysette pictured disappearing each day into her room, leaving Lysette to a succession of nannies. Her father's keenness for her to excel was described in a way that left us in little doubt that any child might have recoiled from his pressurising needs, but Lysette could never allow this sort of emotional connection to be made. Her reluctance or inability to make connections between the difficulties she and Greg experienced, and her previous experience, produced an emotional reaction of extreme frustration as we worked with her. Understanding our counter-transference led us to draw parallels with her childhood and to suggest that the interaction of a beleaguered Lysette faced by a dominating and frustrated father was being recreated in therapy. We also made connections between this dynamic and what appeared to have happened in her first failed marriage, where her husband became too emotionally demanding of her, and to the same dynamic repeating itself with Greg. We explored at length how Greg's need for reassurance fuelled Lysette's anxiety that she was being asked to give more than was possible, promoting her psychological retreat from him.

The exploration of these processes across twelve months produced very little change. Moreover, it became apparent that an uncomfortable and very difficult split counter-transference began to develop between myself and my co-therapist. Faced with a therapy which seemed stuck and going nowhere, my colleague began to give up in the sessions and to show this by getting quite sleepy. Meanwhile, I continued to work away, but began to harbour a grudge against my colleague that I was doing all the work. This rift between us was eventually faced in a painful argument in one of our post-session discussions. My colleague accused me of being too nice to Lysette, and of not confronting both how destructive she was being through her passive withdrawal and of not pointing out to her how her marriage was facing a slow death. For my part, I was angry that my colleague could withdraw into sleepy inactivity and allow me to do most of the work.

This discussion was important for both of us. I heeded what my colleague said and, I think, was able to be more robust and confrontational in the subsequent work. My colleague's sleepiness disappeared and we began to work more as a team again. This process of change had been going on for a few weeks when the couple had a holiday break from therapy. On their return they told us that Lysette had been able to talk about the fact that throughout the therapy she had been seeing a lover. Over the ensuing months this revelation started a process of both Lysette and Greg being more honest and open with each other. They eventually decided to separate.

An attachment commentary

While the 'unresolved/disorganised' classification points to the episodic breakdown in an individual's overall state of mind as a result of earlier trauma or loss, the 'cannot classify' category refers to individuals whose attachment strategy has broken down at a global level (Main and Goldwyn, 1994). This will be shown in individual AAI transcripts where there is strong evidence of two contrasting and incompatible insecure strategies operating simultaneously. For example, the transcripts of some subjects demonstrate high scores for the positive idealisation of parent figures, which is then countered, in another part of the interview transcript, by strong scores for preoccupied anger with the same figures. The degree of dissonance between these two strategies leads to the overall conclusion that the subject has no organised or consistent strategy for managing attachment-related anxiety. It is no surprise to find that this category is well represented in clinical samples. Specifically, the 'cannot classify' category has been associated with psychiatric disorder, personality disorder, marital and criminal violence and experiences of sexual abuse (Hesse, 1996). It is not hard to imagine that someone who simultaneously idealises and hates a parent figure will either enter a turbulent and possibly violent relationship with that parent or give up on attempting to form a relationship at all. If we apply a couple perspective to the 'cannot classify' category, it may help us understand those clinical situations where a quality of non-relating exists.

Greg and Lysette presented us with incompatible expectations about what they wanted from their marriage. When these expectations were not met, Greg became anxious and complained to Lysette. He became preoccupied with what he was missing in the marriage and readily made links with his earlier history of parental absence and neglect. His means of managing his own anxieties about the current failures in the marriage only served to drive his wife away. Her responses to her husband, together with her inability to make emotional connections to her past, suggested that her strategy for managing anxiety was to dismiss her feelings and diminish the significance of her early experience. While, at an individual level, this appears as an organised defensive strategy, at the level of the couple it contributes towards an incompatible and chronically disorganised joint pattern. The inflexibility of the incompatibility was articulated in feelings of hopelessness associated with an absence of emotional engagement.

This patterning of interaction, and the feelings associated with it, permeated the counter-transference and were enacted between the therapists when, over a period of weeks, a gradual breakdown in their capacity to work as a pair became apparent. The identification of this enactment, its working through, and the subsequent change in the therapists' behaviour were, in my view, important in allowing a more direct and forthright discussion to take place in the therapy. My view is that this change in the quality of the weekly discussions, which enabled the parlous state of the marriage to be addressed, helped Greg and Lysette to be more robust and honest with each other. At this point in their relationship they were able to work at the implication of Lysette's affair which had hitherto been a long-standing secret.

In applying the concept of global breakdown in attachment to a couple who are married, living together and seeking therapy, there may be an objection that the categorisation is too simplistic and fails to account for other active processes which are concerned with relating to each other. For example, we heard them describe aspects of their lives outside the therapy room which brought mutual satisfactions. Consistently, these favourable reports centred on their roles as parents. More than this, they could gain some pleasure from each other's company when away on holiday during breaks in therapy. Perhaps the important clinical point is that the idea of non-relating fails to acknowledge that through their angry times together, and when they were emotionally withdrawn from each other, a process of primitive communication *was* operating which needed acknowledgement and interpretation. For example, the times when each was angry with the other could be understood as a primitive way not only of evacuating bad feelings about the self but also of communicating what it feels like to have those bad feelings. There is, in other words, a concrete attempt to make one partner feel what the other's self-loathing is like when words are unavailable to communicate the idea (Ruszczynski and Fisher, 1995). Similarly, times of emotional withdrawal can be understood as ways of unconsciously communicating the feelings of desperation and loneliness associated with impending separation. In fact, work with this couple attempted to address these dimensions of their experience but seemed not to help them. Some relationships thrive on an uncreative and unending form of communication, producing a projective gridlock (Morgan, 1995). In my view this couple did not come into that category. Their difficulties represented more healthy inner worlds, in the sense that both wanted something that they felt was not being created between them. Therapy was a process that went some way to helping them move on and away from an unsatisfying marriage.

Psychoanalytic practice, whether with individuals or couples, relies on the capacities of practitioners to enter into and, at the same time, reflect upon the nature of those relationships in the hope that longstanding and repetitive patterns of behaviour can be understood and transformed. One aspect of the reflective task is to think about the feeling states that are engendered in the therapist or therapists as a result of repeated involvement with the problems of those they see. An important conceptual dimension which may help understand those experiences is the nature of the attachments which individuals form, both with people close to them and with their therapists. The concepts of unresolved and unclassifiable attachment point to the vulnerability of individuals and couples whose strategies for managing anxiety has broken down, either temporarily or permanently. They may be useful tools in enlarging the area of clinical insight as well as indicating research possibilities for broadening the empirical basis of our knowledge about couple relationships.

Chapter 8

Attachment, narcissism and the violent couple

Christopher Clulow

In this chapter I shall bring some aspects of attachment and object relations theories to bear on the complex matter of understanding violence in couples. In particular, I shall consider how organised and disorganised patterns of attachment might contribute to violent behaviour, and whether and how they relate to Rosenfeld's (1987) distinction between thick- and thin-skinned narcissism. For illustrative purposes I will draw on Edward Albee's play *Who's Afraid of Virginia Woolf?*

At the heart of the couple dilemma is the management of difference – between him and her – in encouraging the development of an authentic 'we' as well as two separate 'I's. Difference introduces separateness, and so resonates emotionally with the related existential conundrum for couples who find themselves on the horns of a dilemma between longing for intimacy yet dreading the possibility of loss of self through merger, and longing for independence yet dreading the loss of self through isolation. An escape from the discomfort of difference is sometimes sought through the attempt to kill off both knowledge and feeling, an experience that Bowlby (1988) captured so pithily in a chapter title: 'On knowing what you are not supposed to know, and feeling what you are not supposed to feel'. Sometimes it is sought through the attempt to obliterate or control the 'otherness' of the other.

Fear of loss of self encourages many to err on the side of negative caution. As Skynner put it: 'most of us fear the extremes of pleasure, joy and love far more than hate, anxiety and despair. The negative emotions close us in upon ourselves, tether us safely to the ground, help us to feel clearly defined. They are familiar, repetitive, known, while the most positive emotions encourage us to abandon ourselves and threaten change and growth, even perhaps surrender to others or to causes greater than our petty selves' (1982: xiv–xv).

ON WOLVES AND WOOLF

Albee's play *Who's Afraid of Virginia Woolf?* is a viper's nest of negative emotions. It is a study of a verbally and emotionally abusive marriage, in which the threat and actuality of physical violence is never far from the surface. Set in the boom decade of the twentieth century for getting married, there is a delicious irony in the film using the iconic 1960s married couple, Richard Burton and Elizabeth Taylor, to play George and Martha. The play explores the destructive games couples can play together – 'humiliate the host', 'get the guests', 'hump the hostess', 'bringing up baby' – and their power to involve bystanders in them. Only the final game, 'kill the kid', breaks new ground for the couple by publicly introducing a reality that shatters the private illusion they had nurtured together. In adopting a psychological approach to the play I want to suggest that these violent 'games' have a purpose, and that purpose is to defend against fearfulness associated with intimacy in their marital attachment.

In offering interpretations of literature there is always a danger that the work is reduced to the particular frame of the commentator, without reference to the intentions of the author or other possible readings of the same material. Albee is a political and social playwright who has been located on the fringes of what has been described as the 'absurdist' tradition of post-war dramatists (Esslin, 1980). In this context 'absurd' refers not to the ridiculous, but to a convention of disillusionment with the accepted order of things. Applied mainly to European writers like Sartre, Genet and Camus, the convention fits Albee, who attacked the 'peachy-keen' image of the American Dream (the title of another of his plays that contrasted American ideals of youthful vigour, family life and togetherness with an inner emptiness and sterility of purpose). His intent can be read as an attempt to expose the fantasy in order to challenge audiences to construct new meanings that correspond more closely than the Dream with his view of the human condition as it really is (Cunliffe, 1986). Albee confirmed that his choice of names for the principal couple was deliberately linked to the American archetypal couple of George and Martha Washington, adding that the play examined whether, as a society, Americans had failed to live up to the principles of the Revolution. So, at one level, *Woolf* is a political play.

The political issues are played out on the stage of marriage, that institution-cum-relationship that acts as a perfect vehicle for exploring the ambiguities and interconnections between the public and the private. Early on in the play, Martha is portrayed as the wolf that George might need to fear: 'I've got more teeth than you've got,' she says, to which George replies, 'Two more,' and we know the match between them is going to be fairly even. Similarly, being a 'Pig' is equated with George resisting Martha's wish to be kissed. Need and threat are immediately placed in uneasy juxtaposition and expressed in the language of childhood fable.

What hooks the audience in is a believable, recognisable, albeit savage portrayal of the interior world of a marriage. The portrayal is in real time: we, the audience, live those small hours of the night with the principal couple. The themes touch a personal nerve and allow us to identify, however uncomfortably, with George and Martha's predicament. For couple psycho-therapists, especially those who work in pairs, these themes also touch a professional nerve: they may identify with Nick and Honey, the other couple in the play, who, as so often is the case in referrals, were unilaterally invited into the nightmare by the female partner to witness a conjugal drama. In the event they are sucked into the drama and exposed as a kind of carbon copy of George and Martha: guests cast in the image of their hosts. I shall return to the potential therapeutic significance of Nick and Honey towards the end of this chapter.

The title of the play is ambiguous. 'Who's Afraid of Virginia Woolf?' is sung brashly by Martha early on in the play to try and reverse her attack on George by re-evoking something they had both laughed at during the party from which they have just returned: the line being sung, of course, to the tune 'Who's Afraid of the Big Bad Wolf?'. It is used later in the play to strike up an alliance between Martha and her guests, and by George to drown Martha out. It is returned to at the end of the play, sung gently by George in the spirit of consolation, evoking from Martha the answer that constitutes the closing line of the play: 'I . . . am . . . George . . . I . . . am'.

Much of the drama revolves around the confusion of truth and illusion. Albee is quoted as saying: ' "Who's Afraid of Virginia Woolf?" means "Who's Afraid of the Big Bad Wolf?" means "Who's afraid of living life without false illusions?" ' (Cunliffe, 1986). One critical commentary (Coles, 1980) suggests that the juxtaposition of childhood fable and literary figure contrasts two different but ineffective strategies for managing threat. For those of a Freudian disposition, it is of interest that in some versions of the story the threat is posed by the wolf attempting to enter the piglets' house by coming down the chimney. While this sexual metaphor provides an interest-ing perspective on the play, the point of relevance here is that the piglets that fail to recognise and deal effectively with the threat constituted by the wolf – either by denying its reality or by adopting an outward attitude of confidence to mask their fear – end up dead. In contrast, the commentary asserts, the characters in Virginia Woolf's novels generally fear life too much for their own good, and fall victim of their own neuroses. Whether this is fair com-ment on the characters of Virginia Woolf I am not qualified to say. It is probably a questionable assumption. Virginia Woolf shared common cause with Albee in drawing attention to threatening changes and phenomena (for example, the ambiguities of gender, sanity and historical truth) that indi-viduals and societies often prefer not to acknowledge. Both wolves and Woolf may therefore deserve to be feared.

Be that as it may, I want to use this distinction between avoidance and fearfulness as a bridge into considering the potential relevance of attachment theory for understanding couple violence.

VIOLENCE AND ORGANISED ATTACHMENT

Bowlby (1973) recognised anger as a natural response of the child to situations where the link with an attachment figure is threatened or broken. Protest had the function of communicating with the attachment figure and re-establishing the link by drawing attention to the child's plight. It was functional in the sense that it restored attachment and strengthened the bond between infant and caregiver. Anger became dysfunctional when its intensity or persistence had the effect of weakening or disrupting the attachment bond. Bowlby viewed dysfunctional anger as the foundation of anxious attachment.

As we saw in Part I, the past two decades of research have allowed developmental and social psychologists to capture the organisation of attachment systems in children and adults. Under optimal conditions, individuals will develop secure attachment, resulting in – and from – a trusting confidence that attachment figures are available and responsive and do not have to be manipulated into role. Under less optimal conditions the relationship will become anxious. Absence and unresponsiveness may result in secondary behavioural strategies which, while not as direct and effective as those of the secure individual, are nevertheless organised, and facilitate a level of connection in the attachment relationship.

Developmental psychologists have identified two organised secondary strategies for establishing proximity to a caregiver (see Chapters 1 and 2). These strategies tended to be similar for child and caregiver, as if the child had learned to respond to cues from the caregiver. When anxious, parents of avoidant infants tended to dismiss, deny or minimise the significance of attachment, sometimes in a cruel and derogatory way. They were likely to respond to the activation of attachment by detaching themselves behaviourally and emotionally. In contrast, parents of ambivalently attached children were themselves often preoccupied with attachment figures in a confused, angry or fearful way. Their response to the activation of attachment was likely to result in enmeshed relationships and emotional over-involvement. From a social psychology perspective, Bartholomew and her colleagues (see Chapter 3) have proposed a third organised attachment pattern: that of fearful attachment. Fearful attachment resembles preoccupied attachment in the degree to which others are relied upon for the validation of self-worth, but it also shares similarities with dismissing attachment in placing a premium upon avoiding intimacy. Operating unconsciously, these patterned ways of responding to perceived threats correspond with the psychoanalytic concept of defence. They constitute the 'familiar dance' that George refers to, and are to be distinguished from unresolved/disorganised states of mind to which I shall return later.

Do these categories help us to understand the nature of marital violence as depicted in Albee's play? First, it needs to be acknowledged that violence in marriage is a social and political issue. We are part of a culture that has promoted the interests of men before women, defined women as the property of men and condoned all but the most extreme forms of male violence in the home. The pursuit of equal opportunities at work and at home has created the conditions in which we can register a shocked awareness of the incidence of marital violence. For example, in the United Kingdom, 56 per cent of recorded assaults on women are domestic, as compared with 8 per cent on men (Mayhew et al., 1993). Estimates indicate that one in three women experience severe physical violence from a male partner at some time during their adult lives, while one in ten report such violence annually (Mooney, 1993).

Explanations of domestic violence are various. Particularly prominent have been those that view it as a result of a dissonance between role expectations generated by social conditioning and frustrations in realising these because of changing socio-economic realities. These studies regard the home as the private stage upon which publicly engendered frustrations are acted out (Gelles and Straus, 1988; Gelles, 1994). A similar and related explanation focuses upon conflicts resulting from culture clashes between a movement to break down traditional attitudes towards gender and a force that resists change, seeking instead to continue to structure inequalities into relationships between women and men (Dobash and Dobash, 1979; Pahl, 1985).

Psychological theories have in the past tended to cite individual psychopathology in explaining why people take up perpetrator and victim roles in family relationships (Gayford, 1978; Pizzey and Shapiro, 1982; Roy, 1982). A dimension that is missing from this picture is the influence on individual behaviour of the couple relationship itself. Might, for example, the different attachment styles of spouses act on each other to increase (or reduce) the risk of violence in managing couple conflict? While there are indications from clinical practice that this might be the case, and the link has been made for children in the context of playground bullying (Troy and Sroufe, 1987), the couple dimension has only recently been researched in exploring interactive causes of marital violence.

We have seen from Chapter 3 that there are grounds for believing abusive behaviour can be understood in a relational context, and that attachment status is a key link in this process. The Canadian studies described there highlight the violent potential of pairing fearful and preoccupied strategies for managing attachment-related anxiety. How might they map onto George and Martha's marriage?

George, we might guess, would be classified as either 'fearful' or 'dismissing' in attachment terms, and behave as the one pursued in the marriage. Martha might be classified as either 'fearful' or 'preoccupied'; she behaves provocatively as if she needs to pursue others for attention. Insofar as George protects himself from intimacy through distancing and denigratory attacks, and Martha does likewise through her angry preoccupation with the disappointment she feels him to be, we have the potential for an interactive cycle that, in systemic terms, is likely to result in 'positive feedback' (that is, an unstable escalation of conflict). Her ambivalent push for engagement allows him to respond to just part of the signal – the attack, not the distress – and to remove himself from her and this through his own sequence of retaliatory and pre-emptory strikes. The more he withdraws, the more anxiously she pursues. So the defensive cycle is amplified until it implodes on itself and there is a crisis. Fun and games turn into deadly threatening scenarios. Byng-Hall (1980) refers to such interactive cycles as typifying 'too close–too far' couples. I have come across these pairings in working with violent couples where hitting out has been a desperate attempt to escape from feeling cornered by a partner's pursuit, or has represented a misguided attempt to reassert control when passions were running away with themselves.

To explore domestic violence as a relational phenomenon is a potentially hazardous business in a climate of zero tolerance for perpetrators. It can be misread as colluding with or detracting from what should be condemned as intolerable behaviour, and pernicious in implicating the victim as somehow responsible for what has happened. This constraint on thinking is, I believe, relevant to understanding the phenomenon of violence itself. I know from working with violent couples how difficult it can be to think about what is happening as it happens, and how easy it is to be drawn into a controlling stance to manage the anxiety that things will get out of hand. This response may do no more than mimic the perpetrator's need to gain control rather than restore the checks and balances of reality into a situation dominated by phantasy. The attack on thinking, and the need for control, leads to a second way in which attachment theory can illuminate violent behaviour.

VIOLENCE AND DISORGANISED ATTACHMENT

While Bowlby drew attention to functional aspects of anger, Fonagy and colleagues (1993b) have suggested that the angry outburst of a toddler is not only an attempt to reconnect with the caregiver but also a self-protective response to insensitivity that is experienced as undermining the child's nascent self-image. Normally, anger leads to an intensification of the caregiving response with improved chances for the child's intentionality being recognised. However, it can turn to aggression when insensitivity is continual and pervasive, and we have seen how this can result in secondary strategies for managing attachment-related anxiety.

Observation of infants and caregivers undergoing the Strange Situation Test demonstrated that there were infants who appeared to have no organised strategy for managing separation–reunion anxiety. These infants could engage in contradictory behaviour, for example, approaching a parent with head averted, hitting out when apparently in a good mood, rocking on hands and knees after making an abortive approach for comfort, or moving away from a parent to the wall when apparently frightened by the stranger. Main and Solomon (1987) called this behaviour 'disorganised/disoriented' with regard to attachment. This state of mind can best be illustrated by considering the dilemma faced by children who have been abused by those who care for them. The threat constituted by the abuse activates the attachment system and draws the child to the parent or caregiver. However, when that person is the abuser, he or she is also to be feared. This dilemma is at the heart of disorganised attachment – the collapse of any coherent strategy for managing anxiety when the attachment figure is 'at once the source of and the solution to its alarm' (Main and Hesse, 1990: 163).

It is not difficult to translate this dilemma into the context of marriage and partnership, nor hard to believe that the link between disorganised mental states and violent behaviour is proving to be a strong one (De Zulueta, 1993; Lyons-Ruth and Jacobvitz, 1999; West and George, 1999). In tracking the link Fonagy (1999b) focuses on the capacity to reflect upon mental states, both one's own and those of other people. This process he describes as 'mentalizing'. While his attention was directed towards parent–child relationships, the point transposes well to the process of development in the adult couple:

> The child's understanding of minds critically depends upon a developmental opportunity to find himself represented in the caregiver's mind as a mentalizing individual [an intentional being motivated by mental states, beliefs and desires]. Their parents' mentalizing capacity is . . . a good predictor. Thus, a theory of mind is, first of all the other's theory of the child, then a theory of self and finally a theory of the other. Mentalization, the capacity to understand and interpret human behaviour in terms of the putative mental states underpinning it arises through the experience of having been so understood in the context of an attachment relationship. This, in our view, is a critical aspect of the transgenerational transmission of abuse.
>
> (1999b: 7)

The correspondence between 'mentalising' and Bion's (1959) concept of containment is close. Both describe a capacity to reflect on one's own state of mind in order that the nature of experience in relation to others might be known. Both require an openness to that experience and a capacity to process it in managing the boundary between self and others. Both depend upon the experience of having been held in mind by others, and concern a process that is pivotal to healthy psychological development.

Fonagy's association between mentalising, unresolved/disorganised states of mind and violence follows three stages. The first addresses the incentives for individuals who have experienced childhood trauma to inhibit their capacity to mentalise. For example, children who have been abused are prone to judging themselves culpable, unlovable and deserving of ill-treatment.

There are too few countervailing influences and experiences to offset those imposed by the abuser. Moreover, to preserve a parent as 'good' it may feel necessary to the child to adopt the 'bad' mantle, a process that Fairbairn (1952) described as the child's 'moral defence'. Because maltreatment involves a distortion of experience, the child's intentional state is likely to be denied or distorted, providing a further reason for withdrawing from thinking about the experience. Yet the abuser is still needed and loved by the child. In these circumstances the options may be limited to withdrawing into a private world, or becoming lost in the abuser's world. Neither option fosters the development of an autonomous or reflective self. At its most perverse, an attachment to a sadistic internal object may make it impossible for the child or adult to countenance positive relationship experiences because of the threat they pose to these internal objects: the unconscious pressure is then to evoke a sadistic rather than a loving response from others in order to maintain the original internalised tie (Avery, 1977).

The second stage of the argument links a deficit in mentalising with violent behaviour. Individuals with a limited sense of their own identity may feel less responsible for their actions, may fail to register the psychological consequences of those actions upon others and, in extremis, may reduce others to objects through their inability to hold them in mind. There is little constraint on behaviour because of the absence of identification with the other. Here, one might need to be specific about the domain in which reflective capacities are inhibited, since limitations in one context may not apply to others.

This leads to the third stage of the argument in which certain emotional experiences act as triggers for precipitate action, even for normally reflective people. Traumatic memories, or the fear of abandonment, can cause a dissociative reaction in which frightening elements in the core drama are expelled from the self and controlled in others. Because the trauma cannot be thought about, others (especially partners and therapists in the context of our concerns) are unconsciously manipulated into the state that the self finds intolerable. There is a social enactment of the disorganised internal state in which unconscious efforts are made to externalise the experience of terror into the victim. Violence then both recreates the alien state in the other and represents the attempt to control or destroy it – an attack on fearfulness that in extreme form can result in murder.

Longitudinal studies of childhood disorganisation suggest that the infant's initial disorientation is replaced by brittle behavioural strategies to control the parent either through punitive acts or through caring for him or her (Lyons-Ruth and Jacobvitz, 1999). These strategies appear to be at odds with attachment behaviour because they do not provide the child with care or protection – instead they place the child in control. However, they have a function. There are indications that, for 'disorganised' children, the activation of their attachment system serves also to activate a care-*demanding* bid from the parent rather than a care-*giving* response (George and Solomon,

1999). In these circumstances, punitive and caregiving control may represent attempts to coerce the attachment figure into providing care, or into becoming the object of care so that, through projective identification, the child may be cared-for vicariously. Role-reversal and parentification of the child has been associated with disorganised as well as preoccupied states of mind in recent research studies (West and George, 1999), and the phenomenon of 'asking with fists' (disclaiming need through strategies of aggressive control) is well recognised in clinical practice (Freedman, 2000).

Bowlby's position (1980) concurs with this view. He maintained that severe suffering in childhood could result in a defensive exclusion of experience that was so complete that memories and affect were segregated from consciousness. He saw these segregated systems as key features of pathological mourning, and as representing a continuing internal threat through the risk of uncontrolled attachment-related material surfacing and overwhelming the individual. Feeling left to protect him or herself, the individual tries to control what is feared to be overwhelming. West and George (1999) argue that Bartholomew's 'fearful' category (see Chapter 3) – a category that has been closely associated with abusive behaviour – is, from a developmental perspective, more likely to be categorised as attachment disorganisation than an organised behavioural strategy; the intense approach/avoidance conflict, so often linked with a history of trauma, is the hallmark of both.

Does Albee's play provide any illustration for this theory of violent behaviour? To some degree it does. Both George and Martha refer to past trauma in their lives. George's history, narrated at one remove, is of a teenager who was publicly humiliated by calling bourbon 'bergin', but who found the humiliation also made him a kind of celebrity ('the grandest day of my . . . youth'). This incident provides some grounds for Martha's assertion that he has a masochistic investment in inviting her humiliating attacks. The hero of his story believed he killed both his parents, with the outcome that from the age of sixteen he was locked up in an asylum, not uttering a word for thirty years. This is a prototypical story of both the dismissing and disorganised adult's response to childhood trauma. It constitutes the trigger for physical violence when Martha chooses to expose George as the boy in the story, suggesting both that he is overwhelmed by the exposure and that he has no organised means of dealing with the feelings it stirs up in him.

Martha represents her father as a powerful, demanding and critical figure who entrusted her care to others after her mother's death, who broke up her first love relationship and who is disappointed in the man she chose to marry. Yet she appears to continue to adore him, and use him as the yardstick of success. There are plenty of contradictions in her story that signal insecure attachment, not least the idealised image of a father contrasting with the pain he has caused. One is left to surmise that Martha draws from her experience the conclusion that she has disappointed both her father (perhaps by not being a boy) and her husband (perhaps by failing to conceive a child).

These feelings are projected into George when she says to him: 'I mean you're a blank, a cipher'; or to her guests: 'You see, George didn't have much . . . push . . . he wasn't particularly aggressive. In fact he was sort of a . . . a FLOP! A great . . . big . . . fat . . . FLOP! . . . He didn't have any . . . personality, you know what I mean? Which was disappointing to Daddy, as you can imagine.'

On the face of it, George and Martha have a well-rehearsed 'cat and dog' (Mattinson and Sinclair, 1979) strategy for protecting themselves in their marriage; fighting regulates the emotional distance between them (Byng-Hall, 1985). This is reflected in the games they play with each other and with their guests. Games imply the existence of rules, and prescribe limits on what can be said or done. They tend to be competitive and repetitive, enclosing the players in a closed world for the duration of play. They also allow expression of a level of emotional intensity that might be dangerous in other circumstances, and for anxiety-making situations to be played with and at. The safety provided by the rules of the games accounts for the impression that, as a couple, George and Martha are much less affected by the hurtful things said to each other than the onlooker might expect. Yet the games are deadly. Their repetitive cycles fix George and Martha in prescribed roles that are as constraining as a straitjacket – any attempt to make contact in a different way is rebuffed. They are not of the same order and do not have the exploratory, developmental potential that Winnicott (1974) describes in relation to the creative play of children. They serve principally to maintain a destructive tableau of the marriage.

Insofar as the rules of the games define the parts to be played by the couple they constitute their shared defensive system. In Ezriel's (1956) terms, the games define the required relationship to which both partners must subscribe to avoid the catastrophic consequences that are feared of operating together in another way. George and Martha bring together well-worn yet brittle controlling strategies for defending themselves against underlying anxieties in their marriage. Attack is the best form of defence. What is disturbing for them is when one or other departs from the rules. 'You can't do this' protests Martha in the endgame, 'kill the kid', the culmination of a cycle of increasing betrayals ('book dropper', 'child mentioner') that have resulted from breaking the rules.

The games, while providing a vehicle for shifting alliances to emerge in the face of attack, blend fiction and reality in an ambiguous way. They allow the couple to both play with and protect themselves from what frightens them most. 'Truth and illusion, George; you don't know the difference,' remarks Martha at the point George is about to explode the biggest illusion in their marriage. 'No, but we must carry on as though we did,' he replies. And so he does.

For George and Martha, the central illusion, what might be described as their shared conscious fantasy, concerns their imagined child. This child provides both compensation and outlet for the tenderness and love that cannot be expressed directly between them. It protects them from facing the pain of sterility, loss and inner emptiness in their marriage. The child carries the unsatisfied hopes, needs and yearnings in the relationship – bringing to life the hoped-for child within the partners as well as providing a symbol of creative intercourse between them as a couple. All that is good between them is exported from their relationship and invested in the child. While their images of the child, and their memories of 'bringing up baby', are different (providing further platforms from which to launch attacks), the child survives as the repository of hope for a better future.

In killing off the child, George attacks that hope, and in doing so dismantles a shield that has been protecting them from knowing about the full awfulness of their actual relationship. His action edges them nearer to an awareness of the shared unconscious phantasy (Dicks, 1967; Bannister and Pincus, 1971) in the marriage. This, if you like, is the core psychological bond in their relationship. It can be expressed as the shared fear that they are unlovable people who have either destroyed their attachment figures (George) or failed to qualify for their love and affection (Martha). Rather than perceiving themselves as abandoned children, they are united in believing themselves to be fundamentally flawed human beings, utterly deserving of the rejection they have experienced in the past and are now replaying in their marriage. They are refugees from a world that has, in their estimation, rightly rejected them. It is the fear of facing this phantasy that drives them to cast each other as the outcast.

The games allow them to treat each other as objects, and do not require them to have any sense of the mind of the other beyond that implied by their armoured exterior. Attempts to penetrate the protective armour are not attempts to make contact. They are a kind of psychological mutilation, akin to the bodily mutilation that George so graphically describes:

> We all peel labels, sweetie; and when you get through the skin, all three
> layers, through the muscle, slosh aside the organs – them which is still
> sloshable – and get down to the bone . . . When you get down to bone,
> you haven't got all the way, yet. There's something inside the bone . . . the
> marrow . . .and that's what you gotta get at.

These attacks and intrusions constitute not a quest for truth and intimacy, but the enactment of a sado-masochistic drama, each partner casting the other in roles dictated by their shared internal world. As such they fall into the category of narcissistic object relating.

NARCISSISM AND INSECURE ATTACHMENT

Narcissism is a widely used term in the psychoanalytic literature, and one that has been the subject of extensive debate. Generally speaking, it describes a condition in which there is a turning away from relations with others to adopt the self as the primary object of love. It is pithily illustrated in what must be an archetypal statement of narcissism in the couple when Martha expostulates to George: 'I swear . . . if you existed I'd divorce you.' A lengthier illustration is provided by Nick's response to George exposing his betrayal of Honey's history in the game of 'get the guests':

Nick [*quietly shaking*]:   You shouldn't have done that . . . you shouldn't have done that at all.
George [*calmly*]:   I hate hypocrisy.
Nick: That was cruel . . . and vicious . . .
George: . . . she'll get over it . . .
Nick: . . . and damaging . . .
George: . . . she'll recover . . .
Nick: DAMAGING!! TO ME!!
George [*with wonder*]:   To you!
Nick: TO ME!!
George: To you!!
Nick: YES!!
George: Oh beautiful . . . beautiful. By God, you gotta have a swine to show you where the truffles are.

Psychoanalytic theories differ over whether the turning away is the result of childhood trauma or phobia. Narcissism can be represented as a withdrawal from the vacuum created by an absent or emotionally unavailable object, or from the threat of a frightening parent. Alternatively, it can be represented as the flight from unbearable internal anxiety that is located in others but unrelated to actual environmental threat.

Rosenfeld (1987) distinguished between thick- and thin-skinned narcissism in terms that closely match the distinction between dismissing and preoccupied attachment patterns. Bateman summarised the distinction in the following terms:

In 'thick-skinned' narcissists, the survival of an idealised state is paramount . . . analytic sessions become dominated by defensiveness, a devaluation of external relationships and a wish to destroy the analyst as an object who can be a source of goodness and personal growth. In effect, the thick-skinned narcissist is 'object-destroying'. [He] is difficult to keep in treatment, remains unmoved by breaks in the analytic process, sneers at interpretation directed towards need and dependency, rejects before being rejected, and maintains an impenetrable superiority. . . . In contrast, the thin-skinned narcissist is more vulnerable. He is ashamed of himself, feels sensitive to rejection, and persistently judges himself as inferior to others. . . . In essence the thin-skinned narcissist is 'object-denying', continually abasing himself, looking for agreement and denying difference.

(1998: 14–15)

Balint (1959) distinguished between similar characteristic defences in children. What he described as the 'philobatic attitude' was marked by a withdrawal from actual relationships in preference for self-oriented activities. This was in contrast to the 'ocnophilic attitude', which was most likely to be evident in the child's intense dependence on others. These distinctions also resonate with Britton's (1998) demarcation between attributive ('You are me') and acquisitive ('I am you') modes of projective identification.

Compare these distinctions with Main's descriptions of dismissing and preoccupied attachment:

Transcripts are classified *dismissing* (Ds) when discourse appears aimed at minimizing the import of attachment-related experiences. . . . Dismissing speakers often show subtle to overt dislike of the interview topic, in part by cutting the interviewer and the interview short with brief replies or insistence on lack of memory. In this way, these speakers appear to reject the interviewer . . . they appear, or attempt to appear, undistressed, invulnerable, and lacking in anger. . . . Speakers are classified *preoccupied* (E, for entangled) when their interviews indicate an excessive, confused, and either angry or passive preoccupation with attachment figures or attachment-related events.

(1995: 440–1)

Bateman (1998) cautions that narcissism can take both thick and thin-skinned forms in the same person, and argues that it may be more helpful to think about them as positions rather than types. In this he is in agreement with Britton, who writes:

inside every thick-skinned patient is a thin-skinned patient trying not to get out, and in every thin-skinned patient is a thick-skinned patient who is usually giving himself a hard time and periodically gives the analyst a hard time. There are some analyses where thick-skinned-ness and thin-skinned-ness alternate from session to session, and some where the two qualities alternate in a reciprocal manner between patient and analyst.

(1998: 46)

It is likely that the same caution needs to apply to dismissing and preoccupied attachment patterns, although to be classifiable as an organised pattern there needs to be a discernible continuity in the strategy summoned to manage stressful situations. That condition does not apply to disorganised attachment.

While George appears to operate in a thick-skinned, dismissing and derogatory manner, we occasionally see glimpses of his thin-skinned, angry preoccupation and vulnerability. Likewise, while Martha appears thin-skinned and angrily preoccupied with George, she is clearly also a tough lady. Were both partners to rely on thick-skinned/dismissing strategies, there would be an agreement between them to play down their need of each other and any feelings associated with it. The contract would be, in the terms described in Chapter 1, 'I am not dependent on you and you are not dependent on me'. George and Martha fit more nearly into the endemically conflictful partnership between thick-skinned/dismissing and thin-skinned/preoccupied people, with the preoccupied partner feeling chronically deprived and emotionally abandoned, and the dismissing partner expressing disdain towards the other's expression of dependency needs.

The intriguing dimension added by viewing the couple as a unitary system is that, if an organised classification is assigned, each partner can be said to have an identification with, or an investment in, the defensive strategy of the other. This is the meaning of a shared defensive system. Such systems are evident when partners change roles – as George and Martha do – moving between different positions in relation to each other. This invites the thought that narcissistic positions and attachment patterns are interdependent rather than independent variables: his 'thick-skinned', dismissing stance relying upon her 'thin-skinned' preoccupation and emotional vulnerability, and vice versa.

If, on the other hand, conflict in their marriage is associated with disorganised attachment, the picture changes. Here, as with the 'cannot classify' category, there is either a specific or a global collapse of strategy in the face of a stressful event or episode. What has broken down is the brittle attempt to control that which is feared to be uncontrollable. From an attachment perspective, narcissism is a response to actual trauma in a person's history, and can represent a temporary mental disorganisation in response to stress; in other words it can constitute a 'position' as well as a 'trait'. People who are classified as 'secure' or 'object-relating' in one context, may react in an 'insecure' or 'narcissistic' manner faced with particular threats.

However narcissism is thought about, there is agreement that, as a state of mind, it is antagonistic to self-knowledge. We should therefore assume that it is also antagonistic to mentalising processes. As George casually remarks, after betraying his inattention to Nick and Honey's sensitivity about having no children, 'I wasn't even listening . . . or thinking . . . whichever one applies.' One powerful way of destroying self-knowledge is to project disowned aspects of the self into others, resulting in the boundary confusions that are so commonly seen in couple and family relationships, and which provide a central focus for analytic work. The subject then entertains the phantasy that he or she is in control of the object, and will resist any attempts by the latter to break out of unconsciously prescribed roles.

On the face of it, George and Martha evacuate their anxiety through attacking and shaming each other. It is as if they subscribe to Honey's maxim 'never mix, never worry', although this recipe for getting by often escalates the headaches for all concerned! Shame is intimately associated with wounded narcissism, since it is the emotion experienced when we are exposed as not being all that we wish to portray ourselves as being. It can act as a prompt for a personal reassessment, or it can intensify the struggle to ward off alien and threatening images that are experienced as being imposed by others. George and Martha battle to ward off the threat that each senses the other as being. The mutual and escalating attacks they launch on each other force them more and more onto the defensive, polarising their positions and placing increasing strain on their shared defensive system until it implodes on itself.

Paradoxically, the testing of their shared defence to the point of destruction creates the conditions in which reflection becomes more possible. It is an extreme example of narcissism and projective identification operating to sow the seeds of salvation as well as to reap the harvest of destruction. It underlines the communicative as well as evacuative potential in boundary confusions that are usually more endemic to pathological than so-called normal relationships (see, for example, Ruszczynski and Fisher, 1995). The boundary between what is and is not relational is a difficult one to define. Martha's goading, ambivalent and ultimately unsuccessful attempts to make George claim her, and thereby own his need of her and the marriage, result in the declaration of 'all-out war' and a pyrrhic victory. Yet her sexual conquest of Nick not only makes George retreat even further into his books, but also leaves her feeling the rejected and vulnerable one who then goes on to astound Nick by painting an idealised picture of George and the marriage. Never underestimate the appeal of being wedded to dissatisfaction, nor the fear of declaring love directly.

Of course, the idealisation of George reflects a continuing unresolved split in her representation of the marriage every bit as much as the preceding denigration of it. Yet there is a sense of her being in touch with herself, and of her mentalising capacity, when she drunkenly confesses:

> I cry all the time; but deep inside, so no one can see me. I cry all the time. And Georgie cries all the time, too. We both cry all the time, and then, what we do, we cry, and we take our tears, and we put 'em in the ice box, in the goddam ice trays until they're all frozen and then . . . we put them . . . in our . . . drinks.

This description is interesting since it implies choice and intentionality. George and Martha are not only the victims of trauma or prey to anxiety, they have chosen to turn away from their tears. This links with Symington's (1993) view that narcissism involves choice, and an active renunciation of what he terms the 'lifegiver', a particularly apt term for George and Martha, who are struggling with physical and emotional sterility in their marriage.

George, too, is partially aware of what he is doing in the relationship, although his choice is to turn away from Martha by maintaining her as the threat from which he needs to remove himself:

> I'm numbed enough . . . and I don't mean by liquor, though maybe that's been part of the process – a gradual, over the years going to sleep of the brain cells – I'm numbed enough, now, to be able to take you when we're alone. I don't listen to you . . . or when I *do* listen to you, I sift everything, I bring everything down to reflex response, so I don't really *hear* you, which is the only way to manage it.

As a result, and no doubt, too, because of the context in which it was said, George is not open to Martha's recognition that he has an investment in preserving himself as the victim in the marriage, and that for twenty-three years she has been in the business of satisfying his masochistic emotional needs. George refuses to hear her and brands her as mad. He sifts out what he does not wish to hear.

THERAPEUTIC IMPLICATIONS

I have suggested that the games couples play might be thought of as their shared defensive systems. I have also drawn a link between insecure attachment and narcissistic object relating. I want to conclude with some thoughts about the therapeutic implications for working with such processes. In particular, I want to think about the possible utility of dismissing/preoccupied/disorganised attachment classifications, and the distinction between thick- and thin-skinned narcissism, for therapeutic technique. In doing this I shall reintroduce, as potential couple therapists, Nick and Honey, the invited guests to whom I promised earlier to return.

Holmes (1997) suggests that the aim of psychotherapy is to assist individuals in their search for intimacy and autonomy. This, of course, is the key tension to be managed in every partnership: being involved with another without losing oneself. From attachment theory he takes the key factors predicting security to be consistency and responsiveness. Securely attached children are likely to have experienced consistent responsiveness from their parents. Insecurely attached children are likely to have experienced either consistent unresponsiveness (resulting in avoidant strategies to manage rejection and the experience of loss) or inconsistent responsiveness (resulting in anxious-ambivalent strategies to manage separation anxiety and the prospect of loss).

In his view, the key therapeutic processes are, first, working to be attuned to the communications of patients and, second, containing protest. He suggests that different patient orientations to attachment might have different technical implications, influencing the weight therapists give to fostering attachment as distinct from surviving protest in the therapeutic relationship. He argues that the primary task of the therapist with avoidant or dismissing individuals is to make emotional contact through offering a consistent availability. This might involve giving support, and being ready to depart from the rigours of the therapeutic frame in order to convey that the individual continues to be held in mind, even when absent from the therapeutic relationship. With anxious-ambivalent or preoccupied individuals the primary task is to encourage and survive protest, working with the negative transference through maintaining the therapeutic frame in a rigorous way in order to encourage the controlling phantasy to become evident and accessible to the work.

It is interesting that these approaches almost directly contradict Rosenfeld's technical advice for working with thick and thin-skinned narcissism. While advocating the interpretation of destructive narcissistic elements for thick-skinned narcissism, he warns against this for the thin-skinned variety on the grounds that it may inhibit the patient's ability to build up satisfactory object relationships and puncture a vulnerable sense of self. The contradiction between his and Holmes's position may caution against linking the patterns associated with insecure attachment too closely with those of narcissistic object-relating. They may also indicate real differences in therapeutic technique. But there may be another way of thinking about the discrepancy.

As we have seen earlier, Bateman (1998) is critical of Rosenfeld's schema on the basis that it is too categorical, a criticism that might also be applied to the over-rigid application of organised attachment classifications. He comments that psychological processes can result in the repositioning of narcissism even within the timeframe of a session, making it difficult to know which interpretative approach to adopt. He accepts the intrinsic opposition between the uncovering work of the therapist and the survival of the narcissistically frozen patient, and that interpretative work can be destabilising in these circumstances. However, he argues that while both narcissistic positions are stable in their static and rigid forms, the moment of shift between them exposes a dangerous instability during which both violence and self-destruction are possible. It is at these times that the therapist is allowed to experience the patient's terror, and really to know about the fear of violence or suicide. Because of the anxiety associated with this, it is also at these times that the therapist is most likely to be controlled by the threat, and to have difficulty containing the experience.

It is hard for me to think about the moment of transition between thick- and thin-skinned positions, or the control of the therapist, or the erosion of thinking space and terror communicated through enactment and in the counter-transference, in terms other than those of disorganised attachment. Bateman's account of the process of working with a woman patient who threatened him and herself with a knife can certainly be understood in these terms. He tracks the work through three stages: his enactment of a collusive transference, offering support and reassurance in the face of her apparent vulnerability; his enactment of a defensive counter-transference in the face of the threat of suicide, by which she controlled him; and finally, a third level of enactment in which he differentiated himself from the patient, removing the knife and arranging her admission to hospital. He argues that this third level of enactment was different from the other two in that he was able to think about the patient's experience, and to demonstrate this to her. The enactment was an interpretation of his capacity not to be controlled by the threat in the way that his patient had been by her mother, and a nurturing of the mental- ising function through demonstrating his capacity to represent their experi- ence rather than be drawn into and paralysed by it. For Bateman, the calming, mutative aspect of the work was the process of differentiating him- self from her, surviving the internal threats that dominated their relationship, and doing this in a way that demonstrated his capacity to think about her and his experience of their relationship.

Nick and Honey, George and Martha's invited guests, did not succeed in differentiating themselves from the narcissistic preoccupations of their hosts. They are recruited into George and Martha's escalating cycle of 'games' that attempt to hold in check and provoke a situation that is increasingly spinning out of control. As a couple they are drawn into the enclosed narcissism of George and Martha's relationship as a couple, so that they become like them, the process fuelled by the feelings engendered:

Nick: I'll play the charades like you've got 'em set up . . . I'll play in your language . . . I'll be what you say I am.

George: You are already . . . you just don't know it.

Nick [*shaking within*]:   No . . . no. Not really. But I'll *be* it, mister . . . I'll show you something come to life you'll wish you hadn't set up.

Whatever the actual similarities between their histories and relationships (and the shared internal object of a dominating father is one), Nick and Honey are convenient objects into which the terrors of George and Martha's marriage can be projected. They experience these terrors at first hand.

Guests, like games and therapists, can allow couples to say and do things that might feel unsafe in other circumstances. How they respond to these pressures can make the difference between collusion and containment. Had they been co-therapists, one hopes they would have struggled to make sense of how and why their own relationship was being affected in the way that it was. They would, no doubt, have been drawn to thinking about the meaning of the attack on them as a couple. Perhaps they might have worked with the powerful Oedipal themes in the marriage, the pervading influence of fathers who are both dominating and vulnerable, the destructive phantasies associated with the expression of need in relationships, the fear of rejection, and the absence of space to think about as well as live an experience. Perhaps, most important of all, they would have worked together to try and gain access to the feelings and phantasies surrounding their past trauma and the terror associated with being vulnerable, withstanding the attack on them as a couple as they edged nearer to the claustrum of their shared internal world. George, too, might then have been able to respond to the question posed by the play's title with the answer: 'I . . . am . . . Martha . . . I . . . am.'

Chapter 9

Traumatic loss and the couple

Lynne Cudmore and Dorothy Judd

THE WORK OF MOURNING

This chapter presents findings from a clinical research project which aimed to explore the nature of a couple's bereavement following a child's death. It focuses on the emotional impact of this traumatic rupture of the parent–child relationship upon the parents' relationship as a couple, and the capacity of this relationship to facilitate or impede the partners in their mourning.

We begin by defining how we understand the work of mourning. Freud believed that a significant aspect of mourning is reality-testing: the mourner discovering again and again that the loved person does not exist in the external world. He described how the death of a person frequently prompts 'the painful recollections of past interactions with that individual, heightened by intolerable yearning for his presence, the image, odours, voice and touch of the deceased' (1917: 244).

Klein (1940) described how very early in infantile life, around the time of weaning, the infant is also beset with the work of mourning. She called this stage the 'infantile depressive position' and she believed that the manner in which this position was resolved had a central bearing on the quality of an adult's object relationships in later life. Notably it influenced how later losses were mourned. If the infant has loving parents in childhood, and has managed to establish inside himself or herself these figures as 'good' internal objects, then this will be an internal source of strength and support, enabling the adult to accept the help, love and sympathy of others in later life. Klein said that when faced with loss 'the poignancy of the actual loss of a loved person is greatly increased by the mourner's unconscious phantasies of having lost his internal good objects as well. He or she then feels that his internal bad objects predominate and his inner world is in danger of disruption' (1940: 135). For her, there is a need not only to reinstate the lost loved object into the ego, as Freud described, but also to recover the previously internalised good objects, ultimately the loving parents, in order to restore security. For this to take place the loss had to be acknowledged both externally and internally, and relinquished, in order for it to be re-found internally through the work of mourning. The partners' capacity to mourn then depends on how they have resolved these earlier situations.

In 1949, John Bowlby described the therapist's task in helping troubled families in the following terms:

> Our task is thus one of promoting conditions in which the constructive forces latent [in the family] come into play. I liken it to the job of a surgeon: he does not mend bones, he tries to create conditions which permit bones to mend themselves.
>
> (p. 124)

In this chapter we describe the results of a project that explored what influenced the capacity of couples to mourn the death of a child. To develop Bowlby's analogy, we were particularly interested in finding out why some couples were able to create the conditions which permitted the 'constructive forces latent in the family' to emerge, so that the healing process could begin, while others encountered obstacles to initiating this process. We conclude that an essential condition in this process is the capacity of the couple relationship to function as a psychological container or secure base for each partner, a container within which each partner might be helped *by their relationship* to work through the loss of their child.

The losses that we heard about conveyed the message that the parents, and the dead child's siblings, would never be the same again. For some, the telling of their stories together, often for the first time, was the beginning of a process of mourning. The struggle involved in telling these stories was similar to that conveyed by Paul Celan talking about survivors of the Holocaust – not an exaggerated parallel for the internal holocaust of some of our couples:

> there remained, in the midst of the losses, this one thing: language. This, the language, was not lost but remained, yes, in spite of everything. But it had to *pass through its own answerlessness*, pass through a frightful falling-mute, pass through the thousand darknesses of death-bringing speech. It passed through and yielded no words for what was happening – *but it went through those happenings.* Went through and could come into the light of day again, 'enriched' by all that.
>
> (Felstiner, 1982: 27)

Celan's description of the answerlessness, of the mute phase before the unspeakable can be spoken, and thence, in a way, be worked through in the process of coming out into the open, not only was what our couples were going through, but also conveys an aspect of the difficulty we had in thinking about the often unprocessed, inchoate, unbearable utterances, and then adequately putting them into words for this chapter. The tension between language and silence, and between remembering and forgetting, were at the heart of their dilemma. It seemed particularly important for these couples to feel that their child was remembered, and not allowed to slip away into forgetfulness. They often struggled to hang onto every remembered aspect of the dead child, both in memory and by keeping actual mementoes. This understandable striving was often, paradoxically, an impediment to the mourning process. An inability to *let go* of the actual child, allowing him or her to be truly dead and never returning, prevented the possibility that the child could be re-found, 'alive' in the inner world of each parent and in their relationship.

There is a further paradox. The language they used held the prospect of communication, a possible bridge between their experience and ours. Yet the words they chose meant different things to each of them and to us. The possibility of being understood also contained a reminder of each person's singularity and aloneness. Listening, hearing, witnessing – on our part, and sometimes on the partner's part – involved, at some level, a re-enactment of the original trauma. It also entailed being reminded of our own mortality and the ways in which we deal with it. 'We are called upon to listen back to the point from which the word becomes necessary and speaks itself in its own apartness, to the point at which the word arrives as a gift' (Schmidt, 1998: 747).

We hoped that by telling their story and by our hearing their testament – bearing witness to it, and indeed struggling to *bear* it – we and the couples we saw might understand their predicament in a new way, even, perhaps, helping those whose course had been arrested along the path of 'normal', but no less difficult for that, mourning.

Our understanding of mourning processes draws heavily on object relations theory, and makes only limited reference to Bowlby's contribution in this area. Nevertheless, we think the reader who is versed in attachment theory will have no difficulty relating to the core of this chapter, which is more illustrative than theoretical. For those interested in making theoretical connections there are references earlier in the book to correspondences between the secure base phenomenon and the psychoanalytical concept of containment that we draw upon to inform our work. The therapeutic potential of 'giving voice' to inchoate experience, to which we have already alluded, is central to the task of mourning and fits well with the process of achieving 'narrative competence' that features as one goal of therapy for some attachment theory informed therapists.

THE PROJECT

The research was prompted by discussions with bereavement organisations that helped parents whose child had died. These drew our attention to the profound impact such a loss could have on a partnership, on the subsequent 'replacement' children and on surviving children. These last had to bear the loss not only of a sibling but also of the availability of their parents, who were often unable to facilitate and contain their children's grief because of their own. The discussions also highlighted the anxiety many practitioners had about working with the bereaved *couple*. This seemed partly related to an unsureness about working with couples and being ill-equipped to engage with their complex worlds, and partly to the fear of the emotional impact on them of working with both grieving parents.

Our own work had made us aware of the paucity of psychoanalytic litera-ture on the subject of parental bereavement. One of us had considerable experience of working with children suffering from cancer, and with their families (Judd, 1989, 1994). The other had carried out an extensive literature review revealing a striking absence of clinical research with couples (Cudmore, 1994). The main reasons researchers gave for not exploring a couple's experience in more detail were anxieties about intruding on their grief following a loss as shocking as the death of a child, and concerns about invading the intimacy and complexity of the couple relationship (Cook, 1983; Zeanah, 1989; Bohannon, 1990–1; Hazzard et al., 1992; Dyregrov, 1990). The extreme emotional, social and spiritual crisis presented by the child's death was also cited as placing severe methodological constraints on the researchers (Klass, 1986).

With these findings in mind we aimed to provide a research framework that could offer couples a setting that would facilitate their being able to think and talk about their experiences. Following their initial meeting with us we decided to invite couples to attend up to six one-hour interviews to explore their experience.

As a first step we compiled a leaflet for bereaved couples, directed towards those who felt they were still struggling with their experience, as well as those who felt they had largely come to terms with it, inviting them to come and talk to us. The leaflet was sent to bereavement organisations, hospitals and doctors, and was advertised nationally. Couples responded from all over the country, either by telephone or by letter. Many said that they felt the impact of their loss on the couple relationship was an overlooked area, and that bereavement counselling was usually offered to only one partner.

From these respondents we interviewed twenty-five couples. They were not selected for the project. The only criterion for taking part was that both partners attended. All the couples we saw had lost a child, and in some cases more than one. The recency of the loss varied considerably: one couple lost their baby two weeks before they came to see us, while an elderly couple came thirty-one years after their daughter's death. The circumstances of death were diverse, including perinatal bereavement, cot death, suicide, murder, physical illness and accident. The ages of the children ranged from infancy to twenty-eight years of age. Most of the couples we saw were living together, although some had separated before the child's death and wanted to talk about their shared bereavement.

Although the specific focus of the project was explained at the start of the initial interview, we conducted unstructured interviews, the emphasis being on encouraging the couple to tell their own story. We were interested in how they began to develop (or not develop) their stories, the details given special attention, the order of events, the associated feelings, the tone of voice they used to recount the experience and the way in which they shared or divided the narrative. These factors helped us to have a sense of their emotional experience. We paid particular attention to the way in which the couples related to us and the nature of the contact they made with us. We pieced together in as much detail as possible the atmosphere in the room, the emotions of the two parents, our feelings, positive and negative aspects of their transferences to us and to each other, and our different counter-transferences.

The role of clinical researcher presented its own difficulties. We often found ourselves drawn into acting as therapists despite our research brief. For some couples the research was an acceptable forum for talking about their experience. They brought their immense pain and grief and appealed to us for help in understanding it. When this appeal was unconscious, we often found ourselves in a dilemma about how to respond. At other times we were unsure about the most appropriate way to take the exploration further, especially when couples were still struggling with a difficult issue between them and an interpretative intervention might have helped them understand what was happening. For other couples participation in the research, however brief, seemed to allow constructive processes to operate and our role as researchers – witnesses and interested, attentive observers of their experience – was not compromised. In these circumstances, the research contract constituted a containing environment that enabled couples to think about their experience. As Garland (1998) has described, thinking about a psychically painful experience is a necessary part of laying it to rest.

We will describe the experience of two couples. The circumstances of the child's death were very different in each case. For the first couple, the inevitability of the death had been known about for many years, so the final loss was anticipated. For the second couple, the death was unexpected and the circumstances traumatic. Our intention is not to explore or compare the effects of these different circumstances, although they did have a very different impact and meaning for the parents, but to focus on the emotional experience of each couple as they struggled to incorporate the reality of the child's death into their lives. This is the task of mourning.

Mr and Mrs O.

It was difficult for us to find what might be described as a 'securely attached' couple in our sample. Those we came to know well, who opted for the seven sessions or more, were all what might be described as 'insecurely attached'. In order to convey some characteristics of security in this context, we will describe a couple whom we saw only once. Because of the brief contact, our thoughts and findings are necessarily sketchy.

Mr and Mrs O. appeared to have come through the death of their 22-year-old son, Paul, relatively well. They were a middle-aged couple who exuded a glow of good health and vitality. We hypothesised from Mrs O.'s descriptions of her happy childhood that she had felt secure and contained in her family. From the few details we were given, it was clear that Mr O.'s childhood was more problematic. By 'cherishing' his wife – the word she used – over the long period of their marriage, he had been able to benefit from her stability. Both felt comfortable with this 'unequal' beginning to the relationship. It seemed that through adoring and giving to his wife, he had been able to take in the goodness that he perceived in her. The containment offered by the marriage helped him develop a sufficiently good, sustaining internal object to weather the trauma of Paul's illness and death. His wife said that Mr O.'s support had enabled her to sustain their two well children and to nurse Paul.

Paul had died of a degenerative condition three years before they came to see us. He was the second child, who, although slightly premature, did well as a baby. He was described as 'zestful': he ate a lot and rarely slept. His parents found him trying, but their sense of humour, which stayed with them throughout, seemed to have helped. When he was one year old he showed some odd behaviour which eventually led to his condition being diagnosed. Both parents have to be carriers of this recessive gene, and the fact that the cause was shared between them may have helped them to avoid blaming each other or feeling excessive guilt.

The days succeeding the diagnosis were described as the worst of their lives. Paul was given between four and five years to live. They said that this phase had been worse than his eventual death twenty-one years later. They had made Paul's life as normal as possible, making him part of the family even though 'he looked a mess' and couldn't feed himself; he was tube-fed from the age of four. Their elder daughter was fiercely protective of Paul, and the younger one accepted the situation as part of her life. Strikingly, Mr and Mrs O. felt that life was really worthwhile and rich, and that their children had been changed by the experience, making them kinder to others.

There were a few healthy disagreements between them during the interview with us. One arose when Mr O. was depicting the way their experience of caring for Paul, and then his ultimate death, had changed his life. He said it had made him less ambitious, less materialistic, and more valuing of things to do with the quality of life, such as family relationships and walking in the countryside. Mrs O. put her experience slightly differently. Like her husband it had reinforced for her what was important in life, and when other people complained about little things she thought 'That's trivial!' The subtle difference between her perspective and that of her husband was that she didn't feel the experience had changed her, or been formative, because she had always had that sense of valuing life. It seemed to us that Mrs O.'s benign childhood had given her this great appreciation for life, whilst for Mr O. the twenty-two years with Paul, and the love between him and his wife, had enabled him to respond to their loss in a more secure way than might have been predicted from his relatively troubled childhood.

When Mr and Mrs O. talked about Paul's death they both expressed great relief. Mrs O. said that, if anything, it would have been better if he had died sooner, because there had been no quality of life for him. In his last few years he had been in a vegetative state. As she talked she became more emotional, saying 'They wouldn't leave animals in this state, would they?' They then described the extent of his disabilities. He had been blind since he was very young, had grown into a foetal position with his limbs very rigid, and could not perform most bodily functions without medical intervention. They felt he suffered in the end. They described the nightmare of bathing this 'dead weight', as they called him. We felt they were conveying the truly hopeless and immeasurably heavy burden they had been carrying. Mr O. then described shaving Paul. His wife said she had forgotten about that, and seemed shocked at her forgetting. We wondered, but did not say, if she was seeing him in her mind as a much younger boy or even baby, and that she was reluctant to acknowledge his having grown into a man.

As if on the same wavelength, Mr O. said very thoughtfully that they were not only having to mourn the actual death of Paul, but also all the stages that he had missed out on. He said, 'I can't make sense of what happened and I don't think I ever will. I don't think one can make sense of that kind of a life that has meant nothing to Paul as far as we know, with no quality of life at all. We'll always mourn when we see friends of our other children who would be about the same age as Paul . . . when they reach milestones, like getting married, we wonder what Paul would have been like . . . and we think of him missing out on all this. Only today we were saying, "Paul never made sandcastles, never played on a beach."' Mrs O. said that it left a 'great hole' in her life. They added the positive note that he had packed a great deal into his first year of life.

When we commented on their lack of bitterness, blaming or anger, they questioned this, saying that, in fact, they had had quite a lot of vitriol for the authorities when they were not forthcoming with respite care. Mr O. said he had channelled some of his energy and anger towards them. However, they both felt that theirs had been a good marriage, providing each of them with a source of strength and support that the tragedy had not destroyed. Our impression was that within the 'container' of the marriage (Colman, 1993), their anxieties and feelings about the loss had been well held. Despite the terrible buffeting they had received, each had internalised sufficiently good objects for these to be salvageable and repaired. Perhaps through facilitating each other's mourning they were symbolically repairing their own damaged internal objects. In order to *know* more about their grief, they were prepared to learn about each other's.

Mr and Mrs E.

Mr and Mrs E.'s only daughter, Lucy, committed suicide in her early twenties, six months prior to the research interview. They were seen seven times as part of the project. Following this, and at their request, they transferred to the TMSI clinical service, where they continued to see us.

How they became involved in the project provided an insight into the way each partner managed need in their relationship. The counsellor who had been seeing Mrs E. during the months following her daughter's death heard about the research and mentioned this to Mrs E. She and her husband had found it difficult to talk together about Lucy and were becoming isolated from each other, and the counsellor thought this might help him. Although he had refused counselling for himself, Mr E. was interested in taking part in the research and agreed to his wife telephoning to make an appointment. On the telephone, Mrs E. said they needed help as a couple while her husband wanted to be helpful to the research. For Mr E., the research and his wife were the objects in need, not himself.

This pattern was observable in our first meeting. We were initially struck by their contrasting physical appearances that vividly conveyed their very different states of mind. Mrs E. was heavy looking, pale and sad. She spoke through tears, hunched up and wretched. The word 'despair' came to mind, she looked such a broken woman. In contrast, her husband was alert, almost perky, with a scrubbed pink complexion that gave him an air of well-being. The phrase 'bright eyed and bushy tailed' came to mind, one he used later to describe their daughter as a young girl.

Mr E. began by drawing our attention to the problems they were facing as a couple, and as he described their predicament we were aware of the gulf between them. His description focused on his wife's problems. He felt that following Lucy's death she had been preoccupied and distraught, in a turmoil about the traumatic circumstances of the death and her relationship with their daughter. She agreed with this, and added that she felt guilty that she, and they as a couple, had not done enough to recognise the seriousness of Lucy's problems. They had sought professional help for her, which they later learnt she had found difficult to use, but had been unable to empathise with her desperate despair, a state of which she was now painfully aware in her bereavement.

In contrast to her description of a life that had fallen to pieces, Mr E. thought he was coping well. Returning to work quickly had helped, he said, and now he wanted them to get on with their lives, put the past behind them, 'move onwards and forwards'. He believed Lucy's emotional state had been largely drug-induced, and blamed his daughter for messing up her life. He spoke as if he was a detective on the case: cool, calm and clinically detached. It seemed as if he had not only to keep his distance from his wife's emotional state but also needed to attack and criticise her feelings, which seemed intolerable for him to witness and understand.

Wrapped up in her own despair, Mrs E. was less openly critical of her husband, but she disagreed with his views and felt hurt by his labelling their daughter as drug-dependent. His different views and lack of empathy made her feel very abandoned. They both felt confused about their very different attitudes and ways of reacting to the death as they both believed the marriage had basically been a good one. They had never felt so divided, and their sense of isolation from each other seemed a further loss.

From this initial meeting we understood Mr E.'s self-sufficiency, his matter of fact tone and cut-off response from any feeling about his daughter's death, as a defensive posture, an extreme sensitivity to any expression of dependency and pain. The only emotion that he showed was anger with Lucy for messing herself up with drugs, and he also protested at being left by her in this way. His wife, in contrast, was preoccupied with guilt, self-blame and sorrow. Bowlby (1961) describes feelings of sorrow and anger as characterising every grief reaction. Mr and Mrs E. had split these feelings between them, each expressing what the other could not bear. While Mrs E.'s emotional turmoil was a product of her own intensely complicated feelings about her daughter's death, we wondered if she was also in receipt of her husband's grief – his feelings of loss, shame and blame. We thought that because he seemed unable to bear knowing about these feelings he had projected them into his wife and attacked them in her. The force of this attack made us aware of how violently feelings of this kind were attacked in his internal world. It was more difficult to understand what Mr E.'s detached emotional stance represented for his wife. She had referred to feeling very cut off from her daughter, so we might surmise that there was an aspect of her represented in her husband's wish not to know about the pain – which is, perhaps, why she seemed so accepting of his detachment. Their joint need to put the trauma to one side was expressed in a story they told us. They had gone on a holiday ten days after Lucy had died, but had never mentioned the death to each other or to their fellow passengers. They said they had both enjoyed the holi-day. This extreme denial suggests how the traumatic circumstances of their daughter's death felt quite unmanageable for them to begin with. However, Mrs E.'s defences had broken down upon their return, whereas her husband was trying to carry on as before.

At their first meeting with us Mr and Mrs E. became embroiled in an argument about the causes of Lucy's death. As we have said, Mrs E. believed she had had a mental illness while her husband believed that her death was the result of heavy drug abuse over the years. Each of their explanations implied a singular cause. They both believed they were right and the other was wrong, and they rigidly stuck to their beliefs. They were in a state of mind in which they were unable to listen to each other, to take in anything of what the other had to say or to develop their thinking. The persecuted nature of their interaction defended them from thinking about the relationship they each had with Lucy. It might also be that the anger these disagreements engendered defended them against feelings of loss, guilt and blame, and were a way of feeling they were still alive. For Mrs E. the situation was complicated because she was in touch with self-recriminatory feelings about failing as a mother to protect her daughter, but we saw how easily she could flip into another state of mind and blame other causes.

Over the ensuing months they were gradually able to talk more about, and mourn, their different relationships with Lucy. In her last two years Mrs E. had found her changed, withdrawn and uncommunicative. Her attempts to reach Lucy were rejected, and she was confused and baffled by these changes. As she had never felt really depressed herself she was unable to empathise with her daughter's depression, and she withdrew from her. After the death she felt she had really let her down, and this self-blame and self-reproach left her feeling truly melancholic. She was unable to acknowledge any anger for what Lucy had done to them by leaving them in such a violent way, so perhaps this anger was turned inwards and upon herself in a masochistic fashion. However, in time she was better able to remember the bright, curious little girl Lucy had been, and their close relationship before her turmoil. Remembering her in this way was unbearably painful, but the recovery and sharing of these memories did enable a less persecuting process of mourning to begin. Knowing there was a firm enough foundation to her relationship with Lucy enabled her to modify her grief to a more depressive guilt, as well as feeling concern and regret for what she had not been able to provide. It was in the nature of the vicissitudes of mourning that there were fluctuations between persecutory and depressive states of mind even two years after Lucy's death.

In contrast, Mr E. initially showed a striking absence of any feelings except anger at the way Lucy had messed up her life and deserted them. The difficulties between father and daughter had begun around Lucy's seventeenth birthday. At this time Mr E. had sought help from their doctor, who had said Lucy's difficulties sounded typical of adolescence. This reassured the father, but his daughter's difficulties did not go away. Lucy withdrew, reinforcing her father's lack of confidence in himself as a good father and prompting him, in turn, to withdraw. He found it difficult to talk to Lucy about how she was feeling and behaving, and turned instead to making practical suggestions, which Lucy always rejected. Mr E. said that he had had difficulties with his own father when he was seventeen, following his father's remarriage. Father and son were estranged, so he himself had never had the experience of struggling through adolescent difficulties in that relationship. Talking about this, while unbearably painful, enabled him to acknowledge and think for the first time about the very real problems he had had with the adolescent Lucy. Acknowledging these feelings enabled him subsequently to be more in touch with the joys of Lucy as a little girl, who was then talked about less as a 'drug-dependent' and more as a whole person. This encouraged some grieving for what he had lost. However, he wanted this to remain a private matter, and said that he wanted to reminisce 'in his head' rather than share his memories with his wife. For her part, she seemed accepting of this – perhaps she did not want to be burdened with his feelings when she was so desperately trying to come to terms with her own.

Further light was thrown on the origins of Mr and Mrs E.'s different reactions to loss when we heard about their very different experiences of family life in childhood. Mrs E. described her family as close and supportive. Her mother had died a few years previously and she remained in close touch with her father, who was profoundly affected by Lucy's death. She felt that throughout her childhood her family had always provided her with the security to which she could return at times of crisis. She had three brothers, all of whom had rallied around her following Lucy's death, and she had been able to talk to them about her grief. These experiences of a warm, caring family felt solidly lodged inside her although, as we have described, under the impact of the death her belief in the goodness of her internal world was severely shaken. But the security of that early experience equipped her to begin to struggle with the complicated process of mourning her daughter.

Mr E.'s experience was very different. An only child, his mother had died when he was four. He told us that he returned home from school to find her collapsed on the floor. He cleared up 'all the mess' before calling an ambulance. His mother went to hospital and he never saw her again. He was told by friends at school the next day that his mother had died. Mr E. seemed to be speaking about these memories for the first time, and wondered if his mother might have been saved had he not been so concerned about the mess. We wondered at the crippling sense of responsibility and guilt he must have felt following her death. He went to live with his maternal grandparents, who, of course, had suffered the loss of their daughter and, we surmised, might have found it difficult to support their grandson in his grief. It is likely that feelings related to this early trauma were reactivated when Lucy died, and that Mr E.'s difficulties mourning his daughter were linked to his difficulties mourning his mother. Just as Lucy had blotted out her problems with drugs, it was as if Mr E. had anaesthetised his own mind from the catastrophic feelings associated with his own earlier loss. He often described himself as numb. While he conveyed that he was a good friend to others in trouble, he was unable to ask for help for himself. This applied in the marriage, where he could not bear feeling vulnerable.

The opportunity provided by the research meetings to talk seemed to offer some relief to them both. It was a new experience to tell their story in the presence of each other, as they had been unable to talk about their daughter's death together. Although Mr E. was contemptuous of what he called 'the talking cure', he readily agreed to further meetings.

Over the course of our contact there was some movement in the capacity of their relationship as a couple to function as a place where each partner could think about their loss and be helped along the path of mourning. Mrs E. was better able to protest at what Lucy had done to them by her suicide, and so her husband was not left to carry all the anger. At times, Mr E. seemed more 'moist' than before, less attacking of his wife and better able to tolerate *her* distress as he became able to acknowledge his own. This led to them feeling closer as a couple. But they went backwards and forwards in this process.

At one stage they became very estranged from each other over the subject of Mr E.'s lack of work. He had left his employment some months after Lucy had died, a move that had been planned before the tragedy. The idea had been that he would find another job, but he remained at home and did not look for work. Mrs E. was the sole bread-winner and she felt very aggrieved about this. At first this looked like a disagreement that belonged just to the issue of work, although we had wondered with them whether Mr E.'s lack of motivation might be a symptom of his depression, a thought repudiated by them both. As we explored the work issue further we noticed that Mrs E. related to her husband as if she was admonishing an adolescent son for his laziness. Mr E. laughed off her grievances, and in the meeting it seemed as if he had become the adolescent Lucy, rebelling against and challenging his parents' demands. It was as if they had recreated their relationship with their adolescent daughter between them, each identifying with different aspects of Lucy's problems. We might understand this joint identification as serving the purpose of keeping Lucy close to them and not letting her go.

Despite some fluctuations, the basic system of Mrs E. being the chief mourner and the partner in need of help remained. Mr E. did not think he needed anyone's help. Although his wife was sometimes sad that he did not want to talk much to her, she was more concerned that he looked after her. She said that to help him was probably more than she could manage as she struggled with her own grief. But the nature of her mourning changed. She slowly relinquished her identification with her depressed daughter, and became less blaming and persecutory towards herself – less admonishing of herself and her lost object.

For our part, we struggled to hold on to our capacity to think with them. We felt they needed much more help than either of them was prepared to accept. They chose to space out their meetings with us at monthly intervals, even when they transferred to the clinical service, and we felt that this was a way of defending themselves against the psychological work that remained to be done.

TRAUMA, CONTAINMENT AND THE SECURE BASE

Freud commented at the time of his daughter's death: 'Deep down I sense a bitter, irreparable narcissistic injury' (1920: 331). He wrote at more length about this experience:

> Although we know that after such a loss the acute state of mourning will subside, we also know we shall remain inconsolable and will never find a substitute. No matter what may fill the gap, even if it be filled completely, it nevertheless remains something else. And actually this is how it should be. It is the only way of perpetuating that love which we do not want to relinquish.
>
> (Freud, 1929: 386)

One of the complications for parents in mourning the death of their child is that biologically, psychologically and socially the child is part of the parents as individuals and part of their relationship as a couple. When a child dies, the parents mourn not only the loss of that person but also part of themselves. For this reason the bereavement can be experienced as a vicious assault on the self (Colman, 1988). This confusion of boundaries between parent and child will complicate the task of mourning. Mourning involves separating from the lost object in the external world – accepting the reality of the loss – so that the child can be rehabilitated in the internal world of the individual. For the couple, the child is their unique creation; she or he stands as a potent symbol of their love and creativity as a couple. For many couples, a child's death can strike right at the heart of their relationship and leave them with a profound loss of meaning. Freud described the loss as 'bitter', and this word conveys the sourness and injustice of a child's death. It is a death against the natural order of things, a death out of season (Judd, 1989). For some couples this may turn into a sense of grievance, perhaps linked with earlier, unresolved grievances (Young and Gibb, 1998), which is then played out in their relationship.

The loss affects both partners simultaneously but, as we saw with Mr and Mrs E., the fact that the couple shares the tragedy does not mean that their mourning will be the same. For each partner the death will have a different meaning. They each mourn a different relationship with their child, and they will bring different experiences of previous losses, internal and external, which will inevitably be revived with this loss. They will also bring different internal resources to help or hinder them in their mourning.

A central focus of our work was to find out about the capacity of the couple relationship to act as a container for bereaved partners so that the work of mourning could proceed. Bion's (1962b) work on containment has provided us with a helpful theoretical frame. Bion developed Klein's (1946) concept of projective identification. She believed this was an intrapsychic process whereby unwanted feelings, perceptions and attitudes were projected out of the self and perceived in the object. In the mind of the projector, the object then became identified with those same feelings and attitudes. Although she described this phantasy as omnipotent because the actual attributes of the object were discounted, she described how the external object could be induced to feel or think as if she or he did possess these properties. For the object to take in these projected or evacuated states of mind there must be some degree of fit with something already present in the object, an introjective identification.

Bion believed that projective identification was not only the infant's primary way of dealing with unmanageable levels of distress but also his or her earliest form of communication. It was how the baby let the mother know how s/he was feeling. The mother's capacity to contain her infant's anxieties, without being overwhelmed by them, enabled the baby to order and make sense of experience. Her ability to do this 'detoxified' them, transforming them into something manageable and meaningful. Through her capacity to contain the infant's state of mind the mother transformed what was unthinkable into what could be thought about. The baby with a more or less successfully containing parent eventually incorporated that very capacity to contain his or her own experience.

As Garland (1991) has so vividly described, a traumatic event breaches and floods the structure of this internal capacity to contain:

> Trauma is a Greek word meaning to pierce. . . . It is used most often of physical injuries when the skin is broken – where something once intact has been breached. It suggests that the event which creates the breach is of a certain intensity, or violence, and the consequences for the organism are long lasting. From there it is a small step to the metaphorical use of the concept, to the sense of an event which in the same intense and violent way ruptures the protective layer which surrounds the mind, with equally long lasting consequences for psychic organisations.
>
> (p. 509)

When couples suffer the trauma of their child's death not only does the tragedy rupture each partner's internal capacity for containment (their capacity to symbolise, to think) but it can also rupture the capacity of the couple relationship itself to function in this way for the partners. Partners may turn to each other for help to contain the unmanageable, and find they may not be in a position to provide this because of their own unmanageable feelings. This can lead to an escalating pressure on the relationship.

When they first came to see us, Mr and Mrs E. had been unable to talk at all together about their daughter's death. As we described, Mrs E. was on the point of breakdown. She was completely overwhelmed with feelings of self-blame, recrimination and persecutory guilt. She tortured herself with thoughts of what she had not done for Lucy. She was so much 'in' her experience she had no capacity to think about it; it was as if her mind had broken down. In contrast, Mr E. did not look as if he was grieving at all. There was both an absence of any feeling except anger and an absence of a capacity to think about what had happened.

When anxieties are felt to be totally unmanageable and persecutory the primitive defences of denial, splitting and projective identification can be used between couples as they are between infants and parents. Mr E. was not able to acknowledge any feelings of loss or guilt – these were all projected into his wife and attacked in her. Mrs E. could not bear to know how angry she felt with her daughter, or how deserted she felt by her leaving them through suicide, and these unbearable feelings were projected into her husband. He was then attacked for having them. They were each fixed in their positions and in a rigid pattern of relating. There was no 'give'. They were unable to listen to what the other had to say and had little capacity to see the other as a separate person. This state of mind reflected the very paranoid world they had been catapulted into following Lucy's death. It had not been their way of relating to each other before her death. The horror of their circumstances had activated the most primitive of feelings and defences to deal with the pain of their severed attachment.

As Gibb (1998) has commented, we can all recognise and empathise with the terrible problems in mourning posed for parents when their child commits suicide. The loss is unmitigated by realities such as the natural order of life, accident or fate – all considerations that can relieve feelings of persecution and guilt, and hence facilitate mourning. She points out that for the parent of a child who dies by suicide there is the fear that the dead object is inflicting punishment for the parent's wrongdoings or deficiencies. The E.s' sense of failure to protect their daughter, to look after her and contain her pain, was part of the persecuting nature of their mourning. Their turning away from knowing more about aspects of themselves, both internal and external, posed real obstacles for them in mourning their loss.

A further obstacle was that both Mr and Mrs E. were unable to know about their ambivalence towards Lucy. Freud (1917) writes about the ways in which ambivalence towards the deceased affects the outcome of mourning. Although ambivalence is a part of every relationship, and anger towards the person who has died is often part of normal grieving, if the relationhip was highly ambivalent, and was more on the side of hate and anger than love, then we can postulate that the mourning process will be much more problematic. The nature of Lucy's death provoked a great deal of ambivalence towards her for what felt to her parents like a massive rejection and attack upon them.

This couple's relationship was so severely traumatised by Lucy's death that when Mr and Mrs E. first came to see us it could not offer them any possibility of containment. We believe that their lack of containment, and the massive system of projective identification operating between them, presented real obstacles to their beginning a healthy mourning process. It was only possible for this to begin when the couple began to take back some of their projections and to struggle with previously unacknowledged parts of themselves; in other words, when they could become more separate as a couple and more together in themselves. When Mrs E. was relieved of some of the guilt she was carrying for her husband she began to pine for Lucy. An ability to pine for a lost loved object was seen by both Klein and Bowlby as central to the work of mourning.

Mr and Mrs O. were in a more fortunate position. The buffeting they had received, internally and externally, was associated with a chronic 'natural' condition, and not an acute, self-destructive event. Their relationship was able to offer them a space to think, to process their experience, to offer them the containment they needed to assist them in their mourning. Their healthy son had been lost very early on. They had already mourned the loss of this healthy child and lived with the inevitability of his death for many years. They had time to prepare. This might have helped mitigate some of the pain. Their ability to talk about their son together, to share their memories of him, and to disclose to each other the range of their emotions, led to them feeling their son's death was an experience they not only shared but faced together. They each brought considerable internal resources, which contributed to them being able to experience their relationship as containing, but their relationship acted reciprocally to promote their internal capacity for containment. This function of their relationship strengthened them both. We were moved and impressed by Mr and Mrs O.'s openness and their ability to hold on to what was good and valuable in their lives, despite their suffering. Guilt and blame were strikingly absent from their accounts. There was no bitterness or sense of grievance. Instead there was overwhelming sorrow for what had happened. In order to know about their own grief they were prepared to know about each other's grief: they had a capacity for reciprocity.

In Part I we have seen how secure couple attachment involves an ability to move freely between dependent and depended-on positions. Secure attachment involves a corresponding empathic appreciation of the partners' thoughts and feelings, an open expression of the need for comfort and contact as well as open receptivity to that contact. All the couples we saw who used their relationship to assist them in their mourning demonstrated this flexibility, an ability to take turns in looking after and being looked after.

IMPLICATIONS FOR PRACTICE

It seems likely that at the point of joining the research many of the couples we saw were aware that the capacity of their relationship to function as a container, to function as a symbolic third for the pair, had been lost. Morgan (1999) has developed Britton's (1989) concept of the 'third position' in relation to the couple relationship. She describes this as the capacity of the individuals in a relationship to take a position from which, as well as being participants *in* their relationship, they can also stand *outside* their relationship and *think* about their relationship. It then becomes possible for there to be a 'creative intercourse'. Morgan says that one of the central reasons couples come for psychotherapy is that they feel they need help from a 'third' person. This notion of a 'third' is a crucial element of the couple state of mind which is unconsciously sought in the figure of the therapist. The therapy acts as a container which the partnership is unable to provide. We believe that, through participating in the research, some couples were seeking a relationship in which they could be contained and helped to regain their capacity to think and to process their psychic pain.

Our experience was that couples often found it very difficult and painful to talk about their loss, but the encouragement to do so gave them an opportunity to process their grief in a way they otherwise might not. They began to be able to think about what had happened and to acknowledge their different experiences.

But what of those who help couples to recover the container of their partnership? The experience of listening and attending to the couples' stories was distressing and at times overwhelming for us. As Garland (1998) has described, real listening involves making an imaginative identification with the experiences of the speaker. It is of the essence of a containing environment that the listener is not overwhelmed by what s/he is told, and retains a capacity to process and think about experience. The participant-observer stance involves a difficult balance. We were fortunate in having each other in creating a research and therapy container for the couples we saw. At times, one of us in the research partnership was able to think, whilst the other felt overwhelmed. Upon reflection, this was found to be helpful. By 'dividing the load' between us, the fact that one of us could function and think freed the other to become involved and thus gain some sense of the couple's overwhelmed feelings.

As working with couples in distress can be very upsetting, even overwhelming, it is vital for researchers and practitioners in this field to be well 'held' themselves, either through supervision or by colleagues. We built a consultative relationship into the structure of the project to help us think about the experiences we, and the couples we saw, were having.

The research brief enabled us to have access to certain couples (and enabled certain couples to have access to us) whom we might otherwise not have seen. Yet that brief also constrained us from probing or questioning too much. It was then very important that both we and the couples knew that the research was underpinned with the safety net of therapeutic help for those who might need it. We, as researchers, had to take responsibility for disturbances that the project might create for the couple, and we did this by ensuring that the container of therapy was available for them.

To return to Bowlby's metaphor of the right environment for bones to mend, couples who feel contained internally, and by their relationship, facilitate the mending of each other's 'fractured bones'. For those who lack this capacity, whether it is described as containment or secure-base function, outside help may be needed. Those who provide this help need to address the kind of 'container' or 'secure base' they will need to undertake their work in a responsible manner. The next section of this book goes on to consider some contextual matters that have a bearing on good professional practice.

Part III

A secure base for practice

Chapter 10

Training partnerships: safe haven or secure base?

Felicia Olney

A BASE TO EXPLORE FROM

The world of work has undergone significant changes in recent years within the context of an increasingly turbulent environment. This chapter attempts to consider some of the issues that arise as a consequence of these changes, particularly in the area of providing training and consultation in the field of couple work. My particular perspective comes from working at the interface of the Tavistock Marital Studies Institute (TMSI) and those who use its training services, attempting to attune our organisational responses to a changing professional world. I shall argue that training partnerships can be established to create a safe haven to retreat to as well as a secure base from which to develop practice, and illustrate tensions in maintaining a balance between self-protection and service development in setting them up. The examples I give are based on work undertaken by the TMSI over the last decade.

The TMSI is an organisation that works primarily with couple relationships. Yet it has a history of applying this experience to understanding relationship dynamics that occur in other settings, including the working contexts of practitioners. This thinking has developed and applied seminal concepts such as the *reflection process* (Mattinson, 1975/92); the *deadly equal triangle* (Mattinson, 1981), *institutional defences against task-related anxiety* (Woodhouse and Pengelly, 1991) and the *thinking space of supervision* (Hughes and Pengelly, 1997). They testify to a distinct tradition and methodology that might be described as learning from experience.

AN INSECURE ENVIRONMENT

No consideration of trends in training can take place without reference to the turbulence of the soci-economic environment. The world of work is not what it was. Long gone are the days when employees signed up to a munificent 'good breast' that looked after them, and sent them off forty years later into the sunset of their lives with a golden handshake, a works clock and a large pension. Gone, too, are the days when they could be sure that the welfare state would take over their care in hospitals and old peoples' homes when they could no longer take care of themselves. Enter, instead, a world in which, as a consequence of the introduction of market forces into health and welfare, employers wrestle with cash limits and offer short-term contracts. The work base is less secure than before.

Employees respond to the prospect of serial job monogamy with under-standably mixed feelings. Hedging their bets they may, at best, become polygamous, at worst opt for numerous casual affairs in building up their alternative portfolios. This is likely to be at a cost to all parties since, as anyone who has indulged in affairs will know, the behaviour is both physically and emotionally tiring – especially when the parties are in the wrong place at the wrong time. The organisation finds that loyalty and commitment are in short supply. It pays the price as its increasingly disaffected workforce is committed in other directions and becomes less flexible. The tension and disaffection between managers and the managed can increase.

One response to these pressures involves individuals training to become a counsellor or psychotherapist. This is an enterprise that involves not just those who are in the 'caring' professions – including people from health and education – but many others who feel disaffected by organisational life and who see counselling or therapy as a route to salvation. As the public sector shrinks, the private sector expands, thereby hugely increasing the supply of private practitioners of one sort or another who compete with each other, train each other and compete with the people they have trained. With the growth in private practice have come issues of registration and regulation, as professional associations have replaced employers in providing a collective base for practice. These, in turn, have led to the emergence of extreme and painful differences about standards, and of preferences between registering bodies. In an expanding market of providers, demand diminishes as indi-viduals work harder to earn a living. Quality of life is measured less by relationships and mental health, and more by the ability to keep a job and pay the mortgage. Alongside the increasing supply of, and decreasing demand for, services, therapy is attacked from within as well as from without, adding to the energy taken up defining internal differences within the profession as well as defending it externally.

Yet the public sector remains the bedrock of mental health provision, and provides services through multi-disciplinary teams and in-patient treatment that the private sector, by and large, lacks the resources to do. Furthermore, it offers services to clients who do not have the means to pay for private treatment.

In this increasingly turbulent and competitive environment the client is in danger of getting lost. The invitation is to make claims for this or that way of working, which can be more about the needs of the practitioners than of the service users upon whom they depend. In this climate it is easy for thought-fulness about treatments of choice to be replaced by fervently promoting one's own way of working: a 'have hammer, want nail' approach to mental health. The risk must be that in a decreasingly secure work environment practitioners become preoccupied with issues of their own professional sur-vival and are then unable to offer their clients a sufficiently secure base to which they can become appropriately attached and from which they can develop.

The TMSI has been affected by these changes in a number of ways. Most significantly, the growth in approaches from individuals wanting a market-able training has been accompanied by a decrease in demand from some of the agencies that traditionally sought our training services for the tasks their workers were required to perform in their agency roles. The greatest of these shifts has been the loss of work from the probation service – traditionally but no longer involved in marital work, as the 'delinquency' of divorce ceased to be a cultural paradigm. Similarly, social service departments are increasingly being forced to replace 'preventative' work with families – including work with couples – with child protection work. Specialist centres have been closed, or deal with specific problems or symptoms rather than working with couples. Social work, once a core profession, is gradually seeing its casework services transferring to counselling. Counsellors have generally trained for working with individuals, but often have little or no training in couple interaction or the wider family context. They are cheaper to employ and less professional-ised, but face a difficult task with little support from their own and other professions.

This, then, is the context in which the TMSI finds itself, and in which it has constantly to review its position. The capacity to go on thinking about net-works and primary tasks has depended significantly on the fact that the state has provided a funding base. Nevertheless, the security of that base can never be taken for granted, and worrying about this involves expending resources that might otherwise be diverted to other channels of work. Key questions, such as the balance between core and project funding, contain implicit mes-sages that have an attachment dimension: core funding offering a platform for development while carrying the risk of over-dependence; project funding encouraging enterprise while carrying the risk of insecurity.

In thinking about training partnerships I shall consider two main constitu-encies and the relationship between them. As in marriage, the constituencies are individuals and institutions.

TRAINING AND THE INDIVIDUAL

As already indicated, the TMSI is increasingly being approached by *indi-vidual* practitioners with enquiries about and requests for training. This is

often to help them launch alternative careers. Consulting to them is one
response to these enquiries. A major issue to be explored in these consultations is the perception of the TMSI in relation to the kind of training they are
seeking. Is it to be a secure base that can facilitate appropriate development,
or are they seeking shelter from the storm? There are a number of issues to be
explored here.

As a predominantly post-qualifying organisation TMSI ordinarily offers
training in couple work to practitioners who have either a grounding in a core
profession or considerable experience in the couple work field. Whereas individuals approached us in the past with a view to practising within their
employing organisation, and with that organisation's backing, now the
organisation they have in mind is usually themselves. This raises a number of
issues for training bodies. In order to survive and be competitive they must
provide what people want. The TMSI, for example, is increasingly under
pressure to provide academically accredited and registerable training, with
transferable modules that will enable our customers to build up portfolios of
learning.

You will note that I used the word 'customer' with apparent ease. Yet I
remember that I first fully understood the cultural shift that had taken place
when I was addressed as a 'customer' while waiting for a train on Victoria
Station in London, sometime in the mid-Thatcher years. My internal insistence that I was still a 'passenger', and the tannoy's insistence that I was a
'customer', brought home to me that fundamental changes were taking place.
It was a confirmation of a move to a post-dependency culture in which the
customer has a different relationship with the state and other providers – one
that, at least in principle, implied more choice.

The pressure to be customer-led is one of the issues to be thought about
when people come for a consultation about their future careers. But there are
others. The Institute is often invited by practitioners to help them develop
their clinical practice in an agency, an invitation that can come without any
reference to the employing organisation. They may refer to this as a request
for 'supervision'. It is often difficult to convince them that this is also an issue
for their managers or agency supervisors, and that what we can appropriately
offer is *consultation* to this work. This might complement their in-house
supervision rather than being a quite separate enterprise.

I sometimes wonder whether the boundary encapsulating practitioner and
client is used as a defence against organisational involvement by those who,
perhaps understandably, have had enough of it. It can sometimes feel as if the
TMSI is being invited to have a secret affair with the consultee, one that the
organisation is not supposed to know about. It is as if they are trying to
replace one attachment figure (often failing in its developmental duties) with
another (TMSI) without acknowledging what they are doing, and that our
task might be to support their organisation rather than to replace it. The
need to offer external support to the organisation as well as the individual is

analogous to Bowlby's recognition of the need for services to support rather than supplant caregivers in their role as primary attachment figures (Bowlby, 1988).

The trend to 'disown' the organisation reaches far beyond training for couple work. The TMSI does extensive work with first line managers in social services departments as part of its staff supervision training programme. I am frequently struck by how often managers in field, residential and day settings will say that their staff refuse to be supervised by them, preferring instead to be 'supervised' by someone from outside the agency, often an individual or group psychotherapist. It seems not to occur to them and, indeed, to these external supervisors (who might more accurately be called consultants), that they are accountable to their organisation for service delivery, nor that the manager or supervisor has a right to sanction and work with this external input. It is not a question of whether consultants or supervisors are better, it is simply that they offer different things and need to work in partnership with each other.

As an external training or consulting resource it is important for the TMSI staff to be able to spend time thinking these issues through with prospective consultees. If the dynamic behind this behaviour is not understood, the worker will simply go on to find another practitioner – perhaps in private practice – who will offer the consultation instead. My concern is that unless this work is integrated with the organisational base, service delivery will suffer. If, for example, practitioners go off to discuss time-limited counselling in a particular agency with a consultant who does not understand the constraints of that setting and has no relationship with it, the work is likely to get into difficulties. It is striking how often practitioners – who will refer to containment in their clinical work, and who will assiduously talk about splitting or projective identification in that context – seem not to make the connection between themselves and their organisation in relation to their work. It is as if unconscious processes are thought to stop obediently at the consulting room door. One does not, I think, have to attend a group-relations conference to know otherwise.

Similar issues arise when approaches are made by individuals who want supervision on their private work but have no 'setting' from which to work, no training on which to base it, no code of ethics within which to practice – in fact, very little that would constitute a secure base for their practice. They appear to want the respectability of having had a connection with the Institute, perhaps to appear on a curriculum vitae at some future date, but without the experience of thinking things through. Such 'apparent' rather than 'real' connections provide a false base for professional practice.

It is important to add that I have also come across examples of very good practice where these issues have been thought through thoroughly, where the enterprises have been recognised as complementary, and where supervisors and consultants work together in the interests of good practice. Examples of these include senior representatives of the marital agencies who come to discuss their work with us knowing that the context and organisational dimensions of their practice are vital. Similarly, there is some very thoughtful practice in social services departments and voluntary agencies, from whom the psychotherapy profession could, I believe, learn a lot.

When I consider the future, I wonder whether some of the changes I have mentioned represent a transitional stage. Will individuals with specialised trainings start to think of themselves more broadly as mental health practitioners, needing a range of interventions, and, at least, being knowledgeable about appropriate referral sources? The need for psychotherapy trainings to equip graduates to consider these issues, and to help them to develop their assessment and consultative skills, represents a major challenge to training bodies. I think one of the major losses in recent years (as well as being a gain) has been the practitioner's exclusive emphasis on what goes on in the consulting room at the expense of the context in which s/he operates. Attachment, as a theory of social relatedness, has much to offer in this regard.

This brings me to the third party in the triangle: the employing organisation. Bound by cash limits and demands for head-counts, the employing body often creates situations in which reflective work can be difficult. When processes and dynamics are not understood and worked with, employees are more likely to take flight into the private sector to do the work they enjoy. In the end practitioners will have to create some form of secure base from which to practice if they do not already have one. It becomes increasingly obvious to those who have fled the constraints of organisational life in order to work in private practice that they need to be qualified, registered and supervised, and that this involves re-encountering, in their professional bodies, many of the painful and difficult issues that they had hoped to leave behind. If these matters are not faced and worked through, the alternative organisations will be impeded in providing the necessary secure base from which practice can develop. They will become yet another source of threat from which refuge is sought.

TRAINING AND THE ORGANISATION

In this section I want to think about some of the issues involved in working with organisations by providing a direct service to them, working jointly with them or consulting to them on internal matters. I shall illustrate these issues with examples from recent practice.

A major area of the Institute's organisational work in the last decade has been to provide staff supervision courses to social services departments and voluntary agencies. I see this development as coming from a realisation on the part of organisations and their staff that there is a need to make space to reflect on the dynamics of their work, and on the effects of engaging with children and families whose disturbed behaviour impacts on practice and supervisory processes. The Institute's staff supervision courses aim to help workers think about the needs of the agency, the practitioner and the client, and the tensions inherent in managing to keep these three elements connected.

It is significant that many first line managers have been promoted into management roles without necessarily having had a solid clinical grounding, a situation that they are able to share only when their relationship with the training institution is sufficiently well-established to allow for some basic needs to be explored. Hitherto, these managers may have been invited to emphasise their strengths, and not their weaknesses, a worrying trend born of a competitive environment that can only make for unsafe practice if they feel they are being asked to pretend they can run before they can walk. If the need to depend on others in delivering services is seen as incompetence, rather than as an expression of what is needed to resource the work, the agency environment can come to feel brittle and insecure. In the following examples I will illustrate the developmental potential that can follow from building up securely based training partnerships.

Engaging with the request

The first example, consulting to an organisation, looks at some of the issues involved in responding to an approach from an agency to provide training in staff supervision (Wheeler and Olney, 1999). The request came from first line managers in the children and families division of a London social services department via their training officer. Despite an interest in doing the work, we knew from experience that, without the necessary groundwork, any course on supervision would have limited value. We also knew that supervision, so central to the life of a social services department, needed to be linked with the management structure of the organisation and supported by it, and, as already emphasised, that any programme in this area had to complement existing supervision structures and practices, and not compete with them.

As external trainers we were supported in this by our partnership with the training officer involved. With him we embarked on a consultation process, not only with the first line managers themselves but also with their own managers. This involved a number of preliminary meetings with the appropriate principal officers and assistant director, inviting them to think with us about what they needed and what we might appropriately provide. The importance of this preparatory work in providing a secure base from which to proceed cannot be overstated. The risk, in an increasingly freelance world, is that the time and inclination for this is limited, and the temptation is to do 'hit and run' training that provides what is asked for, promises good results in as short and cheap a timeframe as possible, but may not be in the long-term interests of the organisation.

Work with this department took place over an eight-year period and was extended from the initial intake of field team leaders to include day care and residential managers, specialist workers in fostering and adoption, and new members of staff. This mixed membership eventually offered participants the opportunity to address and dispel many phantasies about their work through the gradual process of sharing their difficulties. Throughout the programme we consistently met with management to try to ensure that it remained complementary to their in-house supervision and to consult with them about appropriate future directions.

Central to the supervision programme was a regular group meeting (up to twelve in a group) at which members were invited to share their supervisory concerns with colleagues, as well as receive relevant theoretical input from ourselves. A hallmark of the work was ensuring that the training (structure, content and process) related to the issues that supervisors and managers had to work with in their day-to-day practice. The use of the trainers' authority was central to this. It was essential to avoid the programme becoming an oasis where thinking was split off from constraints and limitations, so constituting an unreal world.

Attendance at the programme had voluntary and compulsory aspects, offering all concerned the opportunity for learning about different models of authority. In practice this was not easy. When one has been working with a group of people over a number of months, trying to help them make sense of painful supervisory material, it can seem somewhat pedantic for trainers to sit in an empty room five minutes after the start of a session, reflecting on the meaning of lateness or absence and how to respond to it. Social workers are notoriously late, and to wonder about the meaning of this with them may seem trifling. Similarly, to keep chairs empty for absent members who may have been called to court, required to attend an adoption panel, taken annual leave, or gone off sick is to fly in the face of a culture in which people have become accustomed to being forgotten about, in which there is a certain relief at being unchallenged and a collusion that encourages colleagues to be unaccountable in the face of demands made on them by disturbed clients and pressured managers.

In short, faced with these pressures, wondering about empty chairs and time boundaries might seem irrelevant. However, it was our experience that, over time, participants realised that being held in mind and thought about, when they were absent as well as when they were present, had value. Our attempts to understand what meaning their behaviour might have towards us as trainers, and for them as a working group, led very gradually to creating an environment in which real anxieties could be shared and understood. Risks could then be taken, both in thinking about their work and in their relations with each other and us, that could be survived and learnt from. Members frequently commented that knowing the group was there for them to return to with their difficulties enabled them to cope in situations that would otherwise have felt unmanageable. Such learning can only come from actual experience and the parallels with supervision speak for themselves. Creating the framework in which it becomes possible to learn from experience is, in effect, the process of establishing a secure base for practice.

Training the trainers

The second illustration involved collaboration between agencies and concerned an attempt to train the trainers in the area of staff supervision. It involved a partnership between the TMSI and the Central Council for Education and Training in Social Work (CCETSW). The resources of the CCETSW – funding, identification of needs, introductions to appropriate contacts and co-work on the programme – were combined with the TMSI's input of staff resources and development time to design and deliver a regional training programme. This involved seven local authorities and was to result in over 300 first line managers receiving training in providing staff supervision. By entering into this partnership with the CCETSW, the TMSI obtained not only financial backing for the considerable development work involved, but also access to local authority training and staff development officers who were attracted to the venture through the involvement of the CCETSW.

An important area of partnership in this venture grew from our insistence that participants in the programme would be limited to those local authorities that were prepared to involve training officers *and* their relevant managers in the programme. This proved crucial. Over the eighteen-month period of the programme, those local authorities that managed to keep the trainer–management team on board, both during the development work and as partners in delivering the training, were the ones that had long-term success in maintaining in-house supervision programmes. This was so even when some of them were simultaneously coping with internal reorganisation. In contrast, two local authorities where the managers dropped out failed to deliver their in-house training.

This theme of the need for a partnership between trainers and managers will be very familiar to training and staff development officers. All too often they find themselves being asked to deal with some major organisational issue such as 'supervision' or 'managing change' by putting on a training event without linking it into formal management policies. This tendency to split off important aspects of organisational life, and deal with them as separate parts of the system, is analogous to a common situation in couple work where one partner is presented as the problem without the other acknowledging any part in it. It is often very seductive to the training department, or in our case to the external training agency, to leap in and provide what is being asked for, rather than adopt a more considered approach.

The hallmark of this piece of work was the emphasis on consultation. I would refer to it as consultative training. Although a component of the pro-gramme involved participants attending a four-day supervision course run by the TMSI, by far the most important work involved a series of meetings during which staff invited the working partnerships of trainer and manager to think about their organisation's supervisory needs, policies and issues for training. Within this framework they were invited, with our help and with input from other colleagues on the programme, to design their own version of the course they had attended, adapted to meet their own particular circum-stances. In attachment terms, they used the TMSI consultants as a secure base from which to explore their own work and to implement a development programme.

Consulting to marital agencies

An important area of the TMSI's organisational consultancy work involves collaborating with our colleagues in the marital field. For the past fifty years, the major providers of services to couples in the UK have been the marital agencies, which, between them, offer a nation-wide counselling service. While the couple psychotherapy training of the TMSI has been taken up by a num-ber of marital counsellors wanting to work in depth, this is not an appropriate route for the majority. Instead, the TMSI offers itself as a consultative resource to senior managers and trainers. The marital agencies have been dealing with their own particular concerns in a turbulent environment, one of which is the increasing professionalisation of work that has its roots in volun-tary provision. TMSI, with its roots in the core professions, has a role to play in relation to other marital agencies providing consultation that enables them to develop their own secure base for the profession of couple counselling.

The marital agencies occupy an interesting position in the helping profes-sions, and the matters they bring for consultation reflect this. Despite becom-ing more professionalised, some of them still rely predominantly on the input of volunteers, many of whom are women. Like the rest of us, they are having to survive in an environment where demands for accountability are increasing and expectations of training are rising. There are increasing tensions between demands for quality and quantity. The issues that preoccupy their managers and trainers include how to integrate clinical work with management; how to manage authority and accountability when time is given voluntarily; and how to contain difference in organisational cultures that are often not given to expressing conflict. In restructuring their organisations, managers have to engage with the feelings and conflicts surrounding loss in harnessing the potential for growth and change.

They also must work with role conflicts that are endemic to the marital agencies. For example, some of their members occupy different roles at the same time, for example, counsellor, tutor, supervisor, and even member of the organisation's management committee. This presents the organisation and its managers with particular challenges to accommodate flexibility while maintaining role boundaries. Working with these boundaries, and the tasks that they are there to expedite, provides an immediacy and relevance to the learning experience.

Linking practice and academia

For the most part in this chapter I have addressed the partnerships established with individuals and organisations to whom we have consulted as part of our training programme. I want to end with some thoughts about the most recent partnership we have entered into: that with a university for the purpose of providing academic accreditation for our courses at Masters and Doctorate levels.

This is a partnership into which we have not exactly rushed. Rather, we have stood back, somewhat bashfully, as some of our peers have taken the plunge, telling us, rather like the recently married, that it's hard work, and requires considerable compromise, but that they cannot imagine life without it. While cautiously impressed by these accolades we have also been worried about being 'left on the shelf', since clinical trainings are increasingly being offered in university contexts. So we have finally taken the plunge ourselves and found a suitable partner to go with. We still have some reservations about the 'fit' in the relationship between a clinical training and an academic degree, and worry about whether we can maintain a creative tension between different programmes. We are already experiencing the conflict between accountability to students and accountability to clients – for example, needing to attend planning meetings and maintain clinical commitments to clients, and managing the tension between the excitement of being challenged by academic rigour and the comfort of familiar practices. The prospect of adopting different learning processes, assessment techniques, accountability structures and timeframes is both daunting and stimulating. As with the beginning of any partnership, our dilemma is how to confront our differences without being defensive; how to involve ourselves without losing ourselves.

Whilst somewhere in unconscious phantasy there might be a hope that all partnerships have a happy ending, we have been in the relationship business too long to be more than cautiously optimistic. We do know that many of our constituents have advised us to take this route, and that we are joining an institution with a well-established track record: a dowry as good as our own. We both look forward to and fear the challenge of this new partnership and the growth potential inherent in it. We are determined that whatever the gains may be (and we hope they will be considerable) we will not compromise our own integrity or identity. These are core anxieties for all new partnerships

SAFE HAVEN OR SECURE BASE?

In this chapter I have tried to consider some contemporary issues for training organisations, illustrated by examples from recent practice in the TMSI. I have argued that amidst the forces and turbulence of contemporary professional life, training partnerships can form both a safe haven in which to take refuge and a secure base from which to develop practice. Whilst this has involved discussion of well-established agencies and professions, I have also referred to the emergence of relatively new ones – notably psychotherapy and counselling – which have emerged alongside, and sometimes in place of, the core professions.

The examples drawn upon suggest that for a partnership base to be secure it is essential that the parties involved have a relatively clear sense of their own identity and a capacity to know what they can and cannot do. They also need to know when they need help from others, especially when the work involves managing considerable anxiety. The need for a professional identity, for appropriately permeable boundaries and for mechanisms to understand professional defences against anxiety has been well demonstrated by Woodhouse and Pengelly. Their research has shown the temptation to fall back on narrowly defined primary tasks in the face of anxiety, and for boundaries to become 'defensive bulwarks, instead of the definition of secure base for commerce and regulation' (1991: 229).

In all the examples I have drawn on, the importance of knowing one's professional identity, neither making false claims nor denying competence, has been a central theme. The challenge, so similar to that faced by couples, is, in the end, to manage difference constructively. What all the examples demonstrate is the need for appropriate partnerships to help professionals recognise and enhance the different attributes that each individual, organisation or part of an organisation, brings to a common task. Training partnerships then provide a secure base from which the complex process of relating can be learned about.

Chapter 11

Security and creativity at work

Anton Obholzer

On first impression the relevance of the secure base concept for practice, and thus for the practitioner, seems to be an absolute given for any work, whatever the practice and wherever the base. But the more you think about it, the more complex and contentious an issue it becomes. In this chapter I will consider the nature of the relationship between individuals and the institutions in which they work, and reflect on how different understandings of security might work for and against the creativity of both.

As I understand it, having a secure base for the practitioner is the institutional equivalent of having a secure base for a child. In other words, an attachment theory concept is being lifted from the field of child development and applied to organisation and management. While I can see the attraction of this form of application, the basic argument seems to me to be flawed. While it is appropriate, healthy and, in fact, essential to development for the child to be in a suitably dependent state of mind relative to its attachment figures, an equivalent dependence in practitioners seems to me to be a somewhat dubious proposition, more reminiscent of member–institution relationships in the 1970s and '80s than what is required for the twenty-first century.

The concept of a secure base, as we have seen in Part I, relates to the work of John Bowlby and attachment theory (Bowlby, 1969, 1973, 1980). Misinterpreted, it could be said to mean that provision for all needs must be on tap so that the work in hand (in his context, child development) can proceed. But this is to misunderstand the concept, for it is clear that Bowlby was referring to an equation being constantly negotiated between the presence and absence of a secure base, with all the strength and stimuli for growth that comes from riding the roller-coaster connecting these two poles.

It would be more in keeping with Bowlby's intention to speak of a *good-enough secure base*, perhaps calling it a *secure-enough base*, and in the process make the link with Winnicott's idea of the *good-enough mother* (Winnicott, 1971). I believe that this change is not, as might seem at first glance, a minor pedantic semantic, but one that goes to the heart of the issue. So I propose to look at the qualities and characteristics of a secure-enough base and then to contrast that with the problems of having a too-secure, or too-insecure, base.

I also want to keep both parties to the relationship in mind, since practitioners have responsibilities for and obligations towards their employing institution, as well as the employing institution having responsibilities for and obligations towards employees. Just as in the political debate, where it is emphasised that duties accompany rights, so, too, is this a key issue for the healthy functioning of institutions. The question is: what can the practitioner reasonably expect from the institution, and what can the institution reasonably expect from the practitioner? My use of the word 'reasonably' is to make the point that I am referring to what is described, in object relations theory terms, as 'depressive position' functioning, as contrasted with 'paranoid/schizoid' functioning (Klein, 1946). The latter sometimes gives rise to unreasonable assumptions that can lead to enormous problems of institutional functioning.

A SECURE-ENOUGH BASE FOR WORK

As a basic minimum, a secure-enough base entails the opportunity for a continuity of creative work within a psychically envisageable timeframe. This does not mean a job for life with the sort of professional freedom that brooks no accountability. But it also does not mean being on a treadmill of statistics and audit that feeds persecutory fantasies. What, instead, is required is some connection between an individual's sense of self-worth and productive creativity and the context and primary task of his or her institution. This relies upon there being mechanisms for airing views, as honest as can be managed feedback and interchange between individual and institution. Likewise, productivity should be measurable, not as the sole criterion of worth but as a powerful antidote to the process of self or group idealisation that is not uncommon in institutions. For evaluation to be possible requires that agreed systems are included in the annual cycle of the institution. There needs also to be a connection between review/evaluation procedures and the process of being a member, or continuing to be a member, of the institution.

Some might object that this is really the wolf-like visage of orthodox management dressed up in sheep's clothing. I would disagree. My observation, both as Chief Executive of the Tavistock & Portman National Health Service Trust and as an organisational consultant working in the public and private sectors, has shown me that each member of the work enterprise has a life and a professional trajectory of their own, and that without the process of review and re-evaluation there is a risk of both parties ending up in the institutional equivalent of the Sargasso Sea (where sailing ships and their sailors were becalmed for weeks if not months on end, with no breeze or current to move them, stuck in a sea of flotsam, jetsam and seaweed). Individuals caught in such a state are not necessarily burnt out but they are thoroughly stuck. They may then unconsciously perform a function for other members of the institution, doing harm to themselves, their work institution and their personal life in the process. How often individuals change careers only when forced to do so by illness or retirement, having created an impossible situation at work by operating in what Bion (1961) called 'fight–flight basic assumption' mode.

The ongoing question posed for both individual and institution can be expressed as: 'Is this the right place for me and what is the evidence?' It is a question that could, and should, be incorporated into any review of institutional connection. In the helping professions, it is not uncommon for individuals to be connected to several institutions as part of their working week. With time and personal development the worth, vitality and creative interest of these links might vary, leading to a change of cathexis. If this process is countered by the innate conservatism and resistance to change of the individual and institution connections may become emotionally withered, to the detriment of both parties. So, a sense of connection to one's workplace that has, as an integral part of it, a questioning approach that allows either a severance or a positive re-affirmation of the link, is essential for the well-being of all concerned.

A secure-enough base does not only entail time and a contract to go with it. It also entails thought being given to the concept of place. If organisations behaved rationally, the least securely attached members would be given the most secure places in the building. If newness, or being a learner, creates the greatest anxiety and uncertainty, one might expect that for this to be contained (in Bion's sense) implies that newcomers and students should be given the most secure physical environment. I've yet to see an institution where this happens. What happens instead is that the more senior one becomes, the more encrusted in the building one is. Conversely, the more junior one is, the more likely one will end up with a pigeonhole in a dark closet.

The opposite of the right to a place is the practice now in play in cities and financial institutions called 'hot-desking' – presumably a derivative of the industrial revolution concept of 'hot-bedding'. An unexpected result of this process can now be seen in the institutions that have adopted this system: they are calling in institutional consultants to conduct team-building exercises. They wish to stop their staff from joining the institutions in which they do their work on behalf of the parent organisation and where they *are* given a place. Absence of physical space can be as potentially destructive as rigidly defined territory.

In addition to a sense of place, some thought is needed to ensure that the inter-professional, interpersonal and inter-group relations that are inevitable in an institution are sufficiently accommodated. The setting must be conducive to both individual and group work. There should be sufficient opportunities and requirements for a degree of institutional membership. What needs to be avoided is either a state of expectant dependency or a disillusioned version of what a previous head of the Tavistock Clinic, described to me as 'the boarding house' syndrome (Dr Robert Gosling, personal communication). This syndrome promotes a state in which individuals only look after themselves and beyond that make no contribution to communal activities and meeting collective needs. A member in this state of mind pursues only personal interests and activities, and shows no awareness of how their work impacts on that of others in the organisation, regardless of whether their contribution is collectively damaging or enhancing. The essential feature of the boarding house state of mind is that the individual component parts of an organisation do not contribute to a common whole.

SECURE OR DEPENDENT? A DILEMMA FOR TRAINING INSTITUTIONS

It is worth looking at some ideas inherent in the concepts of security and dependence in relation to how they affect institutional membership. The *Oxford English Dictionary* defines secure as 'free from care, apprehension, anxiety or alarm'. I have already commented on some advantages and disadvantages of such a state of mind. Dependent is defined as 'having existence contingent on, or conditioned by, that of something else . . . subordinate'. When looking at the concept of security, the problem can be for a degree of counterproductive comfort and self-satisfaction to enter the individual and institutional state of mind. The problem with dependency seems to me to be a related issue. It might result in processes whereby competence is located out of the individual and, usually by a process of projective identification, perceived to reside only in those higher up in the hierarchy.

For example, it is a common problem in postgraduate training organisations for competent, serious, adult, mature trainees to find themselves deskilled, and behaving as if they had no previous experience whatsoever. This is a great loss to the trainee, who is then at risk of losing the link between past experience and present training. If this happens, the risk extends beyond the training because it negates learning that might facilitate future applications of the training experience. At worst, training can unfit students for the work they have left and only fit them for joining their trainers. Such dependency dynamics are equally disadvantageous to the training organisation and its trainers because they mean that outside perspectives are not brought in as much as they otherwise might be, thus contributing to an 'Ivory Tower' institutional state of mind.

Unconsciously, dependency suits both trainee and trainer, for it means that neither has to integrate a new point of view, and hence adapt and learn from the process. For the trainee, there is no past experience, and so no need to make links that might threaten one's identity and position as a student through challenging the ideas, assumptions and prohibitions of the training institution. For the trainer, there is the pseudo-comfort of not being questioned or challenged, possibly accompanied by the poisonous chalice of idealisation; the offer of having an acolyte can be hard to resist. This collusion can lead to a vicious cycle of unquestioning mutual idealisation, having the by-product of generating the occasional 'difficult' student who develops an equally unproductive counter-dependency state of mind representing split-off and denied aspects of the student body as a whole.

The issue of dependency can be extremely difficult to handle in the context of psychotherapy training and practice. There is a fine line distinguishing between dependency and limited professional experience. There is another fine line dividing work dependence and the dependence students might experience at the beginning of their own therapy (which often happens at the same time as their starting to take on patients). Basic Assumption Dependency (Bion, 1961) is a defensive reaction against intolerable anxiety, and intolerable anxiety is particularly rife at the beginning of therapy. Bion described a Basic Assumption group state of mind as one in which individual thoughts and work-related functioning are submerged by primitive group mentality. In its dependency form, this process manifests itself as a state of non-functioning in which the individual becomes an entirely passive, dependent group particle. Once this state of mind is embedded in institutional functioning it is hard to dislodge. In the long term, it runs the risk of constituting the established way of incorporating new members into the work group and institution.

ANXIETY AND SECURITY

So far my discussion about a secure-enough base can be characterised as follows: two ingredients with both a conscious and unconscious element to them need to be titrated into a mix so that the ensuing blend has enough security to enable the work to be done, and enough insecurity to draw on and stimulate the resilience and vitality of the members of the organisation.

But there is another way of addressing the problem of creating a secure-enough base: through considering the impact of task-related anxiety. In exploring this dimension we are following in the footsteps of Jaques (1990) and Menzies-Lyth (1988), and looking at the innate anxiety inherent in the 'raw material' that an organisation is working with. This approach can be called a psychological health approach to secure practice based on an understanding of unconscious processes. Just as in public health there is an awareness that there are specific risks inherent in certain manufacturing processes (for example, silicosis in miners resulting from breathing coal dust), so, too, one might assume that there are equivalent processes at work in institutions offering to help others. Practitioners are susceptible to, and need to be aware of, the 'psychic dust' that, symbolically speaking, arises from their work. This dust creates anxiety, the presence of which generates the need for a secure base (perhaps even a maximum-secure and thus rigidly defended base).

I have written elsewhere about work-related anxiety (Obholzer and Roberts, 1994). The question here is: what psychic dust might be specific to work with adult couples? It seems to me that it is likely to be related not only to the projective and introjective processes that are essential psychic bonds servicing a marriage or partnership, but also to these bonds becoming unserviceable, and in the process of therapy being re-enacted in the therapeutic system. This, in turn, is likely to set off inner-world dynamics within therapists with a resultant risk to them if not contained. These dynamics have been described by Dicks (1967) and Clulow (1985), amongst others.

What responses might this anxiety engender in practitioners and their agencies? One might be to design a system that has as an integral part of the structure an awareness of the underlying noxious processes, builds in mechanisms to contain and to metabolise the anxieties associated with them and thereby hopes to reduce them to a level that requires only a moderate degree of security in its basic structure. It sounds good, but is it a realistic or sufficient basis for managing an institution?

An alternative approach might be to ensure that all structures (both concrete and symbolic) and tasks are clearly spelt out and directly linked to the primary task of the organisation. This should result in the most containing structure, and therefore create the most secure base. Maybe this would be the case. Maybe, again, it would create a bureaucratic nightmare. These are just two approaches detailing what the layers of an institutional organisational laminate might be. Even if all the positive features were integrated to create a securely-enough based institution, we would still only have a shell organisation, one that lacked spirit. So, is there a third way?

ON CREATIVITY

The test of whether a base is secure enough, to use the language of attachment theory, or functioning in the depressive position, to use an object relations theory term, is whether it encourages creativity for its members and for the institution as a whole. Without creativity in security there is no secure base in the terms that Bowlby implied.

Creativity is a state of mind in which there is a certain release from previous perceptions and solutions in tackling problems, and a capacity to note this emerging freedom, as well as to pursue it in spite of any rising anxiety in self and others about questioning orthodoxy. It is not routine, humdrum activity, nor is it a mindless going along with group and social thoughts and norms. It is associated with thinking independently, and with not being intimidated by received wisdoms. But it is different from being a recluse or a rebel, although, at times, creativity might involve adopting aspects of both.

So, as a concept, creativity has individual, group and societal components, and needs to be understood at all these levels in order for us to be able to provide the optimum conditions for its development.

What are the personal, intra-psychic processes that make for creativity, and can they in any way be fostered or furthered from an institutional perspective? Perhaps less ambitiously, but possibly no less importantly, might they be recognised as part of a recruitment process in pursuit of personnel policy? Are they more likely to be found in mature, intelligent or depressive position people than in those who do not meet such criteria? Are they associated with one age group, or stage of development, more than another?

While there are preconceptions about these matters, evidence pointing one way or another is very hard to come by. Attempts have been inconclusive. For example, the psychoanalyst Elliot Jaques (1990) gathered evidence about the phenomenon of artistic creativity. He studied artists of known stature in order to see whether he could find common factors that might elucidate the matter of their creativity. To the best of my understanding, he found none. While it is very hard to provide evidence about what constellation or configuration of object relationships makes for creativity, I think it is likely that reparation plays an important part.

One major risk to the creative process, and to the creative individual, is the temptation to elicit counter-creative processes in self and others in order to gain some relief from the anxiety of countering group norms and personal conformity. I have referred to the need to be able to stand up to group processes, something that is very difficult for, as Bowlby said in a personal communication, 'we are all, at heart, social beings'. The group of peers or seniors that mocks us when we deviate from group approved thinking, or dare to think thoughts that might be individual and possibly creative, can be as much in the mind as in reality. The difficulty is compounded when external groups, often composed of colleagues, behave in ways that concur with the group in one's mind. This is something that happens quite frequently: transference is not only about perceiving reactions and responses, it is also about making them happen, making them come true.

An example early on in my consultancy career helped me to understand the counter-creative aspect of conformity. I was consultant to a school for physically handicapped children that accepted them from the age of three. In the first few weeks of intake the children, in getting to know each other, would take an interest in those around them and in each other's deformities. They would talk about them. The staff, as part of their institutional defence (against the anxieties thrown up by disability and deformity), discouraged this. Soon, the children learnt not to speak about deformity. The physiotherapists reported that in the first few weeks after intake, the children were much more responsive to physiotherapy than later on. They, too, had been taught never to discuss or focus on the handicap, only to design exercises to address its physical manifestation. In doing so, the link between physical, psychological and social dimensions of disability, and the possibility of harnessing all three in the service of rehabilitation, was lost. Neither children nor staff could learn from their experience, or be creative about their work, as doing so would have meant going against what they had been taught by their respected teachers.

At a psychic level, personal creativity creates social dilemmas. A way out of these is to invite the destruction of one's own creativity by fostering institutional processes that resist change. As I have already indicated, one way is to present oneself as a rebel, or to collude with institutional pressures to turn one into a rebel, thus dealing with the threat of creativity both for oneself and for the institution. Another is to attack creativity in others.

Attacking creativity in others raises the matter of envy. Envy is not much written about in its institutional incarnation. It is, in essence, the attack on a quality or asset that another person has, or is perceived to have. An envious attack diminishes or demolishes creativity, both in the subject and in the person or quality attacked. The worst combination is one in which the envied person, for reasons mentioned above, presents themself as enviable, thus unlocking the envious attack. However, it is at this point that reparation can undo the damage of an envious attack and allow creativity to resurface.

On the periphery of envy there is a lesser and more constructive dynamic that acts to stimulate effectiveness and creativity. Betty Joseph, in a personal communication, made the point that a little envy can energise individuals to compete with, emulate and overtake the objects of their envy. But this can only result in a creative outcome if, in the inner world of the individual concerned, the envy is adequately contained.

Moving from an individual context to that of the institution, two factors often reduce the capacity for being creative. These are what I shall call difference and domesticity. Creativity can generate institutional strife because it causes differentation. When people think differently from each other, the experience can be threatening, unsettling a comfortable but uncreative uniformity of thought. Domesticity manifests itself in a substantial and distracting concern with detail, not only in terms of the fabric of the organisation and its services but also in terms of managerial and administrative processes. It has a very time- and mind-consuming quality about it, and can lead to a haemorrhaging of creativity and thought, ultimately resulting in institutional anaemia.

Countering these processes requires allowing managers to carry out appropriate managerial tasks and practitioners to carry out appropriate professional tasks. Given the often considerable strife between managers and practitioners over the efficient delivery of services, this is not always easy to achieve.

If creativity has as one of its qualities the capacity to resist group norms and activities, where does that leave the concept of the team – as a working concept and as a unit of institutional functioning? Principles gleaned from couple work are particularly relevant here. One of the balances to be achieved for individuals in a partnership is that they give up a degree of personal autonomy in return for the advantages of being part of a couple, a balance that continues to be negotiated as the arrangement develops. The same tension, perhaps with a greater element of dependency, is present in work with families and children. The process of institutional membership, and thus of institutional responsibility, is very similar: individual members have to give up a degree of personal autonomy in order to gain the benefits of institutional membership. Giving up a degree of personal autonomy is not the same thing as falling into a state of dependency. It is, in fact, the opposite. The greater the mature, autonomous independence in the individual who needs to confirm his or her membership of the institution by giving up a degree of autonomy, the more creative the link is likely to be for both the individual and the institution.

Yet the equation is not definitive. One of the great mysteries in the field of human relations is why some individuals who come from the most unfortunate circumstances do well by whatever parameters you choose to name, while others who supposedly have everything going for them fail. Until we have more knowledge about resilience in the field of individual development and human relationships there will be a gap in our understanding of what is needed at an institutional level to provide a good-enough secure base for creative professional practice.

Chapter 12

The sense of connection

Christopher Clulow

Within two months of John Bowlby's death in 1990 the World Association of Infant Psychiatry and Allied Disciplines designated its regional meeting in London as a special memorial event. The title of the conference was *The Effect of Relationships on Relationships*, and the proceedings were published in a special issue of the *Infant Mental Health Journal* the following year. The title is highly significant, and goes to the heart of the contribution attachment theory has made to our understanding of the human condition. It emphasises the conception of individuals as social beings, and of the mind as inter-personal. Self-understanding and the understanding of others are inter-connected in a theory of development that has vital ramifications for our understanding of individuals, couples and society as a whole.

This book has charted some different ways of exploring the process of relating in the adult couple. In Part I we presented some approaches adopted by researchers to examining the quality of couple relationships. The defining feature of attachment security was taken to be the capacity of partners to act, and to use each other, as a secure base in their partnership. An ability to move flexibly between the positions of depending and being depended upon corresponded with 'complex' or 'secure' attachment. In contrast, insecure patterns of attachment were associated with a rigidity and inflexibility in taking up the roles of care-seeker and care-provider, and a detachment or intrusiveness in the style of relating that impeded the process of connecting partners with their own and each other's experience. Some constellations of insecure attachment were shown to constitute a risk factor for abusive behaviour.

While the context of these studies is the couple, it is the attachment security of individuals that is being assessed. There is a conceptual leap to be made in moving from assessing the security of individuals and how this acts on partnerships, to assessing the security of partnerships and how this acts on individuals. The leap involves regarding the resources of a partnership as greater than those of the two individuals who go to make it up, and making the assumption that it is, in itself, capable of supporting partners in carrying out their secure-base function for each other. It involves conceiving of something beyond the individual partners, something that we might describe as a couple membrane – a 'skin' around the couple that constitutes the sense of 'we' in managing the vicissitudes of what happens between 'me' and 'you'. This membrane may be more or less plastic. The security of the partnership might be assessed on the basis of how adaptive the membrane is to the changing balance between 'we-ness' and 'I-ness' required by the predictable and unpredictable changes that occur in the lifetimes of the partners who make it up. How the membrane is identified and measured is a task for the future. While the Couple Attachment Joint Interview, described in Chapter 1, represents a start on this road, there is a long way to go before we have a reliable measure of *couple* functioning, as compared with the functioning of individuals within the couple relationship.

Nevertheless, researchers have provided us with the means of capturing individual attachment patterns in partnerships. Through observing behaviour, triggering representations and inviting self-classifications it has been possible to group patterns and processes operating in the dyadic system and to think about their intergenerational effects. The research relationship, explicitly defined by a task that is designed to activate codeable patterns of response, both influences and provides access to processes of relating between partners. The field of investigation includes not only the relationship between the partners but also the research context within which that relationship is examined. The research method turns to its advantage the knowledge that relationships affect people's ways of relating by creating environmentally induced circumstances that activate patterns of attachment. What is then captured is a dynamic property, not a fixed attribute.

While researchers usually take the initiative in establishing a relationship with their subjects, the reverse is the case when couples seek help. In Part II we examined the therapeutic frame of the practitioner, and explored the rationale and potential for changing dysfunctional patterns of relating in the couple through psychotherapeutic practice and research. This, in common with the preventive work described in Chapter 4, is a very practical applica-tion of the knowledge that relationships have the power to influence patterns of relating. The approaches described here eschew the didactic teaching of communication skills in favour of inviting couples to review their assump-tions about themselves, their partners and others who are close to them. The different contributors share a belief that psychotherapy has the potential to act as a secure base for members of a partnership, providing them not only with emotional support but also with opportunities to explore their intra-psychic and interpersonal worlds.

The process of exploration and the possibility of discovery connect the therapeutic enterprise (whether preventive or remedial, a distinction that I, personally, find unhelpful) with that of research. Neither couples nor the clinicians they consult are likely to view themselves as researchers, yet there is a sense in which that is precisely what they are. Here, the tables can be turned, for as well as the therapeutic relationship having potential to influence patterns of relating in the couple, the couple relationship also has the potential to influence patterns of relating in the therapist. Unconscious communications can trigger actions that become the means by which something is made manifest and available to be understood. The value of the counter-transference as a therapeutic tool is well established in psychoanalytic psychotherapy. Its potential value as an instrument of research has begun to be appreciated only relatively recently.

Whether or not they consider themselves as researchers, those who offer couples help are also in need of a secure base if they are to practise effectively. Their capacity to develop an empathic understanding of the predicaments presented to them by the couples they see will depend on the training they receive, their understanding of themselves and the capacity of their agency to support them. Part III of this book has examined what constitutes a secure base for practice. It has highlighted the need for practitioners to manage a three-cornered relationship in their work, one which connects the needs of the couple with the personal/professional resources of the therapist and the setting in which she or he practises. This triangle constitutes the service delivery system, and provides a further illustration of how relationships can influence patterns of relating for good or ill.

Common to each part of the book is a link between security (as a couple, as a researcher, as a practitioner, as an organisation) and the capacity to think. For partners to operate securely as a couple they need to be able to stand outside themselves and reflect on their relationship, tolerating the discomfort that comes with acknowledging they are part of any problems occurring between them as well as part of their solution. Researchers similarly rely upon a reflexive stance that includes themselves as well as their subjects in their field of investigation. Practitioners try to cultivate a capacity to reflect upon their emotional experience, and to think about their own actions and behaviour in trying to attune themselves to the problems facing the couples they see. Supervisors, trainers and managers likewise face the challenge of processing their experiences in making sense of the many and complex communications to which they are asked to respond. When this becomes difficult, they may call consultants in.

One product of thinking is linking – as, indeed, one product of linking is thinking. An important contribution of psychoanalysis to the understanding of child and adult development has been to focus attention on processes of linking. Fairbairn (1952), Bion (1962a) and Kohut (1977) assert that identity develops from the perception and reflection of oneself in someone else's mind. Bion described the parent's processing of the infant's raw mental state into tolerable, thinkable experience: transforming 'beta-elements' into 'alpha-functions' through linking the infant's preconceptions with a quality of maternal care that allows the infant to form a conception. Attachment research has contributed concepts like 'metacognitive monitoring' (Main, 1991) and 'reflective function' (Fonagy et al., 1991b, 1995) to describe processes of linking and thinking, and devised methods for measuring how far they are present in the way people represent their experiences of attachment. From the outset, individuals are intersubjective beings in that they come to recognise themselves in the images that are reflected back to them by others, and by learning that others have thoughts and feelings that are separate from their own. In developing social understanding they have to make sense of their own experience, and to develop theories about the minds of others. All this is done in a relational context.

One link this book has attempted to encourage is that between the disciplines of research and clinical practice. These disciplines have often run on parallel lines in exploring similar phenomena, with little or no cross-over between them. For practitioners, the classical scientific research method, with its emphasis on objectivity and detachment implied by the gold standard of random controlled trials, has seemed ill-suited to capturing the complexity of human relationships. For researchers, there has been a suspicion that practitioners compress their understanding of relationships to fit the theories to which they are most wedded, and resist any attempts to test those theories in any systematic way.

Yet the picture is changing. Case study, action research and scientific method are evolving rapidly to take account of intersubjective realities, to include researchers as part of the field of study, to access unconscious processes and to focus on hypothesis-building and testing in clinical practice as well as in research investigation. This evolution is reflected in the work of the Tavistock Marital Studies Institute, which based its contribution to understanding the dynamics of intimacy on a rich and prolific stream of case studies (see Ruszczynski, 1993, for an overview), applied this understanding through action research (see, for example, Mattinson and Sinclair, 1979; Clulow, 1982; Clulow and Vincent, 1987; Mattinson, 1988; Colman, 1989; Woodhouse and Pengelly, 1991; Cudmore, 1996), and is now developing an empirical approach to studying partnerships and couple psychotherapy – a development that owes much to influences from the attachment research field. Evolution of this kind serves to close the gap between practitioners and researchers, while continuing to acknowledge the boundary between different kinds of practice and research. Both disciplines share common cause in wanting to do justice to the intricacies of human complexity, and there are now real possibilities for providing a scientific basis for clinical assertion. Practitioners and researchers need to continue building links with each other for their understanding and effectiveness to develop.

Another link the book has tried to encourage is one between the conceptual systems of attachment and object relations theories. Again, there has been an historical tendency to think of these systems as antithetical to each other, a tendency that splits the inner world of object relations from the outer world of social experience – as if each constituted a threat to, rather than an indissoluble part of, the other. Holmes charts Bowlby's own struggle to remain connected with both systems of thought while distinguishing his perspective from those of his psychoanalytic mentors. He comments on developments that have subsequently enabled a rapprochement, or annealing of the split, in the following terms:

> Out of the post-war schisms of psychoanalysis there emerged an unhealthy polarisation between the concern of psychoanalysis with the primary processes and the focus of attachment and cognitive therapy on secondary processes. The paradigm of narrative, a blending of sensation and perception, in which the inner world can be described objectively, while the subjective colouring of the outer world is also held up for inspection, is exciting increasing interest in psychotherapy.
>
> (Holmes, 1993: 148)

From a couple therapist's perspective, development arises from creative intercourse between two different partners who, together, give birth to something new. The analogy applies to the conception of ideas as it does to the conception of people. What is required is that there should be enough security to bring differences into some kind of relation to one another for new ideas to be conceived and gestated. Preconceptions are often aborted when they constitute a threat to an established order of being, or have little chance of development when they find themselves at odds with an environment in which they might otherwise grow up. Orphaned, or compelled to attach themselves to one or other of the parent ideas, they may lack the support and stimulus to come of age.

I want to conclude by identifying three areas of potential disconnection that may adversely affect the security of individuals and the community of which they are a part. The first concerns the actual procreative link between partners and parents. The second relates to the worlds of home and work. The third concerns the relationship between caring and producing. The net is cast widely to serve as a reminder of the relationship of interdependence between the quality of personal relatedness and the contextual frameworks within which it is defined. Each holds a mirror to the other.

A feature of the contemporary family landscape is the increasing disconnection of the issues concerning parenting and child development from those concerning marriage and committed partnerships (Clulow, 1996). From the outset of the parenting cycle informal surrogacy, medical technology and adoption enable people to become parents without being in a partnership. For parents who raise children in a conventional partnership the tension between being a parent and being a partner is not easy. 'Mothering' remains a synonym for 'parenting', revealing the still-prevalent assumption that bringing up children is women's work. Services that are developed to assist parents to give their children the best start in life seldom take account of the partnership between parents. Parenting is viewed as a relationship in which the public has a stake; partnerships are private. The potential effects of partnering processes on parenting is frequently overlooked, even though we know that good partnerships make for healthy child development (see Chapter 4).

It is apparent, even at this level, that security of attachment is connected with triangular rather than dyadic processes. Part of the difficulty for parents in holding parenting and partnering in some kind of creative tension is because third parties can represent an intrusion – either upon the partnership, or upon one parent's relationship with a child. Third parties challenge assumptions of exclusivity and proprietorship in relationships, they may threaten isolation and evoke powerful feelings of envy, jealousy and rage. The differences they introduce generate conflict. But if they can be managed, they offer the possibility of growth and development for adults and their children.

The stability of a partnership is, in itself, no guarantee of this. The couple relationship can support and undermine the best efforts of individual parents. It can check the impulses of children to 'divide and rule' in their dealings with others, or it can encourage patterns of relating that are deceptive, manipulative and exploitative. It can provide an environment in which parents and children are free to test themselves and develop new strengths, or it can confirm the worst that people fear about themselves, inhibiting further exploration. The point is that the relationship can influence processes of relating in both positive and negative ways. That is why one can never make the quasi-Orwellian claim, 'two parents good, one parent bad'. But that, or any other stance towards family structure, should not foreclose on thinking about how couple and parenting relationships interact with each other to fashion experience in both domains of family life.

Couple and parenting relationships are also affected by the wider contexts in which they operate. Here there can be the second of the potential disconnections to which I want to refer: that between the worlds of home and work. Different social values apply to each of these interconnected domains of life. Secure family organisations are perceived to be those that operate on collaborative lines, that are stable and whose members are committed over years if not a lifetime. Mutual commitment and trust are seen as providing a secure basis for the health and well-being of family members. This is in contrast to values that apply in the world of paid employment.

There is a profound contrast between how we think about nurturing secure attachments within families and how we think about creating prosperous economies (Sennett, 1999). At work, competition drives individualism, lack of commitment, constant change and instability. Those who have the power to do so try to protect themselves against insecurity by exporting that burden onto those less able to protect themselves. Organisations 'downsize' their commitments and subcontract work to others as and when it is available. The hierarchical management of uncertainty ensures those least equipped to bear the burden will end up carrying it (Marris, 1991). In consequence, one feature of contemporary economic landscapes in the Western world is the gap that has emerged between the 'haves' and the 'have nots'. Those in work seem to be working harder, while those out of work find it increasingly difficult to find a place. Such segregation can be understood as a product of insecurity resulting from the uncertainties of modern life and cannot but impact on the security of family life.

Marris (1996) observes that attachment theory is a theory of how people construct worlds that are sufficiently predictable for them to survive and prosper in. Economic circumstances, like child-rearing practices, affect the security of the models individuals develop to guide their social behaviour. In social terms, the poor are most likely to end up suffering, having fewest opportunities of which to take advantage and least resources to protect themselves against abuse. The reinforcement of insecurity and deprivation may then result in alternative societies which, like the return of the repressed, boomerang back to threaten those who believe themselves to be secure and in control. It is then the wealthy who can end up imprisoned in high security estates, an analogy that can be pursued at the level of international as well as national politics.

Ironically, the institution of marriage has been held responsible for some of the disconnections that have arisen between home and work over the past three centuries. As traditionally defined, this institution has come under fire for attending to the primary social tasks of 'producing' and 'caring' through the gendered division of labour (Clulow, 1993, 1995). Men worked, while women brought up children and cared for the old and infirm. Of course, things were never as neat as that, but nevertheless the general rule inscribed itself into the collective psyche. In an industrial age, this located men in the public sphere outside the home while women were confined to the private world of domesticity. Men were visible and powerful outside the home, but relatively invisible and powerless at home; women the reverse. In our post-industrial age, these boundaries are breaking down. The 'old' man of the manufacturing world is increasingly unemployable, while the 'new' woman employed in the service industries finds herself in growing demand. Modern technologies allow the employed to work from home, and there is social pressure on men to become more involved with their children as fathers.

Bowlby, himself, gave some thought to the implications of attachment theory for society. He was critical of what he described as the 'topsy turvy' values that placed economic activity at the pinnacle of social usefulness and discounted the vital contribution to well-being made by parents and other carers. He became a target for the feminist movement at a time when his theory was read to imply that a woman's place was in the home, at least for the first five years of a child's life, and that disorders of attachment were her fault. Yet he held to a central principle: that the security of the state reflected the security of the individuals within it, and their security depended on the quality of child-rearing. Formulated between the collective euphoria of a post-war period that saw the foundation of the welfare state and the ascendancy of individual values characteristic of the 1980s market economy philosophy, attachment theory provided a bridge between the personal and the public. It allowed, and continues to allow us to conceive of a society in which individuals matter, and to conceive of individuals for whom society matters.

This brings me to my third and final reflection upon the potential for social disconnection. There is, in Western societies, an ambivalence towards those who care for others and those who seek out care for themselves, one that is sometimes reflected in caricatures of the 'do-gooding' social worker and the 'scrounger' who 'plays the system'. These unfortunates are contrasted with the 'captains of industry', the 'movers and shakers' of free enterprise, who can be relied upon to meet ever-increasing targets of economic productivity. Politically and socially we have fostered parental images of a 'nanny state' that induces a 'dependency culture' which threatens the 'survival of the fittest' imperative coming from exponents of market economy philosophies. Insofar as we are dismissing or ambivalently attached to our representations of 'caring' and 'productive' institutions we betray our insecurity. Security implies recognising the interdependence of welfare and economic activity, the individual and society, the carer and the cared-for, generosity and commitment. It is closely allied with the capacity to manage the paradoxes facing couples in being both 'I' and 'We'. The socio-economics and politics of secure attachment are rooted in relationships of reciprocal commitment, at all levels, and as such, secure attachment constitutes a moral framework (Kraemer and Roberts, 1996).

In psychoanalytic terms, the capacity to attend both to one's own needs and to those of others is a product of having developed an internal capacity that Britton (1989) refers to as 'triangular space' and Fonagy (1999b) as 'mentalising'. At an individual level this capacity fosters concern for others, a respect for autonomy, an ability to request and accept help, the confidence to protest and be tolerant, a resourcefulness to engage with problems rather than evade them, an ability to think before acting, a willingness to tolerate uncertainty, and an openness to learn from past experience and to sustain a sense of adventure about the future. These are qualities that, in turn, contribute to the resilience of couple relationships, building up an emotional capital that can sustain partners, and those with whom they are involved – whether inside or outside families – when times are hard. In summary, secure individuals form secure partnerships that are arguably the principal building blocks of the secure society. The secure society provides the best environment for promoting secure partnerships, which, in turn, contribute to individual security (Blumenfeld et al., 1997). Partnerships can thereby act as a conduit, with the power to create both virtuous circles and vicious spirals of influence between individuals and the society of which they are a part. As a secure base, the adult couple has the potential to fashion the good society – one that connects commitment, dependability and mutual concern with enterprise, productivity and personal initiative.

Appendix I

Table A.1 2 × 2 Analysis of variance: her security (Secure vs. Insecure) and his security status (Secure vs. Insecure) on the AAI with premarital reports of behaviour and feelings in the relationship

Self-report ratings	Mean scores and standard deviations				Her security $F_{(1, 109)}$	His security $F_{(1, 109)}$	Interaction $F_{(1, 109)}$
	Women		Men				
	Secure	Insecure	Secure	Insecure			
Her satisfaction	4.8 (0.8)	4.7 (1.0)	4.7 (0.9)	4.7 (0.9)	ns	ns	ns
Her reports of discord	15.1 (10.7)	17.1 (10.7)	15.6 (8.7)	16.3 (11.9)	ns	ns	ns
Her verbal aggression	17.5 (15.3)	21.4 (21.5)	20.6 (16.1)	15.8 (19.2)	ns	2.66†	ns
Her physical aggression	0.8 (1.5)	1.5 (2.9)	0.7 (1.9)	1.4 (2.6)	ns	ns	ns
Her threats to leave	1.0 (1.9)	2.2 (3.9)	0.9 (1.8)	1.9 (3.1)	ns	3.42†	ns
Her feelings of:							
Dedication	88.9 (7.1)	87.8 (8.8)	87.6 (9.6)	88.5 (7.6)	ns	ns	ns
Constraint	58.2 (9.6)	56.8 (9.2)	58.1 (9.4)	57.0 (9.2)	ns	ns	ns
Passion	43.3 (4.3)	43.2 (4.5)	42.8 (4.7)	43.2 (4.5)	ns	ns	ns
Intimacy	38.7 (3.5)	38.0 (4.1)	38.0 (4.2)	38.4 (3.7)	ns	ns	ns
Commitment	47.5 (2.4)	47.3 (3.3)	47.3 (3.9)	47.4 (2.4)	ns	ns	ns
His satisfaction	4.7 (0.8)	4.6 (0.9)	4.7 (0.8)	4.7 (0.9)	ns	ns	3.3†
His reports of discord	20.0 (14.4)	20.5 (13.4)	18.9 (12.2)	20.2 (14.5)	ns	ns	ns
His verbal aggression	17.5 (15.3)	21.4 (21.5)	12.4 (11.2)	17.0 (17.1)	ns	2.75†	ns
His physical aggression	0.8 (1.5)	1.6 (2.9)	0.7 (1.6)	1.3 (2.2)	ns	ns	ns
His threats to leave	1.3 (0.5)	1.5 (0.5)	0.5 (0.8)	1.6 (3.3)	ns	5.25*	ns
His feelings of:							
Dedication	86.0 (10.2)	85.3 (9.3)	86.9 (7.5)	85.0 (17.1)	ns	ns	ns
Constraint	61.6 (9.0)	57.8 (10.2)	62.3 (8.8)	57.8 (9.7)	3.38†	7.96**	ns
Passion	42.1 (4.9)	42.2 (6.0)	42.0 (4.9)	42.6 (5.2)	ns	ns	ns
Intimacy	38.4 (2.7)	37.3 (4.8)	37.9 (3.2)	37.8 (4.5)	ns	ns	ns
Commitment	46.8 (3.2)	46.7 (4.0)	46.9 (2.7)	47.0 (3.0)	ns	ns	ns

†p = 0.10; *p = 0.05; **p = 0.01; ***p = 0.001

Table A.2 2 × 2 Analysis of variance: her security (Secure vs. Insecure) and his security status (Secure vs. Insecure) on the AAI with reports of behaviour and feelings in the relationship after five years of marriage

Self-report ratings	Mean scores and standard deviations				Her security $F(1, 89)$	His security $F(1, 89)$	Interaction $F(1, 89)$
	Women		Men				
	Secure	Insecure	Secure	Insecure			
Her satisfaction	4.4 (1.2)	4.1 (1.3)	4.2 (1.3)	4.2 (1.2)	ns	ns	ns
Her reports of discord	13.6 (8.8)	14.0 (8.2)	12.5 (7.2)	14.2 (9.1)	ns	ns	ns
Her verbal aggression	11.4 (10.0)	14.1 (13.9)	11.2 (10.4)	14.0 (13.5)	ns	ns	ns
Her physical aggression	0.4 (1.7)	0.6 (1.4)	0.4 (1.3)	0.6 (1.2)	ns	ns	ns
Her threats to leave	0.7 (1.7)	1.0 (2.1)	0.8 (1.7)	1.0 (2.1)	ns	ns	ns
Her feelings of:							
Dedication	86.7 (8.9)	87.7 (11.1)	86.9 (11.7)	87.3 (10.4)	ns	ns	ns
Constraint	67.5 (13.5)	70.0 (12.4)	68.8 (13.5)	68.9 (12.9)	ns	ns	ns
Passion	41.2 (4.7)	40.6 (7.6)	40.1 (7.0)	41.1 (7.0)	ns	ns	ns
Intimacy	38.3 (3.2)	37.3 (6.1)	37.6 (6.3)	37.8 (4.5)	ns	ns	ns
Commitment	46.6 (3.6)	45.6 (7.1)	45.4 (7.9)	45.9 (6.2)	ns	ns	ns
Depression	5.2 (4.1)	7.3 (6.6)	5.2 (4.7)	7.4 (6.4)	ns	ns	ns
His satisfaction	4.5 (1.2)	4.4 (1.1)	4.2 (1.3)	4.6 (0.9)	ns	3.11†	ns
His reports of discord	13.5 (8.6)	15.8 (8.3)	15.2 (8.8)	14.3 (8.5)	3.01†	ns	ns
His verbal aggression	10.3 (10.5)	13.7 (18.5)	8.7 (7.9)	13.7 (18.3)	ns	ns	ns
His physical aggression	0.3 (0.9)	0.7 (1.4)	0.5 (1.0)	0.5 (1.2)	ns	ns	ns
His threats to leave	0.9 (1.9)	1.3 (2.4)	0.6 (1.4)	1.3 (2.5)	ns	ns	ns
His feelings of:							
Dedication	83.7 (11.9)	83.9 (10.6)	83.6 (11.9)	83.8 (10.9)	ns	ns	ns
Constraint	67.6 (12.3)	68.6 (11.0)	68.1 (13.3)	68.1 (10.6)	ns	ns	ns
Passion	40.1 (7.7)	41.1 (7.1)	38.3 (8.1)	42.1 (6.6)	ns	4.3*	ns
Intimacy	37.1 (6.7)	36.7 (5.3)	35.6 (7.0)	37.5 (5.2)	ns	ns	ns
Commitment	44.9 (7.9)	45.5 (6.2)	44.0 (8.3)	46.0 (6.0)	ns	ns	ns
Depression	3.9 (4.3)	5.2 (3.8)	3.6 (2.9)	5.3 (4.6)	ns	ns	ns

†p = 0.10; *p = 0.05; **p = 0.01; ***p = 0.001

Table A.3 2 × 2 Analysis of variance: her security (Secure vs. Insecure) and his security status (Secure vs. Insecure) on the CRI with premarital reports of behaviour and feelings in the relationship

| Self-report ratings | Mean scores and standard deviations | | | | Her security $F(1, 110)$ | His security $F(1, 110)$ | Interaction $F(1, 110)$ |
| | Women | | Men | | | | |
	Secure	Insecure	Secure	Insecure			
Her satisfaction	5.1 (0.6)	4.5 (1.1)	5.0 (0.8)	4.6 (1.0)	6.69**	3.42†	ns
Her reports of discord	13.3 (10.3)	17.2 (9.2)	12.3 (6.6)	17.2 (11.4)	ns	5.26*	ns
Her verbal aggression	13.4 (11.9)	22.2 (19.6)	13.4 (12.2)	20.6 (18.7)	4.29*	3.72†	2.88† I/I < others
Her physical aggression	0.5 (1.1)	1.7 (2.9)	0.7 (1.9)	1.4 (2.7)	6.98**	ns	ns
Her threats to leave	0.7 (1.3)	2.0 (3.0)	0.8 (2.0)	1.7 (2.5)	7.06**	ns	ns
Her feelings of:							
Dedication	89.9 (6.0)	86.2 (9.6)	89.4 (7.5)	87.3 (8.5)	4.43*	ns	ns
Constraint	59.2 (8.7)	55.8 (9.2)	57.1 (8.7)	58.0 (9.4)	5.94*	ns	ns
Passion	44.3 (3.6)	42.1 (5.1)	44.1 (3.8)	42.7 (4.9)	4.68*	ns	ns
Intimacy	39.5 (2.6)	36.8 (4.9)	39.4 (2.5)	37.4 (4.7)	6.20*	5.38*	6.73** I/I < others
Commitment	48.2 (1.4)	46.6 (4.1)	48.1 (1.6)	47.0 (3.8)	4.07*	ns	3.86* I/I < others
His satisfaction	4.9 (0.8)	4.5 (0.8)	4.9 (0.8)	4.6 (0.8)	3.15†	2.96†	ns
His reports of discord	16.6 (13.1)	21.6 (12.0)	16.2 (10.4)	21.0 (14.0)	ns	ns	ns
His verbal aggression	10.3 (10.5)	18.2 (15.5)	9.4 (9.2)	17.4 (15.3)	5.71*	6.88**	ns
His physical aggression	0.5 (1.3)	1.5 (2.4)	0.8 (1.9)	1.1 (2.0)	5.71*	ns	ns
His threats to leave	0.5 (1.0)	1.6 (3.7)	0.6 (1.4)	1.3 (3.3)	3.51†	ns	ns
His feelings of:							
Dedication	87.8 (8.2)	84.4 (9.1)	88.1 (7.7)	84.8 (9.2)	ns	3.01†	ns
Constraint	61.8 (8.9)	57.4 (9.1)	61.9 (9.7)	58.1 (8.6)	4.15*	ns	ns
Passion	43.3 (5.4)	41.7 (4.8)	43.8 (4.5)	41.6 (5.4)	ns	3.86*	ns
Intimacy	39.1 (3.3)	36.8 (4.6)	39.1 (3.2)	37.3 (4.5)	5.51*	3.45†	ns
Commitment	47.5 (2.6)	46.6 (2.9)	47.3 (2.6)	46.9 (2.9)	ns	ns	ns

†p = 0.10; *p = 0.05; **p = 0.01; ***p = 0.001

Table A.4 2 × 2 Analysis of variance: her security (Secure vs. Insecure) and his security status (Secure vs. Insecure) on the CRI with reports of behaviour and feelings in the relationship after five years of marriage

	Mean scores and standard deviations						Her security $F(1, 72)$	His security $F(1, 72)$	Interaction $F(1, 72)$
	Women				Men				
Self-report ratings	Secure		Insecure		Secure		Insecure			
Her satisfaction	4.4	(1.1)	4.0	(1.4)	4.5	(1.1)	4.0	(1.3)	ns	ns	ns
Her reports of discord	12.3	(7.7)	16.8	(13.3)	11.7	(7.7)	14.2	(7.8)	ns	ns	ns
Her verbal aggression	11.0	(11.2)	13.5	(11.9)	7.6	(9.1)	12.1	(10.9)	ns	8.26**	ns
Her physical aggression	0.6	(1.3)	0.6	(1.3)	0.6	(1.4)	0.6	(1.2)	ns	ns	ns
Her threats to leave	1.0	(1.8)	1.1	(2.4)	0.7	(1.7)	1.2	(2.2)	ns	ns	ns
Her feelings of:											
Dedication	89.7	(6.5)	85.3	(12.8)	90.7	(6.5)	85.6	(12.8)	ns	4.99*	4.75*
											I/I < others
Constraint	70.3	(11.7)	68.6	(13.9)	69.7	(11.6)	69.4	(13.9)	ns	ns	ns
Passion	41.7	(4.9)	39.5	(8.4)	42.3	(4.3)	39.6	(8.0)	ns	ns	ns
Intimacy	39.1	(3.4)	36.2	(6.6)	38.9	(3.8)	36.9	(6.0)	ns	ns	3.98*
											I/I < others
Commitment	47.9	(2.0)	44.3	(8.5)	47.5	(2.6)	45.4	(7.6)	3.59†	ns	ns
Depression	5.6	(5.2)	6.1	(3.8)	5.8	(5.0)	5.8	(4.3)	ns	ns	ns

His satisfaction	4.7 (1.3)	4.2 (1.0)	4.5 (1.4)	4.5 (1.0)	2.91†	ns	ns
His reports of discord	13.1 (9.2)	17.1 (6.6)	12.8 (8.9)	16.3 (7.7)	ns	ns	ns
His verbal aggression	7.3 (7.9)	13.5 (11.9)	7.6 (9.1)	12.1 (10.9)	5.35*	ns	ns
His physical aggression	0.2 (1.9)	0.6 (1.2)	0.3 (0.7)	0.5 (1.2)	ns	ns	ns
His threats to leave	0.5 (1.2)	1.1 (1.6)	0.5 (1.3)	0.9 (1.5)	ns	ns	ns
His feelings of:							
Dedication	84.7 (12.2)	82.5 (11.0)	84.5 (12.4)	83.1 (11.2)	ns	ns	4.18* I/I < I/S and S/I
Constraint	67.1 (9.3)	70.0 (11.0)	69.7 (11.5)	67.6 (9.3)	3.10†	ns	3.31† I(woman)/S(man) > others
Passion	41.5 (8.1)	39.2 (7.7)	40.1 (7.9)	40.3 (8.0)	ns	ns	4.33* I/I < S(woman)/I(man)
Intimacy	37.7 (6.8)	35.3 (5.5)	36.7 (7.5)	36.4 (5.5)	ns	ns	3.71† I/I < S(woman)/I(man)
Commitment	45.2 (8.0)	44.2 (7.3)	44.6 (11.5)	44.8 (9.3)	ns	ns	5.06* I/I < S(woman)/I(man)
Depression	3.1 (2.7)	5.0 (3.4)	2.9 (2.9)	4.7 (3.2)	ns	4.68*	2.86†

†p = 0.10; *p = 0.05; **p = 0.01; ***p = 0.001

Appendix 2
Attachment style descriptive paragraphs

Bartholomew and Horowitz, 1991

Secure

It is easy for me to become emotionally close to others. I am comfortable depending on others and having others depend on me. I don't worry about being alone or having others not accept me.

Dismissing

I am comfortable without close emotional relationships. It is very important to me to feel independent and self-sufficient, and I prefer not to depend on others or have others depend on me.

Fearful

I am uncomfortable getting close to others. I want emotionally close relationships, but I find it difficult to trust others completely, or to depend on them. I sometimes worry that I will be hurt if I allow myself to become too close to others.

Preoccupied

I want to be completely emotionally intimate with others, but I often find that others are reluctant to get as close as I would like. I am uncomfortable being without close relationships, but I sometimes worry that others don't value me as much as I value them.

Bibliography

Ainsworth, M. D. S. (1985) 'Attachment across the life span', *Bulletin of the New York Academy of Medicine*, 61/9: 792–811.

Ainsworth, M. D. S. (1991) 'Attachments and other affectional bonds across the life cycle', in C. M. Parkes, J. Stevenson-Hinde, and P. Marris (eds.), *Attachment Across the Life Cycle*. London: Routledge.

Ainsworth, M. D. S., Blehar, M., Waters, E., and Wall, S. (1978) *Patterns of Attachment: A Psychological Study of the Strange Situation*. Hillsdale, NJ: Erlbaum.

Arend, R., Grove, F., and Stroufe, L. (1979) 'Continuity of individual adaptation from infancy to kindergarten: a predictive study of ego-resiliency and curiosity in pre-schoolers', *Child Development*, 50: 950–9.

Avery, N. (1977) 'Sadomasochism: a defence against object loss', *Psychoanalytic Review*, 64: 101–9.

Balint, E. (1993) 'Fair shares and mutual concern', in E. Balint, *Before I Was I: Psychoanalysis and the Imagination*. London: Free Association Books.

Balint, M. (1959) *Thrills and Regressions*. London: Hogarth.

Bannister, K. (ed.) (1955) *Social Casework in Marital Problems*. London: Tavistock.

Bannister, K., and Pincus, L. (1971) *Shared Phantasy in Marital Problems*. London: Institute of Marital Studies.

Bartholomew, K. (1990) 'Avoidance of intimacy: an attachment perspective', *Journal of Social and Personal Relationships*, 7: 147–78.

Bartholomew, K. (1997) 'Attachment processes: individual and couple perspectives', *British Journal of Medical Psychology*, 70: 249–63.

Bartholomew, K., and Horowitz, L. M. (1991) 'Attachment styles among young adults: a test of a four category model', *Journal of Personality and Social Psychology*, 61: 226–44.

Bartholomew, K., Landolt, M., and Oram, D. (1998) 'The West End Relationships Project', unpublished data, Simon Fraser University.

Bateman, A. (1998) 'Thick and thin-skinned organisations and enactment in borderline and narcissistic disorders', *International Journal of Psycho-Analysis*, 79: 13–25.

Berlin, L., and Cassidy, J. (1999) 'Relations among relationships: contributions from attachment theory and research', in J. Cassidy and P. R. Shaver (eds), *Handbook of Attachment: Theory, Research, and Clinical Applications*. New York: Guilford.

Bion, W. (1959) 'Attacks on linking', in W. Bion (1984) *Second Thoughts*. London: Karnac.

Bion, W. (1961) *Experiences in Groups.* London: Tavistock.

Bion, W. (1962a) 'A theory of thinking', in W. Bion (1984) *Second Thoughts.* London: Karnac.

Bion, W. (1962b) *Learning from Experience.* London: Heinemann.

Blumenfeld, J., Bowler, S., Clulow, C., Corbett, M., and Mansfield, P. (1997) *Marriage Support and the Secure Society.* London: Lord Chancellor's Department.

Bohannon, J. (1990–1) 'Grief reactions of spouses following the death of a child: a longitudunal study', *Omega Journal of Death and Dying*, 22/2: 109–21.

Bowlby, J. (1949) 'The study and reduction of group tensions in the family', *Human Relations*, 2: 123–8.

Bowlby, J. (1958) 'The nature of the child's tie to its mother', *International Journal of Psycho-Analysis*, 39: 350–73.

Bowlby, J. (1961) 'Processes of mourning', *International Journal of Psycho-Analysis*, 42, parts 4–5: 317–40.

Bowlby, J. (1969) *Attachment and Loss*, vol. 1: *Attachment* (2nd edn, 1982). London: Hogarth Press; New York: Basic Books.

Bowlby, J. (1973) *Attachment and Loss*, vol. 2: *Separation.* London: Hogarth Press; New York: Basic Books.

Bowlby, J. (1979) 'Psychoanalysis as art and science', *International Review of Psycho-Analysis*, 6/3: 3–14.

Bowlby, J. (1980) *Attachment and Loss*, vol. 3: *Loss, Sadness, and Depression.* London: Hogarth Press; New York: Basic Books.

Bowlby, J. (1982) *Attachment*, 2nd edition of vol. I of *Attachment and Loss.* London: Hogath Press; New York: Basic Books.

Bowlby, J. (1984) 'Violence in the family as a disorder of the attachment and care-giving systems', *The American Journal of Psychoanalysis*, 44: 9–27.

Bowlby, J. (1988) *A Secure Base: Clinical Applications of Attachment Theory.* London: Routledge; also published as *A Secure Base: Parent–Child Attachment and Healthy Human Development.* New York: Basic Books.

Bradburn, I. S. (1997) 'Attachment and coping strategies in married couples with preschool children', unpublished doctoral dissertation, University of California, Berkeley.

Bretherton, I. (1985) 'Attachment theory: retrospect and prospect', in I. Bretherton and E. Waters (eds), *Growing Points of Attachment Theory and Research*, Monographs of the Society for Research in Child Development, nos. 1–2, serial no. 209.

Bretherton, I. (1991) 'The roots and growing points of attachment theory', in C. Parkes, J. Stevenson-Hinde, and P. Marris (eds), *Attachment Across the Life Cycle.* London: Tavistock/Routledge.

Bretherton, I. (1999) 'Updating the "internal working model" construct: some reflections', *Attachment and Human Development*, 3: 343–57.

Britton, R. (1989) 'The missing link: parental sexuality in the Oedipus complex', in J. Steiner (ed.), *The Oedipus Complex Today: Clinical Implications.* London, Karnac.

Britton, R. (1998) *Belief and Imagination. Explorations in Psycho-Analysis.* London: Routledge.

Brookes, S. (1991) 'Bion's concept of containment in marital work', *Journal of Social Work Practice*, 5/2: 133–41.

Byng-Hall, J. (1980) 'The symptom bearer as marital distance regulator: clinical implications', *Family Process*, 19: 355–65.

Byng-Hall, J. (1985) 'Resolving distance conflicts', in A. Gurman (ed.), *Casebook of Marital Therapy*. New York: Guilford.

Byng-Hall, J. (1999) 'Family and couple therapy: toward greater security', in J. Cassidy and P. R. Shaver (eds), *Handbook of Attachment: Theory, Research, and Clinical Applications*. New York: Guilford.

Cassidy, J. (1988) 'Child–mother attachment and the self in six-year-olds', *Child Development*, 59: 121–34.

Clulow, C. (1982) *To Have and To Hold: Marriage, the First Baby and Preparing Couples for Parenthood*. Aberdeen: Aberdeen University Press.

Clulow, C. (1985) *Marital Therapy: An Inside View*. Aberdeen: Aberdeen University Press.

Clulow, C. (ed.) (1993) *Rethinking Marriage: Public and Private Perspectives*. London: Karnac.

Clulow, C. (ed.) (1995) *Women, Men and Marriage*. London: Sheldon.

Clulow, C. (ed.) (1996) *Partners Becoming Parents*. London: Sheldon.

Clulow, C., and Mattinson, J. (1988) *Marriage Inside Out: Understanding Problems of Intimacy*. Harmondsworth: Pelican; 2nd edn, Penguin, 1995.

Clulow, C., and Vincent, C. (1987) *In the Child's Best Interests? Divorce Court Welfare and the Search for a Settlement*. London: Tavistock/Sweet & Maxwell.

Cohn, D., Silver D., Cowan, P., Cowan, C., and Pearson, J. (1992) 'Working models of childhood attachment and couples relationships', *Journal of Family Issues*, 13: 432–49.

Coles Study Notes (1980) *The Plays of Edward Albee*. Toronto: Coles.

Collins, N. L., and Read, S. J. (1994) 'Cognitive representations of attachment: the structure and function of working models', in K. Bartholomew and D. Perlman (eds), *Advances in Personal Relationship*, vol. 5: *Attachment Processes in Adulthood*. London: Jessica Kingsley.

Colman, W. (1988) 'After the fall', *Free Associations*, 13: 59–83.

Colman, W. (1989) *On Call: The Work of a Telephone Helpline for Child Abusers*. Aberdeen: Aberdeen University Press.

Colman, W. (1993) 'Marriage as a psychological container', in S. Ruszczynski (ed.), *Psychotherapy with Couples*. London: Karnac, pp. 70–96.

Colman, W. (1995) 'Gesture and recognition: an alternative model to projective identification as a basis for couple relationships', in S. Ruszczynski, and J. Fisher, (eds), *Intrusiveness and Intimacy in the Couple*. London: Karnac.

Cook, J. (1983) 'A death in the family: parental bereavement in the first year', *Suicide and Life-Threatening Behaviour*, 13/1: 42–61.

Cowan, C. P. (1988) 'Working with men becoming fathers: the impact of a couples group intervention', in P. Bronstein and C. P. Cowan (eds), *Fatherhood Today: Men's Changing Role in the Family*. New York: Wiley.

Cowan, C. P., and Cowan, P. A. (1997) 'Working with couples during stressful family transitions', in S. Dreman (ed.), *The Family on the Threshold of the 21st Century*. Hillsdale, NJ: Erlbaum.

Cowan, C. P., and Cowan, P. A. (2000) *When Partners Become Parents: The Big Life Change for Couples*, 2nd edn. Mattwah, NJ: Erlbaum.

Cowan, P. A., Bradburn, I., and Cowan, C. P. (1999) 'Adding adult attachment to marital interaction and parenting style as predictors of children's behavior problems in kindergarten', unpublished manuscript, University of California, Berkeley.

Cowan, P. A., Cohn, D. A., Cowan, C. P., and Pearson, J. L. (1996) 'Parents' attachment histories and children's internalizing and externalizing behavior: exploring family systems models of linkage', *Journal of Consulting and Clinical Psychology,* 64: 53–63.

Cowan, P. A., Cowan, C. P., Schulz, M., and Heming, G. (1994) 'Prebirth to preschool family factors predicting children's adaptation to kindergarten', in R. Parke and S. Kellam (eds), *Exploring Family Relationships with other Social Contexts: Advances in Family Research,* vol. 4. Hillsdale, NJ: Erlbaum.

Cronin, H. (1999) 'A moment or a lifetime? A Darwinian perspective on sex and parenting', in *Commitment: Who Cares?,* transcript of proceedings of a conference held in London, 25 October 1999. London: One Plus One Marriage and Partnership Research.

Crowell, J. A. (1998) 'Adult attachment and the couple', paper presented at the 50th Jubilee Conference of the Tavistock Marital Studies Institute, London, July.

Crowell, J. A., and Owens, G. (1996) 'Current relationship interview and scoring system', unpublished manuscript, State University of New York at Stony Brook.

Crowell, J., and Treboux, D. (1995) 'A review of adult attachment measures: implications for theory and research', *Social Development,* 4/3: 294–327.

Crowell, J. A., Fraley, R. C., and Shaver, P. R. (1999) 'Measurement of individual differences in adolescent and adult attachment', in J. Cassidy and P. R. Shaver (eds), *Handbook of Attachment: Theory, Research, and Clinical Applications.* New York: Guilford.

Crowell, J., Gao, Y., Owens, G., and Waters, E. (1997) 'Current relationship representations: relation to secure base behavior in marital interaction', presented at a poster-symposium at the Biennial Meeting of the Society for Research in Child Development, Washington, DC.

Crowell, J., Treboux, D., Owens, G., and Pan, H. (1995) 'Is it true that the longer you're together the more you think alike? Examining two hypotheses of attachment theory', poster presented at the Biennial Meeting of the Society for Research in Child Development, Indianapolis, IN.

Crowell, J. A., Pan, H. S., Gao, Y., Treboux, D., O'Connor, E., and Waters, E. (1998) 'The Secure Base Scoring System for adults', unpublished manuscript, State University of New York at Stony Brook.

Cudmore, L. (1994) 'The impact of a child's death on the couple relationship', unpublished literature review, Tavistock Marital Studies Institute.

Cudmore, L. (1996) 'Infertility and the couple', in C. Clulow (ed.), *Partners Becoming Parents.* London: Sheldon.

Cummings, E. M., and Davies, P. T. (1994) *Children and Marital Conflict: The Impact of Family Dispute and Resolution.* New York: Guilford.

Cunliffe, M. (1986) *The Literature of the United States,* 4th edn. Harmondsworth: Penguin.

Davis, M., and Hadiks, D. (1994) 'Non-verbal aspects of therapist attunement', *Journal of Clinical Psychology,* 50: 393–405.

De Zulueta, F. (1993) *From Pain to Violence: The Traumatic Roots of Destructiveness.* London: Whurr.

Dicks, H. V. (1967) *Marital Tensions.* London and New York: Routledge and Basic Books.

Dickstein, S., Schiller, M., Seifer, R., Magee, K.D., St-Andre, M., and Wheeler, E. (1996) 'Marital attachment interview pilot study', poster presented at the International Conference on Infant Studies, Providence, RI.

Dobash, R., and Dobash, R. (1979) *Violence Against Wives: A Case Against Patriarchy.* London: Open Books.

Dozier, M., and Tyrell, C. (1998) 'The role of attachment in therapeutic relationships', in J. Simpson and W. Rholes (eds), *Attachment Theory and Close Relationships.* London/New York: Guilford.

Dutton, D. G. (1995) *The Domestic Assault of Women: Psychological and Criminal Justice Perspectives.* Boston: Allyn & Bacon.

Dutton, D. G., and Painter, S. L. (1993) 'Emotional attachment in abusive relationships: a test of traumatic bonding theory', *Violence and Victims*, 8: 105–20.

Dutton, D. G., Saunders, K., Starzomski, A. J., and Bartholomew, K. (1994) 'Intimacy-anger and insecure attachment as precursors of abuse in intimate relationships', *Journal of Applied Social Psychology*, 24: 1367–86.

Dyregrov, A. (1990) 'Parental reactions to the loss of an infant child: a review', *Scandinavian Journal of Psychology*, 31/4: 266–80.

Elliott, J., Richards, M., and Warwick, H. (1993) 'The consequences of divorce for the health and well-being of adults and children', *Final Report for the Health Promotion Trust.* Cambridge: Health Promotion Trust.

Esslin, M. (1980) *The Theatre of the Absurd*, 3rd edn. Harmondsworth: Penguin.

Ezriel, H. (1956) 'Experimentation within the psycho-analytic session', *British Journal for the Philosophy of Science*, 7/25: 29–48.

Fairbairn, W. (1952) *Psychoanalytic Studies of the Personality.* London: Tavistock.

Feeney, J. (1999) 'Adult romantic attachment and couple relationships', in J. Cassidy and P. Shaver (eds), *Handbook of Attachment: Theory, Research and Clinical Applications.* New York: Guilford.

Felstiner, J. (1982) 'Translating Celan's last poem', *American Poetry Review*, July/August: 21–7.

Fisher, J. (1993) 'The impenetrable other: ambivalence and the Oedipal conflict in work with couples', in S. Rusczcynski (ed.), *Psychotherapy with Couples: Theory and Practice at the Tavistock Institute of Marital Studies.* London: Karnac.

Fisher, J. (1999) *The Uninvited Guest: Emerging from Narcissism towards Marriage.* London: Karnac.

Follingstad, D. R., Rutledge, L. L., Berg, B. J., Hause, E. S., and Polek, D. S. (1990) 'The role of emotional abuse in physically abusive relationships', *Journal of Family Violence*, 5: 107–20.

Fonagy, P. (1999a) 'Psychoanalytic theory from the viewpoint of attachment theory and research', in J. Cassidy and P. Shaver (eds), *Handbook of Attachment: Theory, Research and Clinical Applications.* New York: Guilford.

Fonagy, P. (1999b) 'The male perpetrator: the role of trauma and failures of mentalization in aggression against women: an attachment theory perspective', The 6th John Bowlby Memorial Lecture, London, 20 February.

Fonagy, P., Steele, H., and Steele, M. (1991a) 'Maternal representations of attachment during pregnancy predict infant–mother attachment patterns at one year', *Child Development*, 62: 891–905.

Fonagy, P., Steele, H., Moran, G., Steele, M., and Higgitt, A. (1991b) 'The capacity for understanding mental states: the reflective self in parent and child and its significance for security of attachment', *Infant Mental Health Journal*, 13: 200–17.

Fonagy, P., Steele, M., Moran, G., Steele, G., and Higgitt, A. (1993a) 'Measuring the ghost in the nursery: an empirical study of the relation between parents' mental representations of childhood experiences and their infants' security of attachment', *Journal of the American Psychoanalytic Association*, 41: 957–89.

Fonagy, P., Moran, G., and Target, M. (1993b) 'Aggression and the psychological self', *International Journal of Psycho-Analysis*, 74: 471–85.

Fonagy, P., Steele, M., Steele, H., Leigh, T., Kennedy, R., Mattoon, G., and Target, M. (1995) 'Attachment, the reflective self, and borderline states: the predictive specificity of the Adult Attachment Interview and pathological emotional development', in S. Goldberg, R. Muir, and J. Kerr (eds), *Attachment Theory: Social, Developmental and Clinical Perspectives*. Hillsdale, NJ: Analytic Press.

Freedman, J. (2000) 'Giving as bad as you get', paper given at a conference on 'Love and Violence in Marriage', London, 11 March 2000.

Freud, S. (1917) *Mourning and Melancholia*, Standard Edition, 14. London: Hogarth, pp. 239–58.

Freud, S. (1920) 'Letter to Ferenczi', in M. Schur (1922) *Freud: Living and Dying*, London: Hogarth.

Freud, S. (1929) 'Letter to Ludwig Binswanger', in E. Freud (ed.), *The Letters of Sigmund Freud 1873–1939*. London: Hogarth, 1970.

Freud, S. (1949/53) *Abriss der Psychoanalyse (An Outline of Psychoanalysis)*. Frankfurt am Main: Fischer Bucherei.

Fyffe, C. (1997) 'Empirical classification of adult attachment status: predicting group membership', poster presented at the Biennial Meeting of the Society for Research in Child Development, Washington, DC.

Gao, Y., Crowell, J., Pan, H., O'Connor, E., and Waters, E. (1996) 'Are secure people better caregivers or careseekers in marriage?' poster presented at the XIVth Biennial International Society for the Study of Behavioral Development Conference, Quebec City, Canada.

Garland, C. (1991) 'External disasters and the internal world: an approach to the psychotherapeutic understanding of survivors', in J. Holmes (ed.), *Textbook of Psychotherapy in Psychiatric Practice*, Edinburgh: Churchill Livingstone.

Garland, C., (1998) 'Thinking about trauma', in C. Garland (ed.), *Understanding Trauma: A Psychoanalytic Approach*, Tavistock Clinic Series. London: Duckworth.

Gayford, J. (1978) 'Battered wives', in J. Martin (ed.), *Violence and the Family*. Chichester: Wiley.

Gelles, R. (1994) 'Through a sociological lens: social structure and family violence', in R. Gelles and D. Loseke (eds), *Current Controversies in Family Violence*. Newbury Park: Sage.

Gelles, R., and Straus, M. (1988) *Intimate Violence*. New York: Simon & Schuster.

George, C., and Solomon, J. (1999) 'Attachment and caregiving: the caregiving behavioural system', in J. Cassidy and P. Shaver (eds), *Handbook of Attachment: Theory, Research and Clinical Applications*. New York: Guilford.

George, C., Kaplan, N., and Main, M. (1985) 'The adult attachment interview', unpublished manuscript, University of California at Berkeley.

Gibb, E. (1998) 'Dreaming after a traumatic bereavement', in C. Garland (ed.), *Under-*

standing Trauma: A Psychoanalytic Approach, Tavistock Clinic Series. London: Duckworth.

Gibran, K. (1926) *The Prophet*. London: Heinemann.

Gottman, J. M., Katz, L. F., and Hooven, C. (1997) *Meta-Emotion: How Families Communicate Emotionally*, Mahwah, NJ: Erlbaum.

Greenfield, S. (1999) 'The future is too much fun', Richard Dimbleby Lecture, BBC, 1 December 1999.

Griffin, D. W., and Bartholomew, K. (1994) 'The metaphysics of measurement: the case of adult attachment', in K. Bartholomew and D. Perlman (eds), *Advances in Personal Relationships: Attachment Processes in Adulthood,* vol. 5. London: Jessica Kingsley.

Hardy, G., Aldridge, J., Davidson, C., Rowe, C., Reilly, S., and Shapiro, D. (1999) 'Therapist responsiveness to client attachment styles and issues observed in client-identified significant events in psychodynamic-interpersonal psychotherapy', *Psychotherapy Research*, 9/1: 36–53.

Hazan, C., and Shaver, P. (1987) 'Romantic love conceptualized as an attachment process', *Journal of Personality and Social Psychology*, 52/3: 511–24.

Hazan, C., and Shaver, P. (1994) 'Attachment as an organizational framework for research on close relationships', *Psychological Inquiry: An International Journal of Peer Commentary and Review*, 5/1: 1–22.

Hazan, C., and Zeifman, D. (1994) 'Sex and the psychological tether', in K. Bartholomew and D. Perlman (eds), *Advances in Personal Relationships*, vol. 5. *Attachment Processes in Adulthood.* London: Jessica Kingsley.

Hazan, C., and Zeifman, D. (1999) 'Pair bonds as attachments: evaluating the evidence', in J. Cassidy and P. Shaver (eds), *Handbook of Attachment: Theory, Research and Clinical Applications.* New York: Guilford.

Hazzard, A., Weston, J., and Gutterres, C. (1992) 'After a child's death: factors related to parental bereavement', *Developmental and Behavioral Pediatrics*, 13/1: 24–30.

Heard, D., and Lake, B. (1997) *The Challenge of Attachment for Caregiving*. London: Routledge.

Henderson, A. J. Z. (1998) 'It takes two to tango: an attachment perspective exploring women's and men's relationship aggression', unpublished doctoral dissertation, Simon Fraser University, Burnaby, BC, Canada.

Henderson, A. J. Z., Bartholomew, K., and Dutton, D. G. (1997) 'He loves me; he loves me not: attachment and separation resolution of abused women', *Journal of Family Violence*, 12: 169–91.

Henderson, A. J. Z., Heinzl, C., and Bartholomew, K. (1994) 'A prospective study of attachment representations and psychological abuse', paper presented at the American Psychological Association Convention, Los Angeles, California.

Hesse, E. (1996) 'Discourse, memory, and the Adult Attachment Interview: a note with emphasis on the emerging cannot classify category', *Infant Mental Health Journal*, 17/1: 4–11.

Hesse, E. (1999) 'The Adult Attachment Interview: historical and current perspectives', in J. Cassidy and P. Shaver (eds), *Handbook of Attachment: Theory, Research, and Clinical Applications*, New York: Guilford.

Hobson, R. (1995) 'The inter-subjective domain: approaches from developmental psychopathology', in T. Shapiro and R. Emde (eds), *Research in Psychoanalysis: Process Development, Outcome.* Madison, CT: International Universities Press.

Holmes, J. (1993) *John Bowlby and Attachment Theory*. London: Routledge.

Holmes, J. (1996) *Attachment, Intimacy and Autonomy: Using Attachment Theory in Adult Psychotherapy*. London/New York: Jason Aronson.

Holmes, J. (1997) 'Attachment, autonomy, intimacy: some clinical implications of attachment theory', *British Journal of Medical Psychology*, 70: 231–48.

Holmes, J. (1999) 'Narrative, attachment and the therapeutic process', in C. Mace (ed.), *Heart and Soul: The Therapeutic Face of Philosophy*. London: Routledge.

Hudson, L., and Jacot, B. (1991) *The Way Men Think: Intellect, Intimacy and the Erotic Imagination*. New Haven and London: Yale University Press.

Hughes, L., and Pengelly, P. (1997) *Staff Supervision in a Turbulent Environment: Managing Process and Task in Front-line Services*. London: Jessica Kingsley.

Jaques, E. (1990) 'Death and the mid-life crisis', in E. B. Spillius (ed.), *Melanie Klein Today*, vol. 2. London: Routledge.

Johns, J. (1996) 'Daughters becoming mothers', in C. Clulow (ed.), *Partners Becoming Parents*. London: Sheldon.

Johnson, S. (1986) 'Bonds or bargains: relationship paradigms and their significance for marital therapy', *Journal of Marital and Family Therapy*, 12: 259–67.

Johnson, S. (1996) *The Practice of Emotionally Focused Marital Therapy: Creating Connection*. New York: Bruner Mazell.

Judd, D. (1989) *Give Sorrow Words: Working with a Dying Child*. London: Free Association Books; 2nd edn (1995) London: Whurr.

Judd, D. (1994) 'Life threatening illness as psychic trauma: psychotherapy with adolescent patients', in A. Erskine and D. Judd (eds), *The Imaginative Body: Psychodynamic Therapy in Health Care*, London: Whurr.

Klass, D. (1986) 'Marriage and divorce among bereaved parents in a self-help group', *Omega Journal of Death and Dying*, 17/3: 237–49.

Klein, M. (1940) 'Mourning and its relation to manic depressive states', *International Journal of Psycho-Analysis*, 21: 125–53.

Klein, M. (1946) 'Notes on some schizoid mechanisms', in M. Klein (ed), *The Writings of Melanie Klein*, vol. 3. London: Hogarth, 1975, reprinted 1993, London: Karnac.

Kobak, R., and Hazan, C. (1991) 'Attachment in marriage: effects of security and accuracy of working models', *Journal of Personality and Social Psychology*, 60: 861–9.

Kobak, R., and Sceery, A. (1988) 'Attachment in late adolescence: working models, affect regulation, and representations of self and others', *Child Development*, 59: 135–46.

Kohut, H. (1977) *The Restoration of the Self*. Madison, CT: International Universities Press.

Kraemer, S., and Roberts, V. (1996) *The Politics of Attachment: Towards a Secure Society*. London: Free Association Books.

Landolt, M. A., and Dutton, D. G. (1998) 'Power and personality: an analysis of gay male intimate abuse', *Sex Roles*, 37: 335–58.

Londerville, S., and Main, M. (1981) 'Security of attachment, compliance and maternal training methods in the second year of life', *Developmental Psychology*, 21: 289–99.

Lyons-Ruth, K. and Jacobvitz, D. (1999) 'Attachment disorganisation: unresolved loss, relational violence, and lapses in behavioural and attentional strategies', in

J. Cassidy and P. R. Shaver (eds), *Handbook of Attachment*, New York and London: Guilford.

Magdol, L., Moffitt, T. E., Caspi, A., Newman, D. L., Fagan, J., and Silva, P. A. (1997) 'Gender differences in partner violence in a birth cohort of 21-year-olds: bridging the gap between clinical and epidemiological approaches', *Journal of Consulting and Clinical Psychology*, 65: 68–78.

Main, M. (1991) 'Metacognitive knowledge, metacognitive monitoring, and singular (coherent) versus multiple (incoherent) models of attachment: findings and directions for future research', in C. Parkes, J. Stevenson-Hinde, and P. Marris (eds), *Attachment Across the Life Cycle*. London: Routledge.

Main, M. (1993) 'Discourse, prediction, and recent studies in attachment: implications for psychoanalysis', *Journal of the American Psychoanalytic Association*, 41: 209–43.

Main, M. (1995) 'Recent studies in attachment: overview, with selected implications for clinical work', in S. Goldberg, R. Muir, and J. Kerr (eds), *Attachment Theory: Social, Developmental, and Clinical Perspectives*, Hillsdale, NJ: Analytic Press.

Main, M., and Goldwyn, R. (1994) 'Adult attachment rating and classification systems', Version 6.0, unpublished manuscript, University of California at Berkeley.

Main, M., and Hesse, E. (1990) 'Parents' unresolved traumatic experiences are related to infant disorganized attachment status: is frightened and/or frightening parental behavior the linking mechanism?' in M. Greenberg, D. Cicchetti, and M. Cummings (eds), *Attachment in the Preschool Years: Theory Research and Intervention*, Chicago: University of Chicago Press.

Main, M., and Solomon, J. (1987) 'Discovery of an insecure disorganized/disoriented attachment pattern: procedures, findings and implications for the classifications of behaviour', in M. Yogman and T. Brazelton (eds), *Affective Development in Infancy*. Norwood, NJ: Ablex.

Main, M., Kaplan, N., and Cassidy, J. (1985) 'Security of infancy, childhood, and adulthood: a move to the level of representation', in I. Bretherton and E. Waters (eds), *Growing Points of Attachment Theory and Research*, Monographs for the Society for Research in Child Development, vol. 50, nos. 1–2, serial no. 209.

Marris, P. (1991) 'The social construction of uncertainty', in C. Parkes, J. Stevenson-Hinde, and P. Marris (eds), *Attachment Across the Life Cycle*. London: Routledge.

Marris, P. (1996) 'The management of uncertainty', in S. Kraemer and V. Roberts (eds), *The Politics of Attachment: Towards a Secure Society*. London: Free Association Books.

Marrone, M. (1998) *Attachment and Interaction*. London: Jessica Kingsley.

Mattinson, J. (1975/92) *The Reflection Process in Casework Supervision*. London: Tavistock Marital Studies Institute.

Mattinson, J. (1981) 'The deadly equal triangle', in *Change and Renewal in Psychodynamic Social Work: British and American Developments in Practice and Education for Services to Families and Children*. Massachusetts: Smith College School of Social Work; London: Group for the Advancement of Psychotherapy in Social Work. Republished in 1997, London: Tavistock Marital Studies Institute.

Mattinson, J. (1988) *Work, Love and Marriage: The Impact of Unemployment*. London: Duckworth.

Mattinson, J., and Sinclair, I. (1979) *Mate and Stalemate: Working with Marital Problems in a Social Services Department*. Oxford: Blackwell.

Mayhew, P., Maung, N., and Mirrless-Black, C. (1993) *The 1992 British Crime Survey*. London: HMSO.

McAllister, F. (1995) *Marital Breakdown and the Health of the Nation*. London: One Plus One.

McCleod, J. (1997) *Narrative and Psychotherapy*. London: Sage.

McCluskey, U., Roger, D., and Nash, P. (1997) 'A preliminary study of the role of attunement in adult psychotherapy', *Human Relations*, 50/10: 1261–73.

McCluskey, U., Hooper, C., and Bingley Miller, L. (1999) 'Goal-corrected empathic attunement: developing and rating the concept within an attachment perspective', *Journal of the Division of Psychotherapy*, APA 36: 80–90.

Meins, E. (1999) 'Sensitivity, security and internal working models: bridging the transmission gap', *Attachment and Human Development*, 1/3: 325–42.

Meltzer, D. (1990) 'Gathering of the transference', in D. Meltzer, *The Analytic Process*. Perthshire, Scotland: Clunie Press.

Menzies-Lyth, I. E. P. (1988) *Containing Anxiety in Institutions: Selected Essays*, vol. 1. London: Free Association Books.

Minuchin, S., and Fishman, H. C. (1981) *Family Therapy Techniques*. Cambridge, MA: Harvard University Press.

Mooney, J. (1993) 'The hidden figure: domestic violence in north London', cited in K. Browne and M. Herbert (1997) *Preventing Family Violence*. Chichester: Wiley.

Morgan, M. (1995) 'The projective gridlock: a form of projective identification in couple relationships', in S. Ruszczynski and J. Fisher (eds), *Intrusiveness and Intimacy in the Couple*. London: Karnac.

Morgan, M. (1999) 'First contacts: the therapist's 'couple state of mind' as a factor in the containment of couples seen for initial consultations', unpublished paper, Tavistock Marital Studies Institute.

Murray, L., and Trevarthen, C. (1986) 'The infant's role in mother–infant communications', *Journal of Child Language*, 13: 15–29.

Obholzer, A., and Roberts, V. Z. (eds) (1994) *The Unconscious at Work: Individual and Organizational Stress in the Human Services*. London: Routledge.

Ogden, T. (1979) 'On projective identification', *International Journal of Psychoanalysis*, 60: 357–73.

O'Shaugnessy, E. (1964) 'The absent object', *Journal of Child Psychotherapy*, 1/2: 34–43.

Owens, G., Crowell, J., Pan, H., Treboux, D., O'Connor, B., and Waters, E. (1995) 'The prototype hypothesis and the origins of attachment working models: child–parent relationships and adult–adult romantic relationships', in E. Waters, B. Vaughn, G. Posada, and K. Kondo-Ikemura (eds), *Caregiving, Cultural, and Cognitive Perspectives on Secure Base Behaviour and Working Models: New Growing Points of Attachment Theory and Research*, Monographs of the Society for Research in Child Development, serial no. 244, vol. 60.

Pahl, J. (1985) *Private Violence and Public Policy*. London: Routledge and Kegan Paul.

Paley, B., Cox, M., Burchinal, M., and Payne, C. (1995) 'Security of spouses' attachment stance and affect regulation in marital interaction', paper presented at the

Biennial Meeting of the Society for Research in Child Development, Indianapolis.

Patrick, M., Hobson, R., Castle, D., Howard, R., and Maugham, B. (1994) 'Personality disorder and the mental representation of early social experience', *Development and Psychopathology*, 6: 375–88.

Pianta, R., Morog, M., and Marvin, R. (1995) 'Adult attachment status and mothers' behavior with their spouses', paper presented at the Biennial Meeting of the Society for Research in Child Development, Indianapolis.

Pincus, L. (ed.) (1960) *Marriage: Studies in Emotional Conflict and Growth*. London: Methuen.

Pizzey, E., and Shapiro, J. (1982) *Prone to Violence*. London: Hamlyn.

Rapoport, R., Rapoport, R. N., and Strelitz, Z. (1977) *Fathers, Mothers, and Society: Perspectives on Parenting*. New York: Vintage.

Rayner, E. (1992) 'Matching, attunement and the psychoanalytic dialogue', *International Journal of Psycho-Analysis*, 73: 39–54.

Richards, M. (1995) 'The companionship trap', in C. Clulow (ed.), *Women, Men and Marriage*. London: Sheldon.

Rodgers, B., and Pryor, J. (1998) *Divorce and Separation: The Outcomes for Children*. York: Joseph Rowntree Foundation.

Rosenfeld, H. (1987) 'Afterthought: changing theories and changing techniques in psychoanalysis', in H. Rosenfeld, *Impasse and Interpretation*. London and New York: Tavistock.

Roy, M. (1982) *The Abusive Partner*. New York: Van Nostrand Reinhold.

Ruszczynski, S. (ed.) (1993) *Psychotherapy with Couples: Theory and Practice at the Tavistock Institute of Marital Studies*. London: Karnac.

Ruszczynski, S., and Fisher, J. (eds) (1995) *Intrusiveness and Intimacy in the Couple*. London, Karnac.

Rutter, M. (1981) *Maternal Deprivation Reassessed*, 2nd edn. Harmondsworth: Penguin.

Sameroff, A. J., and Chandler, M. J. (1975) 'Reproductive risk and the continuum of caretaking casualty', in F. D. Horowitz (ed.), Review of Child Development Research. Chicago: University of Chicago Press.

Sandler, J. (1988) *Projection, Identification, Projective Identification*. London: Karnac.

Scharfe, E., and Bartholomew, K. (1994) 'Reliability and stability of adult attachment patterns', *Personal Relationships*, 1: 23–43.

Scharfe, E., and Bartholomew, K. (1995) 'Accommodation and attachment representations in young couples', *Journal of Social and Personal Relationships*, 12: 389–401.

Scharff, D., and Savege Scharff, J. (1991) *Object Relations Couple Therapy*. New Jersey and London: Jason Aronson.

Schmidt, D. (1998) 'Black milk and blue. Celan and Heidegger on pain and language', *Journal of Melanie Klein and Object Relations*, 16/4: 733–52.

Sennett, R. (1999) *The Corrosion of Character: The Personal Consequences of the New Capitalism*. London and New York: Norton.

Shapiro, T., and Emde, R. (eds) (1995) *Research in Psychoanalysis: Process, Development, Outcome*. Madison, CT: International Universities Press.

Silver, D., Cohn, D., Cowan, P., and Cowan, C. (1990) 'The Couple Attachment Interview', unpublished document, University of California, Berkeley.

Sinclair, I., and McCluskey, U. (1996) 'Invasive partners: an exploration of attachment, communication and family patterns', *Journal of Family Therapy*, 18/1: 61–78.

Skynner, A. C. R. (1982) 'Foreword' to D. Scharff, *The Sexual Relationship: An Object Relations View of Sex and the Family*. London: Routledge.

Steele, H., and Steele, M. (1998) 'Attachment and psychoanalysis: time for a reunion', *Social Development*, 7/1: 92–119.

Stern, D. (1985) *The Interpersonal World of the Infant*. New York: Basic Books.

Stets, J., and Straus, M. (1990) 'Gender differences in reporting marital violence and its medical and psychological consequences', in M. Straus and R. Gelles (eds), *Physical Violence in the American Family*. New Brunswick, NJ: Transaction.

Straus, M. A. (1993) 'Physical assaults by wives: a major social problem', in R. J. Gelles and D. Loseke (eds), *Current Controversies in Family Violence*. Newbury Park, CA: Sage.

Straus, M. A., and Gelles, R. J. (1986) 'Societal change in family violence from 1975 to 1985 as revealed by two national surveys', *Journal of Marriage and the Family*, 48: 465–79.

Symington, N. (1993) *Narcissism: A New Theory*. London: Karnac.

Thompson, G. (1960) 'Introduction', in L. Pincus (ed.), *Marriage: Studies in Emotional Conflict and Growth*. London: Methuen.

Tolman, R. M. (1989) 'The development of a measure of psychological maltreatment of women by their male partners', *Violence and Victims*, 4: 159–77.

Trinke, S., and Bartholomew, K. (1997) 'Attachment hierarchies in young adults', *Journal of Social and Personal Relationships*, 14: 603–25.

Troy, M., and Sroufe, L. (1987) 'Victimization among pre-schoolers: role of attachment relationship history', *Journal of the American Academy of Child and Adolescent Psychiatry*, 26: 166–72.

van IJzendoorn, M. and Bakermans-Kranenburg, M. (1996) 'Attachment representations in mothers, fathers, adolescents, and clinical groups: a meta-analytic search for normative data', *Journal of Consulting and Clinical Psychology*, 64/1: 8–21.

Vincent, C. (1995) 'Consulting to divorcing couples', *Family Law*, 25 (December): 678–81.

Wagner, B., and Reiss, D. (1995) 'Family systems and developmental psychopathology: courtship, marriage, or divorce', in D. Cicchetti and D. J. Cohen (eds), *Developmental Psychopathology*, vol. 1: *Theory and Methods*. New York: Wiley.

Walker, L. E. (1979) *The Battered Woman*. New York: Harper & Row.

Waters, E., Hamilton, C., and Sroufe, L. A. (in press) 'The stability of attachment security from infancy to adolescence and early adulthood', *Child Development*.

Waters, E., Kondo-Ikemura, K., Posada, G., and Richters, J. (1991) 'Learning to love: mechanisms and milestones', in M. R. Gunnar and L. A. Sroufe (eds), *Self Processes and Development*. Hillsdale, NJ: Erlbaum.

Weiss, R. (1974) 'The provisions of social relationships', in Z. Rubin (ed.), *Doing Unto Others*. Englewood Cliffs, NJ: Prentice-Hall.

Weiss, R. (1982) 'Attachment in adult life', in C. M. Parkes and J. Stevenson-Hinde (eds), *The Place of Attachment in Human Behavior*. Englewood Cliffs, NJ: Prentice Hall.

West, M., and George, C. (1999) 'Abuse and violence in intimate adult relationships:

new perspectives from attachment theory', *Attachment and Human Development*, 1/2: 137–56.

Wheeler, J., and Olney, F. (1999) 'Supervision within a creative partnership', *Professional Social Work*, June: 10–11.

Winnicott, D. W. (1971) 'The concept of a healthy individual', in J. D. Sutherland (ed.), *Towards Community Mental Health*. London: Tavistock.

Winnicott, D. W. (1974) *Playing and Reality*. Harmondsworth: Penguin.

Woodhouse, D., and Pengelly, P. (1991) *Anxiety and the Dynamics of Collaboration*. Aberdeen: Aberdeen University Press.

Wright, K. (1991) *Vision and Separation: Between Mother and Baby*. London: Free Association Books.

Young, L., and Gibb, E. (1998) 'Trauma and grievance', in C. Garland (ed.), *Understanding Trauma: A Psychoanalytic Approach*, Tavistock Clinic Series. London: Duckworth.

Zeanah, C. (1989) 'Adaptation following perinatal loss: a critical review', *Journal of the American Academy of Child and Adolescent Psychiatry*, 28/4: 467–80.

Index

absence, development of thought and knowledge 116–17
absent sustaining object 116
abusive relationships: attachment perspective 43–50, 60–1; case illustration 58–60; studies of 50–7, *see also* child abuse; violence
academia: clinical training 183; success and ability to articulate feelings 81
Adult Attachment Interview (AAI) xiv, xvi, 2, 15, 18–19, 32–3, 69, 98; classification table 34; Couple Attachment Interview 70–1; marital break-up 41–2; responses to and behaviour with partner 71–3; self-reports of feelings and behaviour 38, 40; case illustration 106–8; and Oedipus complex 91; tables of variance in security status 39, 203–6; unresolved states of mind 124–5
adult relatedness: and primary attachments 15–16; secure base 31–2, *see also* couples; marriage; partnership
affective attunement 103
Ainsworth, Mary D.S. 1, 31; attachment 28, 29; security 2; Strange Situation Test xiv, 94
Albee, Edward F. xix, 133–4
alpha-functions: and beta-elements 196, *see also* detoxification
ambivalence: in mourning 167–8; toleration of anxieties 24–5, 26
ambivalent individuals xvi; infants 17
anger: attachment theory xvii–xviii; communication 131; mother–infant relationship 138; unresolved individual (case illustration) 121–5, *see also* conflict; violence

anxieties: and loss 105–6; practitioner's 189–90; toleration of and ambivalence 24–5, 26, *see also* fearful attachment; fearful individuals
Assaultive Husbands Project 51
attachment: and abused children 140–1; and abusive relationships 43–61; Adult Attachment Interview 18–19; complex attachment 19–21, 24–7; narcissism 144–51; parenting 73; patterns: breaking cycle of 74–82; patterns: transmission of 61–74; security 28–42; Strange Situation Test 16–18; violence 136–43
attachment behavioural system 43–4
attachment representations 18–19, 20; secure base behaviour 28–42, 70
attachment theory xiv–xx, 1–6; object relations theory 5–6, 15, 24–7, 197–8; therapeutic frame 85–104
avoidant individuals xvi, 47; infants 17

Bacon, Francis xviii
Balint, M., thick and thin-skinned narcissism, ocnophilic and philobatic attitudes 144–5
Bartholomew, Kim 68, 141, 208; abusive relationships 43–61; fearful attachment 136
basic assumption, fight-flight 187
Basic Assumption Dependency (BAD) 189
Bateman, A., thick- and thin-skinned narcissism 144–5, 149, 150
Becoming a Family Project 74, 75
bereavement *see* loss; mourning; separation
beta-elements, and alpha-functions 196